Mother Angelica's Lessons on Genesis

Also by Mother Angelica:

Praying with Mother Angelica
Meditations on the Rosary, the Way of the
Cross, and Other Prayers

Mother Angelica on Christ and Our Lady

Mother Angelica on Suffering and Burnout

Mother Angelica's Quick Guide to the Sacraments

Mother Angelica on Prayer and Living for the Kingdom

Mother Angelica on God, His Home, and His Angels

Mother Angelica's Practical Guide to Holiness

Mother Angelica's Answers, Not Promises

A Holy Hour with Mother Angelica

Living the Scriptures

Mother Angelica's Guide to the Spiritual Life

In His Sandals

What Is Heaven?

Mother M. Angelica

MOTHER ANGELICA'S

LESSONS ON

GENESIS

EWTN PUBLISHING, INC.

Irondale, Alabama

EWTN Publishing, Inc.
5817 Old Leeds Road, Irondale, AL 35210

Distributed by Sophia Institute Press, Box 5284, Manchester, NH 03108.

paperback ISBN 978-1-68278-129-6
ebook ISBN 978-1-68278-130-2
Library of Congress Control Number: 2023943921

First printing

Contents

Mother Angelica's Lessons on Genesis

ONE

Genesis Chapters 1 & 2

This evening, we're going to take a look at something a little different. We've been talking about the spiritual life as such, and we've talked about Heaven, suffering—just a lot of things. We just finished a series on John 14–18, and we learned a lot about the spiritual life. Now, I would like to make a series entitled "Bible Stories Spirituality."

Now, there are many, many ways of reading Scripture. There's an exegesis way, which means that you interpret Scripture scholar language, and you look at the thing, and you go back in history, and you find out what the Medes did and the Egyptians did, and so you get a kind of historical explanation. Then there is a symbolic way of looking at Scripture. There's a tremendous amount of symbolism in Scripture, for example, the parables or something like that; they told one story, but they meant something entirely different. And sometimes when the Lord didn't speak in parables, the apostles seemed almost relieved as if, "Now, I understand." They said, "Oh, now You no longer speak in parables and metaphors, but You speak plainly." So, the Lord used metaphors so that it would apply to every generation and to every individual. Then there's the mystical way of reading Scripture; there is a tremendous amount of mysticism in Scripture. The ability to look at Scripture with the eyes of a contemplative.

Well, all of these are wonderful ways of interpreting Scripture, however, it leaves most of us in the dark. I'm talking about grassroots people. It leaves most of us saying, "What'd you say? I don't understand." So, we're going to start a series called "Bible Stories Spirituality," and that's what we're going to talk about; in other words, we're going to take this book, we're going to start with some Bible story, and say, "What we're saying is, how do you apply it to your life? And what do you do with it? What does it mean to you?" So, I want you to turn, and I hope you have your entire Bible ready, to Genesis. And I want you to begin at the beginning.

Now remember, all of you that are either fundamentalists or whatever, scholars, we are not talking about the exegesis of this interpretation or the symbolic interpretation, we're just going to see what's it mean to you? That's what we want to know. We want to know: How do I apply it to my daily life? Let's begin, then.

And it says: *In the beginning, God created the heavens and the earth.* Now, we're not too concerned about *how* He created Heaven and earth. Some people get so upset. They say, "Well, evolutionists say we came from monkeys." Don't worry about how God created. It doesn't matter whether He said, "Be," and it went *zoom.* Or whether He started with a little tiny, tiny, tiny atom. It doesn't matter. It had to be God Who created it. So, don't feel threatened if some scholar comes along and says, "Well, it took billions of years." It's okay, God has plenty of time. A day is like a thousand years. A thousand years is like a day. It is the same eternal thought, eternal power, eternal Lord, Who created everything that is. And He created it in the beginning, created Heaven, created earth.

Now, it says: *The earth was a formless void.* Meaning it was zilcho. Nothing. *There was darkness over the deep. And God's Spirit hovered over the water.* It's amazing, just this one sentence, the spirituality that you can get out of this one paragraph. In the beginning, there was no one but God. No one. There wasn't even an angel. There wasn't a star. There wasn't anything. Only God. And it's difficult for us to imagine how many eons of time because there was no time. Time began with the world. So, it's hard for us to imagine His timelessness. Oh, well, we have a little idea now that we can put astronauts on the moon, but no matter what we do here, there is always something to go to, or we're coming from something that already exists, and so maybe a few physicists have some kind of concept of nothing. And that's where we're at, we're gonna treat where we are on the grassroots. We don't have a physicist's mind. I don't want one, anyway. I'm happy with what God gave me. I want you to be happy with what God gave you. And in the beginning, this is where some beautiful spirituality comes in. You know why, because you were in the mind of God way back in this first paragraph of Genesis, before there was a Heaven and an earth. You were in the mind of God, and He had already decided that in this century you would be and you'd be doing the thing you're doing.

Do you know how many people are in the world? Don't we have a great God? I mean, isn't it wonderful that He thought of us, that He loves us, that He came down to redeem us, and when you think of the mind of God … I can't think of more than one day at a time, and if I try two … I can't be involved in more than one thing at a time; I couldn't give my total attention to more than one thing at a time. But here is God Who knew. First of all, He decided you would be from billions and billions of people who might have been. You know your chance and my chance of being born are so slim. I know what some of you think and you say, "Well, I wish I hadn't made it." Oh, you don't mean that. No matter how miserable life is on earth, eternity is worth it, it's worth every single minute of it. And so, in this first paragraph of Genesis, you have to look at it. Just think: you were there in the mind of God, He already decided that Mary Smith would be in 1986, and that's millions and millions and maybe billions of years after this; He knew you and loved you.

What a God we have, that He thinks that much of you. Well, I have to give you big doses of spirituality at one time, and I'm going to give you a little chance to think about it. Now, I want you to think about how God thought of you and decided to create you when there was nothing but a formless void. There was neither angel nor creation. He knew and loved you. So, think about it.

Okay, we said that in the beginning, before God created Heaven and earth or the angels or the stars, anything—it was all void and formless. And God knew you, loved you, decided that you would be. Decided what you'd be, where'd you'd be, *when*. I'm going to share at this point a little experience I had; I got it in a little mini book called *Before Time Began*.

One morning after Communion, I was just talking to the Lord as I usually do it, and I was very much suddenly aware, as if my spirit was leaving my body and was placed on a sphere—a round sphere—and it was a very kind of strange experience because I was there in the chapel, and yet I was there on this sphere, and I had a deep realization of nothingness. There was blackness out there and a void. It was rather scary. Because first of all, I realized I was very much alone. There was no one around. And there I was. But it seemed like my spirit would cry out every so often, "Yahweh," and I could hear the echo of my own voice, but there was no response. And this experience went on for days. Yet I was able to do my work and talk and do everything else, but there was that other part of me that seemed to be out there experiencing loneliness, nothingness. And then one morning again after Communion, I was very much aware that there were other beings like me, and they were everywhere, just kind of hovering over this sphere, and that lasted for quite a while. And I realized that I wasn't the only one out there in nothingness.

So, that went on another week or so. And then one day, I began to feel a presence, a very gentle, loving, very awesome, majestic presence, but still very kind and compassionate. And this presence seemed to hover over all these beings, and as He hovered over, they seemed to disappear, when He kind of reached the top of them, they all kind of disappeared, and then He'd come over a little more, and they would disappear, and then He'd come up a little further, and the ones below Him would disappear, and He'd come further, and the ones below would disappear. And I realized that those beings would never be.

Something in my spirit told me that this was a time for decisions, and the Supreme Being was making decisions, and I could see all these possible human beings. Thousands of them. And I realized that as the Spirit hovered over them and kept moving, all of those beneath Him would just disappear. And I suddenly one day realized that that Being was beginning to come toward me, and it was a strange experience because my spirit then had no concept of ever having been. I know this sounds a little wacko, but suddenly one day — I think this whole experience must have lasted a couple of months — I could feel this awesome presence slowly, slowly, slowly coming over, and then it stopped over me, and it was just a silence. And I waited. And a voice said, very gently and lovingly, "You shall be." And it went on. I realized then the Lord was giving me an experience of this first paragraph of the book of Genesis. Where in the beginning, there was nothing created, neither angel nor man nor creation itself. We were all in the mind of God, and then God had chosen me out of thousands and thousands and thousands who might have been.

It was a real, definite choice, and I was so grateful, that even with all the crosses in my life, all the problems, heartaches, and pain, when things get tough, when things get rough, it matters that you exist, even if you don't have any feeling of anything or anybody caring or having influenced anybody. It does matter. A lot. Let's go on.

And God said, "Let there be light," and there was light. Now again, don't get bogged down in how He did it. Leave that to scientists and all the rest. You and I are grassroots people. We don't need to know all that stuff. It's not important. What's it mean to you? What a powerful Lord we have. *"Let there be light," and there was light. God saw that light was good, and God divided light from darkness. God called light "day" and darkness he called "night." Evening came and morning came: the first day.* What a wonder it must have been.

Now, we also have to know that this paragraph could also pertain to the angels because the angels are light. They're all in pure intelligence. And suddenly, there came Lucifer, and those who followed him would not obey God, who didn't want the second Person of the Holy Trinity to become man, didn't want His Mother to be over them. And he said, "I will not serve." And God separated the light from the darkness. The first day. So, this is indicative of two kinds of lights and two kinds of darkness: the darkness that was a void until He brought in light, and the light that was angelic until it bred darkness. And He separated them this way. In the physical world, He called the light day and the darkness night.

And then God said, "*Let there be a vault in the waters to divide the waters in two.*" *And so it was. God made the vault, and it divided the waters above the vault from the waters under the vault.* There was the second day. *God called the vault "heaven." Evening came and morning came: the second day.* And this certainly indicates also that when God created the angels, they had to be tested, very much like Adam and Eve. And some said yes, and others said no. Those who said yes, God created Heaven. Those who said no, God separated. So, we have the second day.

And then He said that the *waters under the heavens should come together in a single mass, and the dry land appeared, and He called the dry land "earth" and the masses of water "seas."* And you have here a tremendous amount of symbolism, you have a tremendous amount of reality, a tremendous amount of love and compassion. And what does it all mean to you and to me? Just talk about the power of God, Who merely has to will, and everything begins. We look at Jesus, and we saw Him, He merely had to touch a person, and new skin and new bone and everything new appeared as if nothing had ever been wrong — a touch of His hand, an act of His will. And everybody sensed that, because they would say to Jesus, "If Thou wilt, Thou can make me clean." With the will of God, they knew. They knew their Scripture, they knew He had only to will, and they would be healed.

And then *God said, "Let the earth produce vegetation: seed-bearing plants, and fruit trees."* And you go through this, and you see the marvel of God.

You know, Sr. Raphael has a garden. And yesterday, we went out and unearthed potatoes. And every time that fork went in the ground and pulled up that plant, and I saw all those potatoes, big ones and little ones and tiny ones all sitting there waiting, it was absolutely phenomenal. I think that God put this marvelous thing, like a potato, with so many vitamins on the end of a tiny, little thin root. I was surprised that potato roots are extremely thin. But a potato that big, and you look at all the seeds, and we talked about that before—seeds that don't look like anything, they're just little, bitty things—and all of a sudden, you put them in the ground, and you get a little, bitty sprout. You don't have any idea what it is. If you forgot what you planted, it is a big surprise. And there's squash, and there're different kinds of squash and different kind of peaches, and there're three thousand species of pears.

So, when you look at these chapters, don't read them like you're reading a history of something; read them knowing how marvelous is our God. I'll bet so many of you have trees in your backyard, bushes in the front yard, or somebody else's yard. Did you ever really look at a tree? Did you ever see an acorn, just a tiny little, bitty seed? These mighty trees come out of it. It's so wonderful. We lose sight because we are people of much noise, we're busy about many things, and life is passing before us like it does in a train. I will never forget, I went from Chicago to Denver maybe fifteen years ago in a train, and I looked out that window. I could see fields and houses—fantastic wheat fields—but I could hardly see them. They were all mashed together because that train was going ninety miles an hour. It was just going *choo!* And I realized all of life passes us by. We never see God. We never know God. We never praise Him for His wonders and how many things He's done for us that's just over and abundant. He exaggerates so beautifully. He's so generous. Well, sometimes you get talking about God, you get kind of overwhelmed. Why don't you think about it?

Okay, go down to the fourteenth verse. *God said, "Let there be lights in the vault of heaven to divide day from night, and let them indicate festivals, days and years. Let them be lights in the vault of heaven to shine on the earth." And so it was. God made the two great lights: the greater light to govern the day, the smaller light to govern the night.* He created the sun and the moon, which divide. We know now that the world keeps turning, and so we have all the knowledge of why there is night in some places and day in other places, and sometimes you lose an hour going across the state. So, we have a lot of knowledge of this today, and sometimes that knowledge, the little we have, blurs the reality of God's Creation, His omnipotence, His power. So, let's not let that happen to us.

Those of us that are grassroots people, the majority of people in the world, must save our souls. And it's not necessary for us to get all screwed up in all these incidentals.

Now we come to the fifth day, and we talk about the waters teeming with living creatures and birds that fly above in the sky and every kind of living creature. If you look back at the dinosaur age, you just wonder what happened. Did a big meteorite fall and create darkness on the world for a year or so, and everything just died? What happened that all the dinosaurs are just a blank — you're talking big, huge creatures! And you have to ask yourself a question. Did God have fun? Did He have fun when He created one kind of creature and then said, "Well, let's go to something else"? What did He do, and why did He make them so big? Well, we're all happy, of course, because all the oil you got pumping up from here, there, and everywhere, is partly due to those creatures. So, as we dig into the ground, and we see all the ages before us, let's not lose sight because we have acquired a little bit of knowledge. Let's not lose sight of the Creator.

So, we go down, and the Lord blessed all these creatures. Now we see living things, animals, birds. Well, the Lord is not going around creating all this over and over and over. Instead,

He installed within them mechanisms through which they would recreate themselves.

Do you realize how wonderful that is? You know, we have an outside courtyard, and we found a nest belonging to a red bird. And we could watch this mother lying on three eggs, and we have chickens, and we've seen hens lying on eggs. Did you know that in a chicken egg, the Lord gives these little things inside, these little chicks inside the egg a special beak? And that little creature has to hit against that shell all the way around with this special beak in order to get out. I mean, that little fella is working hard. You know, you don't have a doctor there that cracks it open and says, "Okay, come on." He's got to get out himself, and then the beak falls off. Isn't that wonderful? And don't tell me that's just nature. That's God. It's just wonderful. And the other day, we saw these little chicks, and these little birds can fly. The egg is broken. You know, sometimes I have a hard time breaking an egg — you hit it, and nothing happens, and you've got to hit it again, and by that time it's all over you. But you see the wonder of God. The reason you read this is because you've got to see the wonder in your own life, you've got to make that comparison because you're greater than any creature. And it says here: *The earth produced every kind of living creature, reptiles and cattle, and every kind of wild beast.*

And you just see these animals rather roaming around the earth — suddenly, there they are. Did you ever wonder the first time you knew you were? Can you look back and say, "I know the day I knew I was"? I was not very nice because I was yelling at my grandmother at the age of three. But I knew at that moment I was here on this earth. I knew that.

Well, it says here, on the sixth day, the Lord made man to His own image and likeness. He said, *"Let us make man in our own image, in the likeness of ourselves."* And you have to realize that when Moses wrote this, he had no concept of the Trinity, but the Divine Inspirer—the Spirit—inspired the author of Genesis to say "Us," "We," "Ourselves." *And he blessed them. God created man in the image of himself, in the image of God he created him, male and female he created them.* This is the first account of Creation. *God blessed them, saying to them, "Be fruitful, multiply, fill the earth and conquer it. Be masters of the fish of the sea, the birds of heaven and all living animals on the earth." God said, "See, I give you all the seed-bearing plants that are upon the whole earth." And so it was. God saw all he had made, and indeed it was very good.* That was the sixth day.

Thus, the heavens and the earth were completed with all of their array. On the seventh day God rested after all the work he had been doing. Now, that's a kind of sore spot for many of us today. With all the stores that are opening more and more all over, and we don't have time because we're so busy, and so we do all our shopping on Sunday, and we do all this on Sunday, we do all that on Sunday. We've lost the concept of rest. There we go and run around drinking and doing all the things to calm our nerves, but we make ourselves nervous. The Lord knows that, and this was an example He gave. It says He Himself rested on the seventh day, meaning He did not create anything after that.

But you and I need to rest on the seventh day. You and I *need* to rest. Those of us of the New Testament, our rest is on Sunday, the day of the Resurrection. You say, "What am I gonna do, just lie around the house all day?" For your body, it'd be a great thing, and for your soul, to look at your God, give Him more time. Don't run into Mass or church and run right back out as if it's some kind of obligation. "Well, now I satisfied Him." You see, we lose a lot when we take everything as an obligation that we don't want to do but we have to. You know what Sunday is? It's a day of renewal, it's a retreat day.

It's a day, a family day, and today the family should be home, and you just talk to each other and love each other and talk things over with each other and have a good meal together. And our families don't even know what a meal is together anymore today. Some families don't even cook; everybody is on their own. How are you going to have a family if you're not together? And the greatest time to be together is a meal.

Jesus instituted the Blessed Sacrament at a meal. After the Resurrection, He cooked breakfast for His apostles. He forgave great sinners at a meal. Jesus used a meal as a time for gathering, as a time for family. It's more than the food you eat together, but it's food you eat *together*. And I speak especially to you, that are family, if you ate together and you prayed together, I think big changes would come along — big changes, changes in your family. You would be surprised. I want you to think about it. It may take a little extra work and a few extra dishes. But people that love each other must be together, and it's that relaxing happy time. You say, "Well, it's not happy in my family, and my father's always yelling." Maybe he's yelling because you're not there. Don't look at all the negatives. Try to bring your family back together. The best way is through prayer and a meal.

Let's go on to the second narration of the beginning, which we call the book of Genesis. We're not going to go through the entire Bible, obviously. As we go along, I'm going to pick out various parts of the Bible, the Old Testament right now, and adapt them to your daily life. I don't know how many are going to be in this series, but it really doesn't matter.

So, we come along, and we talk about the Creation of Adam. It says: *At the time when Yahweh God made earth and heaven there was as yet no wild bush on the earth nor had any wild plant yet sprung up. However, a flood was rising from the earth and watering all the surface of the soil. And Yahweh God fashioned man of dust from the soil.*

Fashioned a man. Now, all you that believe that we came from monkeys—well, I have a hard time with the monkey theory. There's such a gap between. I believe, and I think, this book indicates certainly how the first man was created. How long it took, to me, is irrelevant. We know that God created the first man.

Now, don't throw all this archaeology at me, with: "They found one here that was a million years old. They found somebody else in this continent that was three, five million." That doesn't mean anything. We're talking about the world being millions and millions of years old, when continents were closer together, when its whole makeup was so different than it is now. We only know that this man and this woman in this chapter are very important to you and me because God chose them to be the leaders of His creation.

And so, it says Yahweh *breathed into his nostrils a breath of life, and thus man became a living being.* Let's look at that for a minute. When you were in your mother's womb, when God used your mother and father to create you, you were extremely small, not recognizable by the human eye, but an entire person. And God breathes at that moment, in that act of love, a soul into your body, be it ever so tiny. So, at conception, everything happened together. You weren't just body and then soul, you were body and soul together—conception. We have only to look at St. Luke's Gospel to realize that. As soon as Mary said, "Be it unto me according to Thy Word," the incarnate Word became present in her womb—Body, Blood, Soul, Divinity—everything together as He was created in the womb of Mary—His humanity.

So, God breathes your humanity in the womb of your mother. You have to come from God, your soul must come from God. You see how close to God you are; you see why He is your Father. Your natural father and natural mother were instruments in the hand of God in an act of love to give you life.

That's why trying to take away that life for whatever reason is so awfully bad, because you take something of God and destroy it. It's not a small thing anymore. It's putting your finite hand into something that God has created and snatching it away. That's pretty serious, very serious.

And so, in this paragraph here, we realize very, very quickly that Adam had only God, Father. And He planted a garden in Eden, which is to the east. And God took the man here in verse fifteen, settled him in there, and told him, "Take care of it." I can imagine it was extremely lush, extremely fruitful, where there's no fear of animals. Adam never felt this, at this point. Never felt anger. Never felt guilt. Never felt resentment. Never felt anything that was bad. He only felt the presence of God. He only felt awe. He only felt wonder. He only felt happiness. He only felt joy. And then God added a woman. He said: "*It is not good that the man should be alone.*" You've got to talk to somebody. "*I will make him a helpmate.*" *So from the soil Yahweh God fashioned all the wild beasts and all the birds of heaven. These he brought to the man to see what he would call them.* He asked him to call them by name, each one. Isn't that beautiful of God? *And then Yahweh made the man fall into a deep sleep. And while he slept, he took one of his ribs and enclosed it in flesh.* And there was a woman.

I know what you're saying. Some of you, anyway. "Wait a minute! I don't wanna come from Adam." Whatever. You did. It doesn't mean you're inferior to, it means you are part of. Because the first thing Adam said was: "This at last is bone from my bones and flesh from my flesh, so you're a part of me." And that's what love does to married people, love makes a woman and a man part of each other. And so, Adam said, "*Bone of my bones, flesh of my flesh. This is to be called a woman, for she was taken from man.*" It's nothing to do with inferiority. It has to do with union, has to do with being one. So, Love created women, God created woman.

What's the difference if you took mud from the ground and created Adam and rib from Adam to create woman? It's God Who did it. Who cares how He did it? God created you women not to be inferior to men but to be a helpmate, to be an important part of society. So important that without women, there would be no society. Without men, there would be no society. So, you need each other, both coming from God, both understanding their source in God, Father. It's so important that you and I never forget.

And it says here: *This is why a man leaves his father and mother and joins himself to his wife, and they become one body.* You see, you were created by God, for God, you were created by God's love. He breathed the soul into your body; you're there together as one, each having a different function.

Well, I guess that's all for now for our spirituality coming from the book of Genesis. I hope you've learned a lot about God's love for you. Don't forget the freedom that God gave you, the love He gave you, and all the forgiveness and mercy. God bless you.

TWO

Genesis Chapter 3

We continue our series on the spirituality of the Bible, the different aspects of the Bible, because you can't treat Scripture as if it was something of the past that merely has historical value, because Scripture is the Word of God, and every part of it has a lesson to teach, a grace to bestow. It is the Word of God; as such it becomes our food. So, unlike any other book you read—where you read it, you acquire some knowledge, you put it back down—Scripture literally comes within you and influences your life, your thoughts, your actions, everything about you. So, we have to understand now when we speak of the spirituality of the Scripture, when we're reading something in the Scripture, we want to know: What does it mean to me? See, what does Adam and Eve and their Creation mean to you? Previously, the Lord gave us a lot of light on the aspects of Creation; we must adapt to our daily life how valuable we are to God, how are we created, and how we were in the mind of God before time began. So, we learned a lot.

Now, we're going to take another aspect of the spirituality in Scripture and look at the Fall. Now, some of you are kind of traditional—we call fundamentalist—you take everything very literally, some are a little bit more liberal in their interpretation of Scripture. There's a mystical way of interpreting Scripture, there's a symbolic way, and we're not gonna go through any of those ways. We leave those to Scripture scholars. You and I are grassroots. And as grassroots, we must begin at the beginning and make it simple and make it to a point where you and I can not only just understand it but live it. With that in mind, I'm going to let you find the third chapter of Genesis.

So now, we learned that God created everything in six days. Now, we still don't know, but every day may have been two billion years. We're not sure of that, but it's really not relevant. What is relevant is that God created the world. So, don't let anybody get you all mixed up in how He did it and the big bang theory and the little bang theory. It doesn't matter. It matters maybe to scholars and archaeologists and scientists, but it doesn't matter to you and me because we want to get the essence of it. What is God telling us? That is what's important. Nothing else is important, not to you and me. We'll let everybody else argue about those things.

The Fall now is something else, because we need to know. We experienced the Fall. You and I. We need to know, because the enemy of God, who is very, very prominent in the Fall, does the same thing to you and me. He hasn't changed his tactics that work on men and worked all through the centuries. They work now. Why do you stop doing something that works? It's like a man in business saying, "I'm successful, so I think I'll do something else." If you're successful, keep at it.

Well, that's what happened with the enemy. I want you to see a little trick he's performed right here because he does it in your life. Maybe you're not aware of that. If you're not aware of that, then maybe this lesson will help you. The text here speaks of *the serpent*. Now, it's good if you can read your footnote. Some of you don't know how to read Scripture, and you'll find little, tiny letters here, right next to a word. You learn a lot by the footnotes. That's why you need to get a Bible that has footnotes. Now, you can get cheaper ones that don't have footnotes, but you need to have footnotes because you take advantage there of the searching and findings and knowledge of scholars all over the world that have worked out these things for centuries. So, it says that the serpent was used as a disguise for a being hostile to God—it doesn't necessarily mean it was some little, wiggly thing—and an enemy of man. This being is identified with the adversary or devil.

Now today, you see there is a tremendous amount of false doctrine that says there is no Hell, there is no devil. I don't know how in the world you can open up a newspaper or listen to news or go down some of the streets at these pornography places and pass them by and not know. And look at the drugs, the alcohol, and everything else that is going rampant all over the world. How in the world can you possibly say, "There isn't an enemy?" There is someone who is trying to subdue you because he hates God, he doesn't want you to enter the Kingdom. Why would the enemy of God want to bother with me? It's the only thing he wants. He hates you. He hates me. He hates everybody. Because we're human beings graced by God and because His Son became man. He hates every individual, and if he can keep you from entering the Kingdom of Heaven, he then feels he has a victory—he's taken someone away from God. Now, when you believe all this false reality that there is no Hell, there is no devil, then you leave yourself wide open. The evils in the world today, the lack of compassion, the lack of sympathy and pity, the abortion, the euthanasia—you cannot look at the world today and be realistic and say there is no enemy of God.

Now, if you don't believe in God, well then, you've really got a problem. Because then it's just Hell from beginning to end.

You see, just common sense tells you that man himself, as bad as he can be in his own beliefs, believes at least enough to know he can't always do these horrible things unless he's mental. You see, the world today is full of greed, gluttony, lust. Those three things. *Greed*—materialism. *Gluttony*—we overdo everything, drugs, alcohol, even medication. And *lust*—immorality.

You say, "Well, I don't believe in God, so I don't think everything's Hell. I'm having a good time." Are you? Examine your conscience. Examine real down deep. You've got to have a reason. You have to have some kind of reason outside of man's innate evil tendencies that come from the consequences of sin, which we're going to read about in a minute. But you have got to understand that man himself, tempted by the world, the flesh, and the enemy of God, needs God, needs a Supreme Being to survive, to have that peace and joy. So maybe your concept of God is different, and maybe you don't express your love for God in ways other people do, but that's okay.

You know there is a God, you know He is a Father, you know He takes care. From that, other things will grow. Now, let's look at this, and you'll see. *The serpent was the most subtle of all the wild beasts that Yahweh God had made.* And you say, "Well, why does it say a snake if it meant a person like it says here, a being?" Well, have you ever called somebody a snake in your life? I know that he's a *snake*, but not a snake—he's a human being—but maybe things he has done are so deceptive, so mean, that that image is what comes to your mind. So, let's not get bogged down in that, though, because what is important is what comes next.

It asked the woman, "Did God really say you were not to eat from any of the trees in the garden?" See, that's deceit. "Did God say from *any* of the trees in the garden?" Well, that wasn't true. *The woman answered the serpent, "We may eat the fruit of the trees in the garden.*" She's indignant. "No, we can eat. *But of the fruit of the tree in the middle of the garden, God said, 'You must not eat it nor touch it, under pain of death.'*" Now, let's just stop here a minute.

Some people say, "What right did God have to say that?" He has every right. And that's one of the bad things we have today. We have forgotten God's sovereign rights. God has a right to tell you to do one thing and not another. Why? Because He created you. That is His right. Your father and mother have parental rights, and as long as you're under their roof, they have a right to tell you this or that, that you have to come in at ten o'clock or eleven o'clock and you have to do this and you have to do that. They have a right. It's not unjust. As long as you're eating their food and wearing their clothes and benefiting by their hard work, then you owe obedience. This is life. You just can't go around and do as you please, when you please, how you please and not have any concept of how it affects other people—you can't do that. And if you do, you're going to suffer the same consequences.

So here is Eve, and she's saying, "No, wait a minute, we can eat of the trees except one." Now, let's see ourselves in this. We know that there are the Ten Commandments. We know that. And one time, the Pharisees said to the Lord, "Is it right you have to honor your father and mother? What happens if ...?" See, they're looking for excuses. What happens if the money that I was supposed to give to my father and mother in their old age I give to the temple? And the Lord said, "You hypocrite." See, that's the same thing. It's that deceit, trying to cheat God and trying to cheat your mother and your father.

And so, the woman is saying, "No, we can eat." And he says, "Oh. Well, now, wait a minute. I don't think you're going to die. No, I don't think so." Like you get tempted to commit adultery, and the enemy will whisper in your ear, "Oh, is it true?

I mean, is it really true that even though you have a wife and children, and this beautiful secretary of yours or this beautiful woman comes along, and all of these thoughts … Is it really so wrong as that? I mean, after all, who are you hurting?" He does the same thing to you.

Well, after you begin to reason it out, your heart begins to blind you, because maybe you had an argument with your wife this morning, or you're tired of doing nothing but educating your children and doing the same thing over and over and over and over and over. And so, what happens?

Or you have a date. So, you decide you're going to have more than a date, so you just check into some motel, and you say, "Well, after all, I am young."

You see, the serpent is saying to you, "But after all, it's your life. I mean, you can do what you want with it. God understands. I mean, you *are* loving, you're not doing anything bad, you're not influencing anybody, you're not hurting anyone." The devil says the same thing to you. We look at this thing in here, and we say, "Oh, that was stupid of Eve." Well, what about you? Maybe you shouldn't drink. The enemy says to you, "Oh, now, who said you shouldn't drink?" "My doctor says I shouldn't drink." "Well, now, are you telling me that if you just have one drink tonight, that's going to hurt you?" It's all of these things that come up. And let's go on.

Now, what did the serpent say to Eve that convinced her? He said, "*God knows, in fact, that on the day you eat, your eyes will be open, and you will be like gods.*" He didn't say "God." He said, "*like gods, knowing good and evil.*"

Now, let's stop here a minute. What does the word *knowing* mean in Scripture? It means to experience. In this case, it doesn't mean that we acquire some knowledge we store in our memory and we just bring it out when we want it. It's not that kind of knowledge. It's an experience. I feel it, I do it. So, what the devil is saying is that once you eat of that tree, you will feel evil. You don't feel evil now, but you will know what it means to do something wrong, you will know the punishment of disobedience. And that was true. But the way he cloaked it was so deceptive because it made it seem like, "Oh, now, God is jealous of His own prerogatives and attributes, He doesn't want you to be like Him." Well, God doesn't have the experience of evil, but He knows the result of bad actions. He didn't want Adam—or you and me—to ever experience disordered passions, lust, gluttony, greed, adultery, anger, hatred, jealousy. He didn't want us to experience those things; He wanted us to only experience His love, His joy, to experience a Heaven on earth and a Heaven in Heaven.

There was one test. And that is: Will you be obedient?

Let us go back, and we'll find that the serpent himself fell from the realms of the antechamber of Heaven, where the test was for the angels, because he said, "I will not serve." So, God said, "This is what's going to happen. The eternal Word shall become man." And Lucifer said, "Oh no, no." There was that, "No, I will not serve. I will not obey." Now, that same tactic that did him in, he's using it on Eve, and he says, "Oh, no, I mean, you're going to know good and evil, you'll be like gods." So right away, she began to think and said, "That isn't right of God to keep that knowledge from me." And so, it says: *The woman saw that the tree was good to eat and pleasing to the eye.* Now, let's look at that a minute. You see here the devil is working on what? Senses. He's working on her feelings, her touch, her taste or smell, her eyes—all her five senses.

He's working on those to try to get her to be what? Disobedient. A lot of you young people out there are being caught in a web of deceit planted by the world, the flesh, and the enemy, and they basically tell you the same thing: you don't need to be obedient. You're going to be your own person, and so you can run and do as you please. And once you start, you begin to know not good but evil, and you know it in one of the worst ways. You're getting drunk at fourteen, you've had I don't know how many affairs by fifteen, your whole world can be just torn to pieces because you get tempted to experience all the things you read about and see. You know, a lot of people get all mixed up when people say, "Well, I've got to be my own person." But what is that? What does it mean? What does it mean to say, "This is my life?" Is that true? Or is it a time given to you by God to cooperate with Him? Once it's "my life and I'm gonna do what I please, when I please, how I please," you're going to destroy yourself. It happens all the time, because you can't give yourself grace, and only the grace of God within me can give me peace and joy and happiness and help me to overcome and not give in to myself and give in to others over and over and over until, like Eve, you can't tell the truth from the lie. And you'll do anything to get your own will.

You're not happy. Oh, you say, "I'm very happy." No, you're not. Because you're running from the experience of being miserable, and so when the woman saw that it was good, she did away with her will, which was united to God's up to that moment. If she would have thought for a minute and said, "Well, maybe you're right. But God knows best, He doesn't want me to know evil." The enemy told her the truth. *"You will know good and evil."* That's why when you say, "I am my own person," that's true. "This is my life," that's true. Nobody questions that you're your own person, nobody questions that you've your own life, but we do question why you want to destroy it and destroy others with you.

See, it's just like this incident here in Scripture. You think, "Well, Eve thought it was a good idea to know good and evil. How else do you recognize it?" But the enemy never said to her, "You will *recognize* good and evil." He said, "You will *know* good and evil," you will *experience*. That's the hitch. That's the catch. God knows good and evil, meaning He knows what happens to you when you become disobedient. He's never experienced it. He doesn't want you to experience it. He doesn't want Adam and Eve to experience it. He didn't want you to know evil. He wants you only to know God. In fact, He didn't say anything about knowledge. I know, for example, that there is much evil in the world, but you can't always and shouldn't ever want to experience it.

For example, I know there is an Italy. I'm just talking about plain knowledge. I know there is an Italy, or, say, a Switzerland. I know there are mountains in Switzerland, this is good knowledge, but I've never experienced the cold wind up on a mountain or walking on crackling snow or skiing down a mountainside. I've seen pictures of it. It's like a person saying, "Well, I've seen people drink, but I've never been drunk." So, now you decide one night you want to experience being dead drunk. But what have you experienced? You're out of it. You've destroyed part of your brain cells, part of your liver, you've humiliated your own dignity, you've humiliated your family. What did you learn? Every time you begin to experience evil, the reason seems to go right out the window, the knowledge goes right out the window. So, you don't reason anyway.

People say, "I can stop drinking." No, you can't. But you won't admit it. So, Eve knew that this tree would give her knowledge, and that God didn't want her to have it. In other words, she knew if she touched it, she would die. It meant death. Not physical death, only death of the soul. And so, the Lord told her, *"The day you eat from this tree, you shall die,"* meaning your grace will leave you. That's death. That's the only death there is. Death of the body can release us to Heaven, and there is no death of the soul. You kill grace in your soul, and your soul then goes from grace to evil. It's a death that has nothing to do with immortality. You don't cease to exist, you're not annihilated, but Jesus looked upon sin as a death because Hell is a death, meaning an absence of life. And what is life? God is life. Grace is life. Jesus is life.

Without that, there's nothing. And so, the opposite of that is death. Though you live — your soul is immortal — you're still dead. Meaning you are absence, a total absence of love, joy, peace, companionship, all the things that make life beautiful. That's that absence. And the Father was saying to them, "Don't do that. You will die the death."

Well, the serpent goes on to explain what it meant. *And the woman saw that the tree was good to eat and pleasing to the eye and desirable for the knowledge that it could give.* She said, "I shall know." That's how some of you youngsters get into lust. You hear about sex in school, you see it on television — it looks so romantic, and so you think, well, you're gonna try it. Just keep going down and down, and the first thing you know, you're either pregnant or you have some disease or something. You want to experience, and what have you got? *So, she took some of its fruit and ate it. She gave some to her husband, who was with her, and he ate it.*

Now we're going to see what Adam did. He ate it. He had to make a decision. He made the wrong one. Don't you ever wonder what would have happened if Adam would have said no? Or Eve would have said no? Where would we be today? Well, if we'd not failed the test, it would be phenomenal. Just absolutely phenomenal. Someday, maybe we'll talk about what might have been.

The eyes of both of them were opened and they realized that they were naked. Something new happened. What was looked upon as good suddenly became evil. You see what happened? Isn't that what happens to you? You watch movies, and you watch all of this stuff, and it looks so good, and when you do it, it's evil, you see it for what it is — evil. See, the Lord knew exactly what would happen to them once they became disobedient, proud, and jealous of God's authority and sovereign rights. They didn't want anyone telling them that they couldn't do something, so now they knew evil. They knew they were naked.

We previously looked at Genesis 1:27–28. It says: *God created man in the image of himself. In the image of God, he created him.* It says: *God blessed them, saying to them, "Be fruitful, multiply, fill the earth, and conquer it. Be masters of the fish of the sea."* Sex was not the Fall. It was the disobedience; it was after they became disobedient that suddenly an ordinary way of life became evil. Do you see what happens? When we become disobedient to God's commands, we experience guilt, we experience anger, we experience shame, we want to hide. Most of the great sins in the world are committed at night. Did you ever wonder why? Because man himself, in an act of sin, wants to hide, he wants the cover of darkness, he doesn't even want to see himself.

So, they sewed fig leaves together to make themselves loincloths. It's funny, they were running around sewing fig leaves. Before, they didn't need to. They didn't have an evil thought, they didn't have a disobedient thought, they didn't have anything that disturbed or distressed them. It was like Heaven on earth. It was Paradise.

But they wanted to experience evil. All of you, young people, some of you've got one foot in the grave, and you run around doing some of the craziest things that are sinful. Why do you want to do that? Why do you want to just blow it all away at this stage in the game? Doesn't make any sense to me.

Well, let's look on. *The man and his wife heard the sound of Yahweh God walking in the garden in the cool of the day, and they hid from Yahweh God among the trees.* Not only did they become ashamed and go around looking for fig leaves that they could sew together and cover themselves, they hid now. Do you see what happened to them? I mean, here's a couple that walked with God in the cool of the night, talked to Him as a friend, and suddenly you get fear now. See, there were none of these things before the Fall, before they said, "I will not serve." Adam did the same thing as Lucifer did, which means "You're not gonna tell me what to do." Then they had to take the consequences.

See, if you give a child a knife to play with, you can't be surprised if he cuts himself. It doesn't make sense to say, "Well, why did he cut himself?" You gave him a knife to play with. Those are the consequences. Everything has consequences. Even those hidden things you do have consequences. Why? Because your guilt, your resentment, all of that influences your family, it influences you. They all have consequences. You can pretend they don't, but they do. You only have to speak to one woman who has had an abortion and look at the consequences.

Yahweh was walking in the Garden in the cool of the day. And they hid themselves. And Yahweh called. Can you imagine what a dramatic moment this was? *"Where are you?" he asked.* I can imagine Adam saying in a very scared voice, *"I heard the sound of you in the garden, and I was afraid because I was naked, so I hid."* But he walked with God in the cool of the night perhaps for years. Why was he suddenly afraid? You see what knowledge of evil did? To experience evil made him afraid. *"I was afraid."* That word never entered his mind or heart or vocabulary before.

Some of you girls that are thirteen, fourteen, fifteen, that are pregnant, reading this, and no one knows you're pregnant—you're afraid you have made a mistake. Don't make two. If your parents are going to be angry, find a pro-life center; they'll help you. Don't add despair to fear.

The Lord God said, *"Who told you that you were naked?"* See how innocent they were? *"Have you been eating of the tree I forbade you to eat?"* And the man—oh, you and I do this all the time—he blamed God, and he blamed the woman. He said, *"It was the woman you put with me."* You know, some of you people drinking, you say, "It's because of my wife, it's because of my children, it's because of my husband that I drink." No, that's not what it is.

And then he said, *"She gave me the fruit, and I ate it,"* as if he had absolutely no will, no intelligence, and no memory as to the law of God. So, he pushes the whole blame on Eve—"It's the woman's fault, and You gave her to me"—so in other words, just bounce back that guilt a little bit.

The Lord said to her, *"What is this you have done?"* And she said, *"The serpent tempted me, and I ate."* At least she was truthful. *"The serpent tempted me, and I ate."* So, now she knows, and she knew she was being tempted to be disobedient, just as you're tempted to do a lot of things in your life that are not right. And this is what the Lord God said to the serpent, *"Be accursed beyond all cattle and wild beasts. You shall crawl on your belly and eat dust every day of your life, and I will make you enemies of each other, you and the woman."* Oh, here it is—it wasn't Eve He was talking about. Because Eve had just become disobedient, she had wanted to experience evil. He said, *"I will put enmity"*—that's another word for it—*between you and the woman, your offspring and her offspring. It will crush your head, and you will strike its heel.*

So from now on, man would have to fight the enemy, he would have to fight against the enemy to survive. There would no longer be that peace within himself. From then on, unless he fought, they'd do him in, and it's going to be an everyday experience. Anger, hatred, lack of forgiveness, lack of compassion, deceit, drunkenness, orgies, lust — all those things — depravities of every kind. You have only to read St. Paul to get a whole list of all the feelings we know now after the Fall.

And to the woman, God said, "*I will multiply your pains in childbearing, you shall give birth to your children in pain. Your yearning shall be for your husband, yet he will lord it over you.*" Well, Adam didn't get off too hot. God said, "*Because you listened to the voice of your wife and ate from the tree of which I had forbidden you to eat, cursed be the soil because of you. With suffering shall you get your food from it every day of your life. It will produce brambles and thistles for you. With sweat on your brow, you shall eat your bread until you return to the soil, as you were taken from it. For dust you are, and unto dust you shall return.*" They forgot from whence they came. Well, think about that. Look into your life.

Well, it doesn't take long before we come to understand that everything we see Adam and Eve do, we have done. You say, "Well, if Jesus came (and He did), and He died for us (and He did), and He redeemed us (and He did), why do we have all this stuff? Why do I have to struggle with anger and patience and all these other things?" Well, the Lord did something more than suddenly make all the world a paradise. He did something that was going to do His enemy in and give us great merit because we would have the opportunity and the grace now to make the right choices. So, what Jesus purchased for us was the grace of His Holy Spirit, the divine indwelling.

Now, all of this, this kind of man, this kind of woman that we are, is suddenly filled with the Spirit of the Lord God Himself. And so now, we can say no to these temptations, we can say no to these passions, we can say no to all the temptations that the world gives, that my own flesh gives, and that the enemy gives. Not only do we have the power now to say no, but we have the power to rise above. Because of two people: the Son of God and the woman. The Son of God, Who redeemed us by His life, His death, His Crucifixion, and His Resurrection. And the beauty of His Mother.

Now, you see why I've said that when Jesus called Mary the *woman* — "Woman, behold your son," "What is it to you and to me, Woman?" — He was planting that seed. It goes way back to Genesis. The woman. *"Her offspring will crush your head."* Jesus crushed the head of Satan on the Cross.

So, the man named his wife "Eve" because she was the mother of all those who live. And Yahweh made clothes out of skins for the man and his wife, and they put them on. They had just upset God's whole plan for humanity. It's amazing. He corrected them, and He had to. You say, "Well, that's rather severe." He had to. And now, He looks at those fig leaves, and I don't think they looked too hot, so he kind of felt sorry for them. And He said, "Well, you don't even know how to make clothes." So, He took skins — must have killed some animals — and then Yahweh said, *"See, the man has become like one of us, with his knowledge of good and evil. He must not be allowed to stretch his hand out next and pick from the tree of life also, and eat some and live forever* in this terrible state." *So, Yahweh expelled him from the garden of Eden to till the soil from which he had been taken. He banished the man and in front of the garden of Eden he posted the Cherubs.*

Well, much of this is symbolic of man being an outcast because of this knowledge he desired of evil. He could no longer stay in Paradise. Why? Because it was difficult for him now to be loving and kind and compassionate. There was a struggle now, where before he had been compassionate by nature and loving by nature and good by nature. Now, there was this struggle, so he could no longer live in Paradise. He had to be thrust out in order to fight against these things, but then Jesus came as He promised. And now you and I live the life of Jesus resurrected. We may be tempted, and we may be harassed on every side. We may have temptations within and troubles and everything without. But the grace within us is greater. And now we have something that Adam and Eve never had. The Son of God became man and died and shed His blood for us. We have such a proof of His love. The Church says, "O happy fault" on Holy Saturday, meaning what blessings the Father has given us. So, you see, no matter how sinful you are, know that the Father is loving and compassionate in the midst of our sin and sinner condition. He gave us His own Son to be like unto us in all things except sin.

Well, next chapter, we will continue, and we will see exactly what happened after that to others that were born of Adam and Eve. We're not going to run through the whole Scripture. We are going to choose different parts of Scripture. They will be able to teach us some of the things we need to know about ourselves and how to live in this particular world. In the meantime, read this over for yourself, try to remember what I've said, and know that you are loved by a great God. When temptations and everything else get more than you can handle, just say, "Lord Jesus, let Your Precious Blood fall upon me. Jesus and Mary, I love you. Save souls."

God bless you. And remember, He loves you so very much.

THREE

Genesis Chapters 4–6

Well, we were looking at Adam and Eve and the Fall. And we found out a lot of things. So, now we have to start out with them being literally thrown out of Paradise. Paradise, meaning a state of perfect life where there is no evil, never felt the passion of anger or revolted against God. It is very difficult to think that there might even be such a time in our life, and we want that time, that peace. We want that transforming union to occur, where we feel that presence of God, but we know that in the middle of all that, there is that constant struggle. And sometimes, the Lord says, "Now, I want you to grow." And so, what He does is expand that vehicle so our capacity can grow in the meantime, and we get all the wrenching of bones and sinew and spirit. So there is a constant struggle between what we want and what we are. Somewhere in between, we arrive at patches of peace. They are patches. Well, now that man wanted to know and to be like God, knowing and experiencing good and evil … now he knows.

You know, a lot of you have spent time and effort—time that was ill spent—to arrive at some degree of ambition. Glory. And when you got there, I know what you said: "Now what?" "Now I know what it means to be president," or, "I know what it means to be this," or, "I've got that million." "Now what?"

And there is always a "Now what?" at the end of every journey, and if you haven't found that out yet, you haven't lived.
Because part of that is necessary. As we make one mistake
after another, God permits it to teach us a good lesson: there
is something greater to come.

So, now we get to what effect did Adam and Eve's sin have
upon their children? Well, there's big patches of years in between all of this that's not written here, because God is giving us the essence of salvation history. He's not taking it day
by day, year by year, or we'd have books that would fill the
whole world, but we need to understand this is where you and
I come in, because you and I are still suffering from the effects
of Original Sin, though Jesus redeemed us. Now, you're saying,
"That doesn't make sense." You say, "Jesus redeemed me, and
here I am still full anger and hatred and lust and greed and
gluttony," and all the other things that harass us all day long.

So, you're saying to yourself, "Well, what did Jesus do for
me?" When you and I say yes to God, when we combine our
will with His — as weak as we are in our human nature — we
overcome a great enemy who's more powerful than we are,
more intelligent than we are. But we give God within us the
power to overcome His enemy and overcome our enemy and
raise us above ourselves and the things of this world.

And so now, we're coming to Adam and Eve's children.
"*I have acquired,*" *Eve said, "a man with the help of Yahweh." She
gave birth to a second child, Abel, the brother of Cain. Abel became a
shepherd and kept flocks, and Cain tilled the soil. Time passed. Cain
brought some of the produce of the soil as an offering for Yahweh,
while Abel, for his part, brought the firstborn of his flock and some
of their fat as well.* So, now we're finding two different kinds of
individuals; we're finding one who gives more than he should.
And I have to wonder here, when Cain brought some of the

produce, if it was the best produce? From his disposition, you kind of get that "one for you, one for me, but mine's the best," and maybe Yahweh got second best. Whatever it was wasn't too hot. We're beginning to see a disposition of mind that we call selfishness, and we begin to see something else we call generosity, and you've got to examine yourself here. If you were going to give first fruits, what would you give? When you give to the poor, for example. You have some old clothes in the house that are full of holes. What are you going to do with them? If you can't wear them, do you think they're going to wear them? If you're going to give food, do you give all those dented cans? Do you give your leftovers? When you give to God, when you give to the poor, remember that it is Jesus you feed.

It is Jesus you give something to. It is Jesus you clothe. What are you giving Him? You say, "Well, I can't afford to go around buying new stuff for the poor." What I'm saying is don't throw it away because you can't use it anymore. If you want to give, give so that the person who receives has dignity, so it doesn't feel like you threw something at him from underneath a garbage heap. Now, you say, "Well, if I were poor and in the streets, I'd think something were better than nothing." Well, they may have to wear it because something *is* better than nothing. But do you give three-day-old bread away, or if you had a choice between three-day-old bread and fresh bread, would you give the fresh loaf of bread to someone who came to your door? Would you give them something that's the very best? You see, it's not so much, really, what we give, and it's not so much how we feel about it, but the love we have for our unfortunate brother. After all, you and I could be in the same disposition, the same place, in the same atmosphere.

You know, there's no question in my mind what I would be today if God hadn't gobbled me up and made me a nun. I know what I would be. I know where I'd be. I'd be in bad shape. I'd be bitter, angry with God, because coming from where I came from, I don't think by this time, if it hadn't changed, I would have loved God as much as I hope I do now. God was merciful to me. God was good to me.

Now, let's go on. *Yahweh looked with favor on Abel and his offering, but he did not look with favor on Cain and his offering. And Cain was very angry and downcast.* You say, "Well, Cain and Abel came from the same loaf of bread, Adam and Eve." Well, you look around in your family, and you all came from the same loaf of bread, but there's not two of you alike. And when we reach the use of reason, some go this direction, and some go that direction, and some go straight ahead. We do have choices. We do have light.

And Yahweh said to Cain, "Why are you angry and downcast?" Do you ever wonder? You would say to yourself, "Oh, if God would only speak to me with a voice I could hear, my whole life would change!" No, it wouldn't. Because you still have to have that faith that it's God Who's speaking to you. It didn't help Cain. You can't look for the mystical, you can't look for the unusual, because God is in the ordinary, God is in the simple things of life. That's why we miss Him. We miss Him a lot. We miss Him all day long. God seeks to speak to us, but our minds and our hearts are so busy, so self-oriented, we don't hear. And so, the Lord said to him, *"If you are well disposed, ought you not to lift up your head?"* So apparently, Cain was even angry when he gave the fruits. Did you ever have somebody give you a gift and just kind of throw it at you? That happened to me one time. I wanted to push it down his throat. Well, that was before I knew Jesus, but I'm still not too sure that even after I knew Jesus I'd do any differently. There's just something so insulting about somebody who literally says, "Well, here it is." You want to say, *"Keep it."*

So, the Lord was really telling us what was wrong with Cain. He said, "If you wanted to give Me something, should you have not lifted up your head, should you not have given it to Me with joy?" When you give to your church, when you give something to your family, do you give it with joy? When your wife has a birthday, do you bring home some flowers or candy or buy her something nice and have joy on your face like you really, really wanted to do this?

You really love this person. And I don't mean you have to feel joy, we don't always feel joy, but if you love someone, you look forward to doing something for them; it shows in your eyes. You know you don't have to have a smile from ear to ear, but it shows in your eyes. It shows in your gestures. It shows in your love. It's no longer for the reason of obligation that you do this. It's out of love.

Now, the Lord said, "If you are ill disposed, is not sin at the door like a crouching beast hungering for you?" You know, some of you are on drugs, some of you are alcoholics. Some of you have adultery problems. Listen to God's description of sin. Just listen. He says, *"Is not sin at the door like a crouching beast hungering for you, which you must master?"* Now, you see the beauty of God's correction. When we correct, we just lay them out flat, we never say why, we never say what was wrong, and we never say what to do about it. We just look at the thing, we correct it hard, and when we let them just fall down, flattened out, we walk over them. That's how we correct. Many, many times.

But the Lord, first of all, said what was wrong. Then He described what happened to Cain. And now, He said, "You can master it." And I've had a lot of people tell me, who are in really bad conditions of sin, and they keep saying, "I can't master it. I can't help it." But when the Lord God Himself says that sin was like a crouching beast at your door and you must master it, you've got to say *no* to temptation. See, that's why Jesus came. Jesus came so that the grace He merited for you through the pouring out of His Precious Blood and His glorious Resurrection, that kind of grace, that participation in the very nature of God, would give a poor, weak human being like you and me the power to say no to all demons in Hell, to the flesh that gnaws at us in the world, that crouches around us like a roaring lion. After redemption, you and I can never ask and never complain that we didn't have what it took.

And Cain said to his brother, Abel, "Let's go out." Can you imagine, now, this kind of hardness of heart? He absolutely, totally ignores God's word. He is so filled up with jealousy at this point that he doesn't want to hear God, he doesn't want to hear that he can master this terrible evil—jealousy.

And so, he said to his brother, *"Let's go out,"* and while they were out in open country, he killed him. Cain killed Abel. Suddenly, with his brother on the ground, blood probably flowing out of his head, *Yahweh asked Cain, "Where is your brother, Abel?"* And now we find the first lie, the first murder, the first act of jealousy. *He said, "I do not know. Am I my brother's guardian?"*

I wonder, my friends, if you and I have said that to God many times. Am I my brother's keeper? Am I my family's keeper? Am I my parents' keeper? Am I my children's keeper? "Where is your brother?" We have to say, "I don't know." There are many ways of killing people. In some ways you kill them, they don't really die, but they wish they were dead, because we make them so miserable. We're so hard to live with, we're so jealous, or so envious, or so mean that is so difficult to live with us, and we make people die a thousand deaths. Just like Cain did with Abel.

Well, I want you to think about that for a moment. Kind of sobering. But there are times we have to have sober talk in order to look at ourselves and say, "I've got to stop doing this."

I say it to you with love and words that God Himself has given to us in Scripture, not to torment you and not to make you feel guilty, but so that they bring you up short and say, "Hey, hold it. You're going the wrong direction."

I think before we go on, we need to hit a little subject here that's so strong in this chapter, and that is jealousy. Jealousy is to dislike someone because of what they possess in talent or possessions, what they have, their looks, or whatever. And not only envy them, which would be saying that you wish that thing was yours, but you believe in your heart that the fact that person possesses that virtue, that gift, that talent, those beautiful looks, that big house, or whatever, it is somehow yours, and they have it unjustly. That's really the essence of jealousy—to believe that what somebody else has is your rightful possession, and by the fact that it is your rightful possession, you should have it, and so God Himself is unjust by giving this to them.

We can see an example of this in the life of St. Bernadette, the seer of Lourdes. Her novice mistress was extremely jealous of Bernadette. Because her novice mistress fasted, while Bernadette could never fast. Her novice mistress stayed up night after night in prayer until her eyes, she said, burned. Bernadette couldn't do that; she had bad asthma; she was very frail. And so, the mistress hated Bernadette because she felt that the visions she had of Our Lady, she had no right to, she had not merited them, she had not earned them. They rightfully belonged to her, and so she hated Bernadette. What stirred up then is what I would say was the sin of Lucifer—jealousy.

I think we need to look at this ugly, little thing called jealousy and look at it for what it is. You know, a lot of people are jealous of other people's love. I have known people, for example, who are getting along great together in their married life until they have children, and suddenly, the children become an object of jealousy. The wife becomes jealous of the husband's attention to the children. So somehow, she feels that that child has taken away something from her that is rightfully hers. Attention, affection, time. Some marriages break up because we've never understood something: We can love a thousand people. We'd never love two people alike. Love is different. A love a man has for a wife and vice versa is totally different than the love they may have for a child. If it's the same love, then we're in a lot of trouble. When a woman loves her father so much that she tries to marry a man that is exactly like her father, she's in trouble. We have to understand the freedom of God's love: He loves us all, He loves us all individually, He loves us all with an infinite love—that's the only way He can love. But it's different for everybody.

Now, you say, "Well, I've heard God is a jealous God. What does that mean?" Well, it's kind of a bad word for an attribute of God. God knows what is for your good, and so if you love the world or yourself more than Him, He knows it will destroy you, and so He will do everything in His power to detach you from this thing, because He knows that only in loving Him can you arrive at ultimate happiness. So, His jealousy does not create evil, it creates good, and the jealousy we speak of is evil. God has a love of preference for us by the very fact you've been created, and now He wants you to prefer Him. That's the first commandment: you shall love the Lord your God with your whole heart, whole mind, whole soul, and all of your strength.

This kind of jealousy created anger, hatred, murder, and lies. If you have any of that jealousy in your heart, any of that envy that makes you so miserable inside and makes your family miserable, so suspicious, if you're Catholic, go to Confession this week. Will you do that? Say, "Father, I'm guilty of jealousy. I want to overcome myself; I want to live in peace.

I want everyone around me to have whatever God wants to give them." You know a good way to get rid of jealousy? The Lord said to Cain, "You have to master this." The good way to master jealousy is to praise God for all the things you're jealous of. Here's Mrs. Smith, and she's got this fantastic home, and so you envy that. You say, "Somehow, that should have been mine," or you drive your husband crazy trying to arrive at that position. Say, "Lord, I thank You with all my heart for all the gifts other people have that I don't have." You know what? You get the merit of all those gifts without having them.

In this morning's Gospel, we learned that he who accepts the holy man or prophet because he is holy or because he's a prophet gets a prophet's reward. So, what I need to do is thank God for the wonders He does in everybody else's life. I get as much merit as they get without doing a thing. Isn't God generous? If I see a holy priest, I can say, "Lord, I thank you for this holy priest." I get all the merit he worked for. God is so generous, He doesn't want us to be so petty, so small.

Let's go on and see the results of not only Cain's disobedience, but his lack of repentance. You see what we do to ourselves?

Well, after Cain had said, "Am I my brother's keeper?" the Lord said, "*What have you done? Listen,*" He said, "*to the sound of your brother's blood crying out to me from the ground. Now be accursed, driven from the ground that has opened its mouth to receive your brother's blood at your hands. When you till the ground, it shall no longer yield you any of its produce. You shall be a fugitive and a wanderer over the earth.*"

And Cain was devastated. He said, "*My punishment is greater than I can bear. See! Today you drive me from this ground. I must hide from you, and be a fugitive and a wanderer over the earth. Whoever comes across me will kill me!*" "*Very well, then,*" Yahweh replied, "*If anyone kills Cain, sevenfold vengeance shall be taken for him.*" So,

Yahweh put a mark on Cain to prevent whoever might come across him from striking him down. Now, you say that mark was evil. No, it was a sign of protection, which means *hands off.* Do you realize, my friends, what Jesus has done for us? Do you realize how God had to treat a very primitive, hard, stiff-necked, stubborn people? He had to deal hard. Do you realize what Jesus has done for us? He has brought down the Father's mercy in such a wondrous way that we take it for granted. People sin, and they're not even afraid. They do have all kinds of terrible things, they have no fear of God in their heart, and you wonder today why it is that after Jesus did so much, especially the Eucharist, why we still have to struggle so hard. I think it's because we're indifferent to God's gifts.

We're so self-oriented. Did you notice Cain never said, "Lord Yahweh, I am so sorry I offended You. I'm so sorry I killed my brother"? He said, "I can't bear this punishment." It's all self-oriented. "They're gonna come after me." That's all he thinks of. He didn't care about his brother; he's now worried somebody is going to kill him. You see what sin does? If you say, "When you sin, you don't hurt anybody," you're badly mistaken. Because you see sin here taking Cain and drawing him down further and further and further, with God speaking to him right over his head. This is a fine example of the horror of sin. Some of the saints like the Curé of Ars, Don Bosco, Catherine of Siena, Angela of Foligno, Padre Pio — some of those great saints had such a horror of sin that they would say over and over, "I would rather die than commit one sin." They knew what it did to the soul.

So, let's go on. It says here that Cain had intercourse with his wife, and she conceived and gave birth to Enoch. And this is beautiful. He became a builder of a town and gave the town the name of his son, Enoch.

You go all through, and you find that they became tent dwellers, farmers, they became metal workers. And you find God helping all of them with more talents and more gifts and more reasons to change, to improve, and you find them going the other direction over and over and over again. You and I, though we seem to fall many, many times, we should never be discouraged. God hounds us. He is just constantly after us, He's after us every day. He runs after us. He inspires you. Never, never give up. You can't read this without realizing that although these people hurt the Lord, and they have done terrible things, He's constantly running after them, giving grace upon grace, talent upon talent. And though some of them didn't take advantage, many did. You and I, as we go through this lesson, need to understand that the first part of this lesson is to learn how terrible jealousy is. How it can twist our minds and our hearts and make everybody around us miserable. The second part, we learned that although we are punished by God — sometimes just by the fact that we feel the way we feel, we bring on our own punishment — God is constantly hounding us, telling us how much He loves us, giving us everything we need to survive, to know Him, to love Him, to be repentant.

We're going to go to Genesis 6. I'm going to look at Noah. The title of this chapter is the "Corruption of Mankind," and it isn't something we like to look at, but it seems like today is one of those days when we're going to look at a lot of things that we don't like to look at it. That's good and healthy because as a religious, every Sunday I look back over the week and say, "Well, Angelica, you weren't too hot in some areas." So, you look at yourself, as objectively as you can, and say, "Well, I think I could improve this next week." Be honest, that's all. And that's what we're doing here. We're not trying to scare you to death.

So, it says here: *Yahweh saw that the wickedness of man was great on the earth, and that the thoughts in his heart fashioned nothing but wickedness all day long.* That's sad. And it says, *Yahweh regretted having made man on the earth.* We have to look at that because God really can't regret anything. And when we regret, we mean we're sorry we did something. But God knows ahead of time; He knew from the time He created Adam and Eve everything that would happen to the end of time, to everybody and everyone who might have been.

What it means here is that He was so grieved at our reaction, our indifference, the disobedience, us thinking what an awesome thing it was to desire to know the difference between good and evil. And so, it says His heart was grieved. In the Catholic Church, we have a great, beautiful devotion called the Sacred Heart of Jesus, and some people have found fault with that, saying, "Well, you can't adore an organ." Well, you don't adore an organ, you adore the love of Jesus that's symbolized by a heart. What is Valentine's Day, except lots of hearts running around? It symbolizes: *I love you, and you love me.* So, the heart is the seat of our emotions. If you're excited, it beats fast. If you're angry, it beats fast. If you're peaceful, it beats slower. So, your emotions affect your heart. So, when we speak of love or any other emotion, we look at the heart. In fact, they can tell whether you're lying by the way your heart is — whether your heart beats faster. So, when we say His heart was grieved, we see the same thing that the Lord said to Margaret Mary when He showed her His heart, and He said, "Behold, this heart that has so loved man and is loved so little in return."

If we only knew we grieved the Lord! Because He knows what we might be, He knows what we could be, and He doesn't want us to just throw our lives away as if they were nothing. You know, a lot of you young men and women out there may be on drugs tonight, and you've lived it up, you've lived it all. And you're sad, you're depressed, and suicide seems to kind of creep in. Don't. *Don't.* God has made you great, God has made you beautiful. God has made you someone special, and I think if we were to just say we're sorry, God forgives and forgets, and all your sins and all your weaknesses are like a little drop in the ocean of His mercy. And I'm afraid as we read here about Noah, we have to understand that when we talk about this flood—what did the flood do but wash away our sins off the face of the earth? Well, the flood of God's grace is waiting for you at Confession at this moment. Some of you haven't been to Confession for years, and you carry on your shoulders the burden of past sins that is so heavy. That keeps you from having peace, keeps you from having love, keeps you from everything that is enjoyable in this earth because you wake up with it, and you go to bed with it, and you think about it during the day, and your life is just hounded by something in the past. See, what the flood did here is renew, to give mankind another chance, and that's what God wants to do with some of you tonight. Those of you that don't have this great Sacrament of Reconciliation, kneel down right now in your living room, and just say, "Lord God, I'm sorry for all my sins. Come into my heart, wash away all my sins. Wash away all this weakness I have. Heal me, give me grace, give me power, give me love." I want you to keep that in mind when we look at God's infinite love and mercy. That although there was so much evil in the world, He had mercy. He kept it going. He said Noah was a good man. A man of integrity, honesty. And he walked with God. That's the third time. We heard Adam and Eve walked with God, and Enoch walked with God.

Now, we find that Noah walked with God. What does it mean to walk with God? Seems to me they were aware of God's presence, and this is all before Moses; there wasn't a law to follow. No, there were no commandments yet. There was nothing. So, they walked with God, meaning they were aware of His presence, and they did everything knowing they were in the presence of God, and sometimes when you're tempted, it might be nice for you to think of that. With God standing right here before me, do I really want to do this? You can't cover yourself with darkness, because God sees in the dark. So, sometimes when the temptation is so strong, and you think you're going to fall, think of the presence of God around you. Maybe that'll help you.

He saw the earth was corrupt and filled with violence, and He said to Noah, "*The end has come for all things of flesh, and I have decided this because the earth is full of violence of man's making and I will efface them from the earth. Make an ark for yourself of resinous wood. Make it with reeds, and line it with pitch inside and out. And this is how to make it.*"

God gives instructions to Noah on how to make a boat, how to make the roof, put a door on the high side, and three decks. Now, you've got to realize what this meant. It took an enormously long time to build this boat. Can you imagine a neighbor of yours building a boat, and I mean, this thing gets bigger and bigger and bigger and bigger every day, and it gets taller and taller and taller, and all of a sudden in your backyard, you see all these animals collecting? Now, if you wouldn't think he was one kind of wacko because he keeps talking about a flood and he's building a boat on dry land, and you're saying, "You gotta be crazy." And I'll bet his wife gave him a fit, and she was saying, "Do you realize what the neighbors are saying about you?" He goes on his way, getting another squirrel, another bird. And he tells his son, "You gotta help me with this boat." Well, in those days, you obeyed. So, they're running around, they're cutting down trees, they're cutting them up, they're putting them on for what? And it isn't like it happens in three, four weeks, three, four months, a year. Generations come and go, and Noah is still building his ark. Must have been the joke of the world.

You can imagine somebody saying, "Hey, you hear about this guy building an ark on dry land? I mean, he was building it when my grandma was born." Well, the longer he lived and the longer it took to build the ark, it got to be old. So, outside of ridicule, nobody paid attention to Noah. Now, you gotta look at Noah. Man, did he go out and catch the animals? Did he buy them? I mean, how much did pigeons cost? And how did he make a living while he was making this boat? You say, "Well, Mother, it was symbolic." I don't care what it was, symbolic or real. What am I supposed to be learning? Don't give me this exegesis business that I'm supposed to say, "Well, it was just a story." It doesn't matter if it's a story, the message is what's important. Because in your life, in my life, God asks us sometimes to do some rather ridiculous things that other people don't understand, like why should you be chaste when everybody around you is being immoral and having a good time at it—or at least they think they are—and this goes on and on. Why should we believe the messages from Fátima or Medjugorje or anywhere else? I mean, after they've been telling us this for years, and nothing has happened … then one day, *boom.*

You realize it must have rained a lot during all those years, and every time it rained, Noah must have thought, "This is it, get in the ark!" Three hours later, it was dry and sunshine, and everybody was going, "Oh, ha ha!" But you know, there came a day when it rained and never stopped, and it rained and rained and rained. And the first thing you know, the boat began to lift. Well, I'm a great believer in Our Lady of Fátima, and she warned us that if we didn't pray and if we didn't say the Rosary, if we didn't do all those things, then we would suffer the same consequences.

Here's Cain and Abel. The beginning of good and evil. Evil went out and got worse as century passed century. But in the midst of all this violence and evil in the world, there was a man who walked with God, and he saved mankind because he listened and was obedient. And when the world was also in the same predicament, when man no longer cared for his neighbor, the Father sent His Son. And another flood occurred. Only this was a flood of grace through His Precious Blood, and it once again washed away all our sins.

So, Cain and Abel teach us why it happened. Noah teaches us of God's mercy, His love, His compassion, and how He turns all things into good. So, I want you to remember that no matter how sinful you are, just throw yourself in the ocean of God's mercy, and know that in the end, no matter how evil things are around you, God will triumph. The power within you is greater than any power outside of you. The Lord God loves you as if no one else existed. We must overcome ourselves; we have the grace to be like Jesus, we have the grace to stand tall against our peers, against the flesh, against the enemy. You and I are sons of God with a great dignity that nothing but sin can take away from us.

So, I hope you've learned a lot from these two incidents in the beginning of our salvation history. Remember, no matter what you read in Scripture, it's happening today. Let us learn from the past, so that our present may be fruitful and our future peaceful. We hope you enjoy these lessons.

FOUR

Genesis Chapters 11 & 12

So often when you read the Bible, you're just looking for inspiration, something that's going to help you for the present moment, maybe get over some tragedy, endure some cross. But we've got to use the Scriptures for our spiritual life. It's a growth. It's got to lead you, and you've got to be able to really compare your situation, your life with something that has happened, and many, many times, you get the solution to your problems. Now, you say, "Well, isn't that kind of like fundamentalism?" Well, there's nothing wrong with taking the Bible literally, except you just can't take it *all* literally.

For example, the Lord says we should honor our father and our mother—it's a commandment—and yet in another place, He said, "He who does not hate father and mother for My sake cannot enter the Kingdom." Now, we have to interpret that, otherwise it's a contradiction. So you can't take the literal meaning; you've got to interpret. What does it mean? It means preference. The word *hate* there means you don't prefer everything that is dearest to you—family, friends, land, positions, your very self—God has to be preferred to all of that.

So, you have to understand that you can't take every dot and every comma and every colon as literal. And yet you do have to take some things as literal—the Commandments we must take literally. So, I think it's impossible, really, to be a total fundamentalist without really tripping yourself up. And it's impossible *not* to be a fundamentalist in some areas; for example, the Catholic Church takes the Eucharist in a very literal fundamental sense. We take John 6, we take the Eucharist, we take the Mass literally. We don't take the vine and the branches literally because we know it's depicting a dependence upon the Lord, so I am not a branch, and Jesus is not some kind of a little, thin vine. It's a symbol. The fig tree was a symbol. That's why you need the Church to define for you what to take literally and what to take as symbolic and what to take as mystical and what to take as something that's a lesson, a parable.

And you can't know it all. If any one person thinks they know it all, then I would have to question that, because we just don't have the mind, the education—we just don't, none of us do. You can have twenty-five doctorates, you still wouldn't know it all because when you're reading the Word of God, you need the Spirit of God. Only the Spirit of God penetrates the Word of God.

I'd like you to turn to Genesis 11. It's a very short part here I want to take. I think it depicts a lot of what's happening today, and I want you to see what God did about it and then ask yourself a question: Will He do the same to us?

Let's look at it. It says: *Throughout the earth, men spoke the same language, with the same vocabulary.* And that would be great, I think. You know, you wouldn't have to worry about all these languages. So, they move eastward, but they had a plan. You see, this common bond—instead of making them more loving, more brotherly, more of a family—it began to build up their pride.

Pride is so terrible. And so, they said, "*Come let us make bricks and bake them in the fire....*

Let us build ourselves a town and a tower with its top reaching heaven." And you say, "Well, we've got an awful lot of skyscrapers," but they don't scrape any skies, you know that. So, you have buildings like the Empire State Building that's hundreds and some stories, the Sears Tower that's one hundred and some stories, and there's just so high you can go. So, you say, "Well, what's the difference between the Sears Tower or the Empire State Building or all these other tall, tall, tall buildings—what's the difference between them and the Tower of Babel?" I really don't know. Maybe there isn't much difference. But I think the reason for all these buildings we have today is not so much pride—maybe it is—but it is office space, more space, whatever. But here it says: *"Let us make a name for ourselves so that we may not be scattered about the whole earth."* It was an act of pride. They wanted to be great. This tower had really little purpose except to glorify the people who built it, so pride had come to the sons of men; they were all a single people with a single language, and you see their pride had made them think there was just nothing too hard for them to do.

You know, it's amazing how they could be proud with the primitive situation they were in. Primitive. And we're the same way today. We're so proud of our technology, we're so proud of all the things that we put up into the sky and over, all the satellites and all the things that we do, all the computers and the robots and everything, we're so proud of that, that we're so advanced. Yet one hundred years from now, we may look like peanuts. The very thing we take pride in today, the very thing that would make you lose your soul, the next generation will laugh at you. Laugh, because they will say, "Can you imagine it took all these tons of fuel to get up out of the atmosphere, to go around the universe or the world?" My grandmother would have never believed if I had said to her one time, "Grandma, there'll be men on the moon, and you're gonna be able to look at an instrument, a mechanical electronic instrument, and it's gonna give you a picture we call television."

She'd laugh at me. But just as she would have laughed at me, future generations may laugh at us. So, the very thing that's so attractive to you, that you put your whole heart and soul and mind and body into, may be looked upon as primitive. And so, we learned that pride is a very serious sin, because it has only self in view, it's very shortsighted.

Now, there's such a thing as good pride. I can take pride in my work because I do it well. But that kind of pride isn't really pride, it's a desire to do well for the person you work for, for the Lord God, and for yourself. So, this kind of pride is a wholesome thing, but the kind of pride we read about in the Tower of Babel, the kind of pride we see today is "I will not worship, I will not even bow to the Lord God." Now, that kind of pride, my friend, is very serious. When you know something is sinful—or if you're a teacher and you don't teach something that is sinful as sinful—then you become the occasion of other people committing a sin, thinking it's right. I think it's one of the saddest things in the world today. You get so many people, even ministers, that approve abortion, that approve all the things that are sinful, and it's a sin against God, against His Commandments, against the teachings of His Church. And they teach them as right. We need to pray for people like that because all the people they are teaching, they just go into a sinner condition and a sinner state in life, thinking it's right. It's such deception.

And these people in the Tower of Babel were building that tower. They wanted to be great, they wanted men to know they were great, and they didn't want anybody else around. "There's nothing hard for us. There's nothing we can't do." Well, the Lord Yahweh says, "*Let us go down and confuse their language on*

the spot so that they can no longer understand one another." Well, did
the Lord really come down and just confuse their language?
Well, I'm certain He did. But you know what else I think He
confused? I think they began to squabble about the height.
About the depth. About the bricks. About the mortar. All
these things they got so confused. And then when they started
to talk, they couldn't understand each other, they couldn't
understand each other's spirit, they couldn't understand each
other's ways anymore. They were no longer one mind.

"We will make a name for ourselves." It wasn't *ourselves*
anymore, it was a name for *me*, and once you begin to say, "I
wanna do this for me," and you knock everybody else out of
the box who were once your family, you become an individual
who thinks of nothing but what affects you. What you like
and what you don't like and how everybody else is wrong
but you're right. Once you get into this Tower of Babel, your
language is going to be confused. Why? Nobody's going to
understand you. Some of you parents don't understand your
kids, and the kids don't understand you. You're speaking the
same language, but nobody understands. You're living in a
Tower of Babel, because the essence of our life today is, "I will
not serve, I want my freedom." But what is the freedom that
people want today? It's the same freedom that people wanted
then. The freedom to sin without guilt.

Well, I've got to ask myself a question. I hope you ask yourself this question. Will the Lord God look upon us today as
He did then? Since we're doing the same thing, we live in the
days of the Tower of Babel. We built bigger and bigger buildings and greater and greater satellites. It is only for the honor
and glory of man. We will not serve. We shall make a name
for ourselves. Well, think about that, huh? And let's pray that
the Lord God doesn't have to scatter us as He scattered them.

We've been talking about the Tower of Babel and how pride led them to want to build. And we learned that there's a similarity today, and as much as we want to build, we want to be great, we want to have a name for all centuries to come. We want the right to sin without guilt, and so we pattern the gospel, we pattern the Commandments to meet everyday permissiveness. You could say what you want, but that's the way it is. So, we know now what happened at the Tower of Babel, the confusion of mind, the confusion of heart, the confusion is here today. Our Catholics, they're confused. "What do I believe?" This one is saying this. This one is saying that. I've heard this rule. I've heard that regulation. They're all different. It's a Tower of Babel.

And it's in society. People get caught robbing, they commit the most terrible crimes, and you find they get free, and instead the policeman is arrested, or the policeman is at fault. There's such confusion in the world today. Isn't that a Tower of Babel? Then if we can admit it is, and believe me, it doesn't take me long to admit it, is it not the same thing? Have we also not yielded to the sin of pride—that is, wanting to be like the Most High?

Well, let's pass over to Genesis 12 and see another man who lived in perilous times as you and I do. Very similar times, in fact. Not all the modern gadgets and technology and knowledge, but I'm talking about spirit, I'm talking about your interior attitudes and life. They may have used arrows made out of stone, whatever, but it's this attitude that was very similar to us. We've made tremendous advances in electronics and technology and science, but we've gone backward inside. So, I want to give you an example now of a man who did not succumb to his times.

Well, the Lord God Yahweh appeared to Abram.[1] Now, his name at this point was Abram. He said, "*Leave your country, your family, your father's house for the land I will show you.*" It's interesting, we say this when a sister gets professed, when she takes her vows in our religious order. But He asked him to do all of these things before he even saw the land He was going to give. The very first words that the Lord Yahweh spoke to Abram were words of faith, where he had to take that unknown step. He said, "I *will* show you." He didn't say, "Here it is. See what I'm giving you?" This meant they had to take that leap forward before the Lord showed him this land.

Now, you're going to ask, "How do you know it was the Lord Yahweh? How did he know it was the Lord God?" Well, I think he would have had to be awful sure. Just the same way you're sure today. I think you're pretty sure when your own voice is talking to you, when you're talking to yourself, and when the Lord God speaks to your heart. This could have been an audible voice that Abram heard or could have been some very definite inspiration of thought that goes into our mind, just very much like the angels speak. The vocal-cord type of speech is not the only way to speak, and you don't always speak through your vocal cords.

How is it sometimes that you know how a person feels, and they haven't said a word? How is it sometimes your child walks through the door, and you know he's not feeling well? He hasn't said a word. How is it your husband comes home, you know he's had a bad day, and he hasn't said a word? There are things you know. There are other ways of speaking. So, we're not too sure. I would have thought in my own mind that this

---

[1] Mother Angelica seems to use the name Abram and Abraham interchangeabley. God changed Abram's name to Abraham in Gen. 17:5.

is a rather audible voice that he heard with his physical ears, and then I think when you hear the voice of your Creator, the One from Whom you came forth, you know the voice. He said, "*I will make you a great nation; I will bless you and make your name so famous that it will be used as a blessing.*" So, men from then on would say, "I bless you. May the blessings of Abram be upon you."

Well, here's a paragraph here that is phenomenal. You have to ask yourself, since we've been talking about pride, what kept Abram from getting so puffed up? Oh, we're going to learn that as we go along. The uncertainty of his walk certainly worked wonders for his pride.

Because the Lord said, "*I will bless those who bless you. I will curse those who slight you. All the tribes of the earth shall bless themselves by you.*" Now, we see the beginnings of faith. You say, "Well, was Abraham uncertain?" No, he was certain of what he heard. He was not certain how it was to be carried out, and that was his point of humility. You could say to me something very nice, but if it is so far in the future, and I'm in a precarious position at this point, I could care less about your wonderful prophecy because I'm living in a situation now that's not too wonderful. And so, God gave him that balance, the balance of faith that says, "I will give you this, and I will make you great." There he was in the middle of the desert in a tent. Nothing. No children, nothing. He had a wife, he had a few cattle, had to work hard to get a cup of water. That was his point of humility. It's when you begin to possess what your heart has and when that future goal becomes so obsessed in your heart and mind that pride grows. It's like a fungus.

Well, he didn't have that. Thank God. The uncertainty. And the certainty of faith. The positive and the negative. The positive that God said it: "I heard Him." The negative: "Where is this land? Why would anybody use my name for a blessing?" He must have asked himself that question. "I don't even have children." So, Abram went as Yahweh told him. Now, we find something else about the faith — immediate action. Immediate action to carry out what is at present unseen. To carry out immediately that which you do not see, that you're not sure of. That's faith.

Abram was seventy-five years old when he left Haran. Now, you've got to look back and look at the prophecy. Here is a man that's seventy-five years old, and the Lord God said he will be so famous that his name will be used for a blessing and that he's got to leave this place. Had he been a proud man, he would have used his reason and said, "That's ridiculous, I'm seventy-five years old, I'm on my last leg, where am I going to travel? Where am I going into uncertain land, and who wants it in the first place?" See, reason could have very easily talked him out of it. Seventy-five years old.

Now, we see another aspect of faith. You see that these people at the Tower of Babel didn't even get close to finishing. They were only thinking of themselves, they wanted their own honor and glory, they wanted something certain, they wanted power. But Abraham was willing to leave his father, his home, security, contentment at seventy-five. For what? *He took his wife Sarai, his nephew Lot; all the possessions they had amassed and the people they had acquired in Haran. And they set off for the land of Canaan.* Think about that a minute, will you? Just imagine what it means in your life. Make a choice tonight. Where are you? Are you with the Tower of Babel people who have only one thought: me, myself, and I? Or are you with Abram, listening to the Lord God in His Commandments, His Church, and saying, "I go an uncertain way, but my Lord leads me."

One thought you might have had is: "Well, you know when Jesus called the disciples, He said, 'I want to send you out without scrip or shoes or coppers in your purses—nothing. Go.' Well, we see Abraham here, he's taking his life, he's taking the people he accumulated, the animals, sheep, goats, whatever—he takes everything, even his nephew." Well, it's a mistake, first of all, to relegate the New Testament to the Old. By the very fact that it's new, God demanded more, because He had sent His Son. Once He sent His Son, you and I can see the Body and Blood, Soul, and Divinity. Then more is demanded. Here we're talking about the beginning of salvation history, the very beginnings where God could go just so high and demand just so much. Because we're talking about a primitive tribal people that had one thought: themselves. They had some idea through tradition, through word of mouth that there was an Adam and an Eve, that there was the Lord God. But they all had gods. There were so many. Which one was the true God? And this is another marvelous thing about Abram, that he was able to discern the true God.

Are you able to discern the true God today? Are you able to discern which God you follow? Do you follow the god of lust in the flesh and drink and drunkenness, permissiveness, the god of total freedom that's so independent that no one can tell you anything, without discipline? Is that the god you follow? Of all the gods that are presented to you today, which god do you follow? The God Who asked for everything, no scrip, no shoes, and nothing in your purses? Or the god who gives you everything in this life, cuts you off from eternity? Permissiveness, lies, cheating—they're not gods, they're idols.

So, Abram passed through the land as far as Sichem, and the Lord God appeared to him again, and He said, again an encouraging word to a man who is seventy-five: "*It is to your descendants that I will give this land.*" Now, we have two problems as far as common sense is concerned. Common sense says, "Wait a minute, I'm seventy-five. My wife can't even have children. And now You're telling me to leave my father, my home, my land for something my kids (that I don't have) are going to possess?" That's an ordinary common reason. But you see, faith rises above all this. Because Abraham so believed the voice of God, he built there an altar to Yahweh. He built an altar there as a memorial that at this spot, this place, the Lord God promised him descendants that would be blessed.

Well, problems began to arise. There are times in our life when we just reach great heights of faith, I mean, they just seem to bubble up. And you're so sure of everything. And you go your way. You've heard the Lord; you responded. You see Him acting in your life. Everything seems to be falling in place. You know what happened? *A famine came to the land, and Abraham went to Egypt to stay there for the time, since the land was hard pressed by the famine.* What a blow! What a tremendous blow to your ego, to your whole life. You wonder how he kept humble? Well, here is a voice Who's giving him the moon. He's seventy-five, and now a famine wipes out everybody. Do you see how faith pushes you beyond human endurance sometimes?

Now, he goes into Egypt, and Abram was a smart man. He looked at his wife, and she was a very beautiful woman. So, he realized that something is about to occur, and he said, "Look, you're a beautiful woman," but she must have been sixty-five at least. If he was seventy-five, and she was ten years younger; so here's a sixty-five-year-old woman that was very beautiful. So, he said, "When the Egyptians see you, they're gonna say, 'Oh, here's a beautiful woman.'" He said, "Just tell them you're my sister, so that they may treat me well because of you and spare my life out of regard for you." You say that's an outright lie. Again, you've got to understand, though, it wasn't a lie; it's only a lie by our standards today. This is a lie according to the New Testament. In those days, that was permissible. You're talking about times that were primitive.

Now, I remember the old cars—a Ford. I think my uncle got one once, and it was really old. Model T, they called them. My mother told me that my father broke his arm trying to crank one of these things. Well, it would be ridiculous for me to try to use one of these things today when I've got big cars. Do you understand? So, you're doing the same thing, you just can't bring the New Testament into the Old, you've got to put yourself in the times of the day. Now, in today's world, we lie because our morals have deteriorated. It would be extremely wrong today because after Jesus came, He gave us light to see how wrong these things are, and He says, "No, no, no, you can't do that."

But as far as Abraham's day, he owned people, there were slaves, there were enemies that you could kill, or your own slaves you could kill. You are living in a time, so keep yourself in the time, but the difference is you cannot imitate the time, you must get the message for you at this time, in this age in the enlightenment that you have. People say, "Well, Abraham did it, so I could do it." Oh, no, you can't. The Ten Commandments weren't even known at this time. There were no Ten Commandments in Abram's time. So, you're talking about progression of faith, progression of knowledge of God, progression of salvation history.

Some of you Scripture scholars out there are going to say, "Now, wait a minute, Mother. Sarah *was* Abram's half sister." I don't care if she was his uncle. She's still his wife. Sarah was Abram's wife. Unfortunately, I guess in those days, it didn't matter because there weren't that many people around, so you could marry your relative. At this point, she was his wife.

Well, the Egyptians indeed saw the woman, that she was very beautiful, and so *when Pharaoh's officials saw her, they sang her praises to Pharaoh and the woman was taken into Pharaoh's palace. He treated Abram well because of her, and he received oxen, donkeys, men and women slaves, she-donkeys and camels.* I mean, the man got wealthy overnight. But see, this is a very strange story because Pharaoh, who was deceived, was the poor guy afflicted. *Yahweh inflicted severe plagues on Pharoah and his whole household because of Abram's wife.* So, Pharaoh got suspicious. *He summoned Abram and said, "What is this you have done to me? Why didn't you tell me she was your wife? Why did you say, 'She's my sister,' so that I took her for my wife?* Now, here she is. Get out of here!"

Even though this was a primitive society, it was still wrong. God was giving Abram light, and Pharaoh too, and so He made it known that this was Abram's wife. There is no beating around the bush with the Lord. So, Pharaoh even gave men to him to escort him to the border. "I wanna be sure you're out of here."

You see a loving Father, God, teaching His people very slowly, very lovingly, and sometimes very hard. Some people say, "Well, I find the Old Testament extremely hard." Well, you're talking to people who don't know their right hand from their left hand. And sometimes, we all, even today, learn hard. How many lessons have you learned the 'hard way'? It's a very common expression: "I learned everything the 'hard way.'" What is the hard way? It always entails some kind of pain, some kind of distress. Sometimes many mistakes.

Now, Abraham was human. He had great faith; he was a man who would respond to Yahweh immediately. But he was human, and he wanted to protect his life and his possessions. And in those days, there was no knowledge of commandments.

He just did what he thought the present moment required. So, he took his wife, his cattle (which increased), his slaves (which increased), and left. Took Lot with him. And it says Abram, who was at this time a very rich man with livestock and silver and gold, went to Bethel and pitched his tent, and that was the place, if you remember, where the Lord God told him his descendants would receive all these blessings, and he went to that altar and invoked the name of Yahweh.

So, we see so far that struggle between our human nature and wanting to be like God, our sinner condition, and the ease with which we can succumb to that sinner condition. And you have to admit that hasn't changed much in that area and will probably never change in that area that much. You say, "Well, what did the Lord do, then, when He came and redeemed us?" He gave you what Abram didn't have. He gave you His own Son. He gave you redemption, and He gave you the power and the light and the knowledge to know how to live and how to please Him. You see, the Lord used something that Abraham did wrong—a lie. He was very displeased with that lie, and I'm sure that Abram's humility grew very deep at that moment because he learned something that he didn't know before, that a lie is displeasing to God. And so, it was important for him first to learn the lesson. The fact that he accumulated so much more wealth while he was there was something God permitted to happen for the things He wanted him to do, but He didn't ordain it.

But there's no way Pharaoh would not have plunged all kinds of wealth on him just to get rid of him. Wealth was something that just kind of plunked in his lap. This wasn't something he did on purpose to get it. He lied to save his own life, and probably his wife, and all his slaves. But Pharaoh learned that he lied. So, he learned what happens when you lie.

And Pharaoh made reparation for it, for the fault he committed by taking another man's wife. He gave Abram everything he needed, escorted him out, and then you come to the point where you just can't explain it. It was a bad mistake. Abraham managed somehow to get wealthy, but that doesn't take away the mistake at all. What we have to understand here is that, when you make mistakes that are sinful mistakes, you can be assured that, although they may be displeasing to God and hurt your soul, God in His infinite love somehow will bring great good out of it. We see this in Abram. We see this in the beginning, as people were created by God and lost the concept of the Lord Yahweh. So, He began to teach them. He began to manifest Himself to them by teaching them, by their mistakes. That's how you and I learn.

FIVE

Genesis Chapters 13–15

We talked about Abraham in the previous chapter and discussed the Lord's first promise to him. The first time, He promised him a son. And then we find that because of a famine, he has to go to Egypt. Well, now we're going to see the aspects of Abraham's life that make us consider Abraham as the man of faith—the example. In fact, the Lord Himself said his name would be used as a blessing and anyone who cursed Abraham would be cursed in return. So, you know, you can hardly get any higher than that. But with the faith that Abraham had, there were tremendous difficulties.

See, today we think faith takes away all your difficulties, that if you have faith, you're going to be healthy, wealthy, and wise. It's just not realistic. You're going to have problems. And even with all his faith, he had problems, but he had his faith that kept him persevering and believing. So many today have the kind of faith that God has to just come up and answer every prayer, do everything you want, take all your aches and pains away, give you all kinds of money and everything else—the abundant life.

That's not abundant life. The abundant life is faith. And now we're going to see Abraham come up against some new difficulties. Now we're going to see how faith not only made him persevere, but also how faith was the basis of his generosity and gentleness; we don't often think of faith being a basis for generosity and gentleness. You have to really believe in an afterlife, in Jesus and the Lord God, for you and me today to be generous, to be gentle, because there's so much violence, so much selfishness. So, as we look back into the Old Testament and the spirituality there, we're going to find that it's pretty similar to what God demands of us today. It's so similar that it's almost like the New Testament is kind of invisible and visible in the life of Abraham.

Now, let's go to Genesis 13, and we're going to start as we always do, in the name of the one God—Father, Son, and Holy Spirit. So, there's one God, three Divine Persons in one God. Now, it says: *From Egypt Abram returned with his wife and all he possessed and Lot with him,* his nephew.

By this time, Abraham is a very rich man with the livestock. He had silver, he had gold. So, he pitched his tent between Bethel and Ai, and that's the very place he was before he went to Egypt, and he built an altar there to the Lord God. Now, here comes just ordinary, plain human nature. The very same thing you have—the very same thing you have in your family and your relationships with your relatives, with your neighbors, with those you work with—is exactly what Abraham had. I want you to see how Abraham's faith led him and affected his virtue level. He believed in what the Father said to him. He believed enough to make it affect his entire daily moment-to-moment life.

For example, *Lot, who was traveling with Abram, had flocks and cattle of his own, and he had tents too. But the land was not sufficient to accommodate them both at once, for they had too many possessions to be able to live together.* You see what begins to happen. Well, we'll see. *A dispute broke out between the herdsmen of Abram's livestock and those of Lot's.* So, they began the good, old family feud. Arguments. The servants quarreling with one another, saying, "You've got our sheep and our cattle." Then they said, "No, no, this is *our* cattle. You're taking too much water, you're not leaving us enough water, you're not leaving us enough feed." And jealousies and hatred began to brew. And so, Lot, and Abraham also, I would imagine, began to look at each other with a little anger because their servants were quarreling.

Now, it's significant that Abram went to Lot. Lot did not go to Abram. Lot, if I have any knowledge of Lot, probably agreed with his herdsmen that Abraham's herdsmen were just taking too much. So, Abraham's faith that we talk about so much has led him to do something beautifully unselfish. He gently says, "*Let there be no dispute between me and you, nor between my herdsmen and yours, for we are brothers.*" Do you realize, my friends, if you're having difficulty in your relationships, with your relatives and family, just remember this one sentence this evening if you remember nothing more than that.

It was Abraham's faith that made him say, "Hey, wait a minute, I don't wanna fight with you. I don't want my servants to fight with your servants. I mean, we're brothers." Some of you, I bet, you people in our audience have brothers and sisters, mothers and fathers, that haven't spoken to each other in a long time.

Have you ever thought this isn't right? We're brothers, we're sisters, we're relatives. We're friends. It's not right. Go to them first. That's what Abraham did. This is the type of faith this man had. He went first; he didn't wait for Lot and say, "Well, after all, I'm the elder and I'm the uncle. He's only a nephew, and I have much more riches than he, as I have more herds, more gold, more silver. This kid has a few oxen." Lot obviously was not wealthy.

So, when you look at it the way we look at things today, I think Abram should have waited for Lot to come along and do nothing but apologize. But you see, that isn't what Abram did. And many of you have held grudges and resentments for years over that very same principle. "Well, let him come to me. I didn't do anything to him. Let him come to me. Why should I go to him?"

Well, let's see what happened. Abram said, "*Is not the whole land open before to you? Part company with me. If you take the left, I will take the right. If you take the right, I will go left.*" Now, here is the virtue of prudence. Here's Abram. He knows. I mean, practical, common sense tells Abram that this dispute is not going to be settled except if they separate, because there're too many people involved. There may have been hundreds of herdsmen and thousands of cattle, I mean, there's just so much you can do. So, he said, "Let's not argue. I mean, if being together like this is just creating all these problems, look at the land around you. And if you wanna go right, I'll go left. If you wanna go left, I'll go right."

Now we see in Abraham some other fruit of faith. And that is a tremendous amount of humility. Do you realize what humility it took? Not only did he go to Lot first, but he allowed Lot to make the first choice. I mean, there was no reason for him to do that. You know, later on, when the Lord came among us, He said to go that extra mile. But you can see Abram going that extra mile. He went an extra fifty miles, because he should have said to him, "Look, I am the elder, I am the one who has most, so I'll pick and you have what's left." That would have made common sense today. But now we talk about a man who is a man of faith, so you're beginning to see, I hope, that faith is more than just a belief or confidence that God's going to give you what you want—that's sometimes the only kind of faith you hear about today. The faith that says to believe that you're going to get it, and you're going to get it. Well, there're a lot of things you believe you're going to get that you don't get because they're not good for you. You can't have that much pride to think that every single thing you pray for is positively, absolutely for your good. You've gotta be kidding if you think that. We don't have enough light, we don't see the future, we don't know really — we only think we know — what's for our good.

Now, you see, when we admire Abram, you have to know what you're admiring. His gentleness, his perseverance, and now his humility are all an effect of his faith. Well, let's see if we can read Lot a little bit.

Looking around, Lot saw all the Jordan plain irrigated everywhere. He looked at it, all green, grass and trees and shrubs and fruit trees and fig trees. I mean, it was all irrigated. And it says: *This was before Yahweh destroyed Sodom and Gomorrah. It was like the garden of Yahweh or the land of Egypt, as far as Zoar.* And guess what? The selfish Lot, the squabbling Lot, the irritating and irritable Lot chose all the Jordan plain for himself and moved eastward. Can you imagine, I mean, if it wasn't for Abram taking him to Egypt, he would have probably starved to death in the famine. Not grateful. He says, "Well, old man, if you're dumb enough to give me that opportunity, I'm going to take advantage of it. I will take the fertile land; you take the desert. I mean, you've got more cattle and everything. If you lose a few, it won't matter. If I lose a few, it matters. I am going to the fertile land." You have some more selfish common sense. The kind that looks after me, myself, and I.

Well, they parted company. Abraham settled in the land of Canaan, Lot settled in the towns of the plain, pitching his tents on the outskirts of Sodom. Now, he had to know what kind of people were in Sodom. The people inside were vicious men, great sinners against Yahweh. They were, as we learn later on, homosexuals. The immorality in Sodom and Gomorrah was unbelievable. So, Lot in his selfishness really didn't care what he was getting himself into. You see, a lot of you today do the same thing. Some of you youth, you don't know what you're getting into when you go out and are so immoral, you open yourself up to the enemy, you open your soul up to the enemy, you open your mind, your memory, your imagination, and so you're lost from morning to night.

You have no control. And this happened to two towns — Sodom and Gomorrah. You know, I have to ask myself today: Is it not happening today all over the world? You see thousands of youth acting like there was no tomorrow, acting as if immorality, homosexuality, and all these other things were just a way of life. It's exactly what they did in Sodom and Gomorrah. And Lot chose it. It was green. I wonder if that isn't a symbol also that immorality on the large scale, that gets to be habitual, can look very green, very fertile, very Paradise-like. See, you have a tremendous amount of people today who make immorality look so good, you have these so-called role models that are teaching you — and unfortunately some are priests and ministers — they teach you that immorality is okay. It's life. It's human. It's love. It's good. And it's all wrong. The grass looks so green. It looks like a paradise. It all looks so good. But we know the name of the town. Sodom and Gomorrah. Think about that.

As you read the Old Testament, you begin to realize how great these men were. They didn't have the grace as you and I have. They didn't know Jesus. They didn't have the Spirit as Jesus gave Him to us. For Abraham to have this kind of faith when things were just beginning is phenomenal, and it's a faith that just broke out into so many areas of beauty. It was like a diamond that's been cut so perfectly that you put it into a light, and oh, it just sparkles all over. And that's what Abram's faith was. And you, my friend, and I too, have *more* grace than Abram. We live in a greater age than Abram, and God expects more from us than He did Abram. To whom much is given, much is required. To whom much is given on trust—I think that includes Catholic priests, nuns, religious ministers—even more will be required. You can get this from St. Luke's Gospel.

Now, let's go and look at what happens. *Yahweh said to Abram, after Lot had parted company with him, "Look all around from where you are toward the north and the south, toward the east and the west."* That includes where Lot just went. Lot went eastward. The Lord said, "You should look all the way around." And so, He said, *"All the land within sight, I will give to you and your descendants forever. I will make your descendants like the dust on the ground; when men succeed in counting the specks of dust on the ground, then they will be able to count your descendants."*

Do you realize what the Lord did? The Lord was so pleased with Abraham's faith and hope and love and his humility and his total unselfishness. Giving a man like Lot, who was a character to say the least, first choice—not wanting to argue and be violent and going all the way—pleased God so much. He said, "I'm going to give it all to you." You see, so many of you are so afraid to be generous with God. Oh, I'm not only talking about your money or tax deductions or whatever. I'm talking about your generosity with your time—your personal time, your prayer time—and generosity with your neighbor, and whether you give out of humility, and generosity, whether you give them your forgiveness. These are the things that matter to the Lord. I think for some of you, you are so generous to big organizations, you give thousands and millions away, but at home, you're like a bear. I don't think that money does you any good. Maybe it puts a plaque up there for you somewhere, but then who's going to look at that plaque? Did anybody look at it with love? Does anybody say, "Oh, what a great man built this building"? Let me tell you, the wind blows and the rain falls, and the snow and the cold, and it gets tarnished. Nobody sees it. If you gave for that reason, you might as well forget it. If you gave for love and generosity, humility of heart, giving to God, then I think you have something.

So, the Lord continues. He says, "*Come, travel through the length and breadth of the land, for I mean to give it to you.*" I mean to give it to you; I want you to go everywhere. You can go as far as you can see. Of course, the more you travel, the farther you see. I'm going to give it all to you. The generosity of God. So, Abram went with his tents to settle in Hebron. And there again, he built an altar to God. You see, we find qualities in Abraham that are so wonderful.

Now we have another one: thanksgiving. The man was so grateful that there was a promise, you know, when all he had was his patch, and he was on desert, probably had to dig for water and find water for his cattle. He had a much harder time than Lot. There was nothing irrigated where Abram was, although the Lord said, "I'm going to give it to you."

Well, you gotta say, who wants a lot of desert? But you see, he trusted the Lord. He didn't say, "Well, thanks a lot. What have I got here? A bunch of cacti?" No. The man is phenomenal. And he didn't have Jesus like you do. He didn't have the Spirit like you do. How do you like that, huh? Doesn't that kind of make you feel about that small when you read about some of these Old Testament people that had so little and worked so hard with it, and you and I have so much, and we work so little with it, we work as if we had nothing? We don't take advantage of the treasures that God has given us. We don't take advantage of the grace and the power. You and I should never question the Lord, no matter what He does or permits in our life, after we read that. And you and I, we all have our deserts. We are all in a desert sometime, whether the desert of prayer, we don't feel like praying, whether it's a desert of life and nobody seems to be around you or care or love you, whether it's a desert of just people—that nobody likes you or you think they don't—that you can't get along with.

We all live in deserts at some time or other, we all hunger and thirst for the good things. I think where we part company is where it takes trust. God will make good out of it. And we're not grateful. Abram was grateful for his desert.

Well, we learn now that in the fourteenth year there was a battle at the edge of the wilderness, and a survivor came to tell Abram, who was living at the Oak, that Lot had been captured. I bet you anything that Lot never paid any attention to Abram. He enjoyed his lush grass and his cattle, probably enjoyed Sodom and Gomorrah. But the conquerors seized all of the possession of Sodom and Gomorrah and all their provisions and also Lot. Suddenly, now, he loses everything.

Do you know what? You can't believe this man, Abram. This man, Abram, went to battle. He must have supported the members of his household from birth. He had 318 men. 318 isn't a lot of men. You talk about herdsmen and all. We're not talking about a huge amount of men, we're talking about a pretty good household, a nice, little business. And it said they heard that his kinsman had been taken, so he pursues the enemy as far as Dan.

Now, they defeated them and recaptured all the goods and Lot and all his possessions together with all the women and the people. Pretty good warriors for shepherds. Herdsmen.

There again, though, you say, "Well, why would Abraham do that?" But you've got to go back to the man of faith. Faith made him compassionate, forgiving. He was humble, he was thankful, obedient, and now we see him zealous, compassionate, and forgiving to Lot. Because you have to remember that all this time and years passed while Abram was in the desert. That must have been very difficult for him to feed his cattle and feed his family. It wasn't easy. Lot took all the good stuff.

So, you and I would have said, "Well, he had every reason to be bitter and say, 'Good riddance. He deserves to be captured by the enemy. He deserves to lose all his possessions. Here I am struggling, and he had all the lush and all the fertile land, and now he's taken captive. Good riddance.'" It would be hard for you and I not to think that way.

I think I could make a bet we'd think that way. But now we see what faith did to, and with, Abraham. Soon as he heard that Lot was captured with his wives, women, children—everybody—he just took off. He didn't have a lot of people either. What was it, 318 men? And these are not fighters, these are not warriors. These are herdsmen. What did they go with? Forks, staffs, what? We really don't know. So, I'm going to let you think about Abram. I want you also to think about yourself. How would you treat your relatives, family, parents, children if you knew they're in trouble? Would you just sit there and say, "My God, I knew it would happen. They deserve it"? Or do you have enough faith to go help them out? Next time you look at faith, my friends, there's an awful lot to it. See what you need faith to do for you. Think about it.

Now, Abram comes back after the battle, and along with the kings that had been on his side, the King of Sodom came to meet him in the valley.

Now, we find something rather strange happen, but it begins to prefigure the New Testament way back here, because Abram runs up against Melchizedek, the King of Salem. Melchizedek did a very strange thing. He brought bread and wine because he was a priest of the God Most High. Now, bread and wine were not what was ever offered to the God Most High, the Lord Yahweh. So, for the first time, we begin to get the image and symbol of the Eucharist, and that's why in our Faith, when a man is ordained a priest, the bishop says, "You're ordained according to the Order of Melchizedek." The man came out of nowhere. And disappeared. Because he was a king, normally he would not be high priest too. So, there's that mystery about Melchizedek. Where did he come from? Where did he go? You never hear another word about this man, and he was King of Salem. You put "Jeru" and "Salem" together, and you've got Jerusalem later on. The King of Salem, from which would come sacrifice, and the sacrifice would go on until the end of time. And this is what Melchizedek said to Abram: "*Blessed be Abram by God Most High, Creator of heaven and earth, and blessed be God Most High for handing over your enemies to you.*"

So, Abram did two marvelous things. Forgave his nephew, delivered them all—even the king of Sodom—from the enemy. And just returned home. But God was going to make this man known and loved. It was almost as if Abraham was a symbol of the Eternal Father. The Eternal Father's beauty, gentleness, compassion, forgiveness, His mercy, His total giving. He symbolizes to me the Eternal Father, and now comes Melchizedek. And you begin to see the symbols of the Eucharist, offering to God bread and wine. And today, in our churches as Catholics, we offer bread and wine, but this time it is offered as the Body and Blood, Soul and Divinity, the great sacrifice, the one and only sacrifice on the Cross perpetuated forever. So, God blessed Abram through Melchizedek, a priest forever. Jesus is that priest according to Melchizedek. A priest forever. The high priest forever.

And the king of Sodom said to Abram, "Give me the people and take the possessions for yourself." But Abraham replied, *"I raise my hand in the presence of Yahweh God Most High, Creator of heaven and earth. Not one thread, not one sandal strap, nothing will I take of what is yours; you shall not say, 'I enriched Abram.' For myself, I take nothing."*

What a man was Abram. What faith did to this man is unbelievable. Not only is he compassionate and forgiving, but he wants absolutely nothing for his deeds.

"Nothing for myself," he said. *"There is only what my men have eaten and the share belonging to the men who came with me. Let them take their share."* He wanted nothing. He did this fantastic deed. Asked nothing in return. My friends, you and I must ask ourselves a question.

I think at this point, you know, you just can't look at Abram and say, "Wow, yeah, he had lots of faith. He was going to have a child; he had a son. That's the end of that." He had a lot more. A lot that you and I should not only imitate but we should possess. Can you imagine what Abram would have done had he lived in the time of Jesus and believed in Jesus and knew Jesus? Can you imagine the kind of faith he would have had? You imagine the humility and obedience and gentleness? All this comes from faith. If you don't have that real faith, you cannot possess these things, because they don't come from selfishness, they don't come from greed, they don't come from gluttony, they don't come from lust. They come from faith. And if you don't understand that, then, well, you just have to wonder, don't you? Just have to wonder. I think the greatest thing the Lord did for Abram was to send to him Melchizedek, because you see, it was the sign of the Lord. You can't create faith. We say, "Well, it's a gift from God," but it's a gift God gives to everyone. Lot could've stayed with Abram and learned from him, but no, he was selfish. He was, perhaps, immoral himself. So, you and I, as we look at Abraham, must respond with great humility of heart and say, "Lord, increase my faith." Say to Him, "I believe. Help my unbelief." Think of that, will you?

I hope you learned a lot about Abraham. I never cease to wonder at this man. There is so much to learn about this man. Most of all, to learn how faith goes way deep into your daily life and daily existence. It isn't just saying, "Oh, I believe in the holy Roman Catholic Church. I believe in the Resurrection." It goes deeper than that.

You see how God had to prove Abraham? He had to prove him. "Is this the man I'm going to choose? Whose name would be used as a blessing?"

It says: *The word of Yahweh was spoken to Abram in a vision. He saw the Lord. And He said, "Have no fear, Abram. I am your shield. Your reward will be great."* Oh, now we've got something. Fear can go with faith. And I want you to hear this. Fear can go right along with faith and be mixed in with it. Today, if you say, "I'm fearful," people will say you gotta have more faith. Well, I want you to look at Abram. If you can tell me that you or anyone else you know has this kind of faith that Abraham had, I want to see them. But He says, "Have no fear." Abram was afraid. He was getting older and older, and his wife was getting older and older, and he had no one to leave all this to, no one with his name. So faith and fear can go together, and don't you let anyone say they can't. And if they do, say, "Look, the Lord had to come in a vision and say to Abram, 'Don't be afraid. It's okay. I am your shield and your reward.'"

And Abraham looks, and he pours out his heart, and he says, "*My Lord Yahweh, what do you intend to give me? I go, childless.*" That's all he wanted. He didn't want the king's booty. He didn't want anything from the kings that he just saved. He didn't want anything from Lot. Only a son. The older he got, he waited with confidence and love, but his faith and fear went together. "*You have given me no descendants; some man of my household will be my heir.*" See, he says: "Some ordinary man's going to be my heir. I have nothing of myself. I have no one that belongs to me. One of these servants is going to be my heir." Then the words of Yahweh were spoken: "*He shall not be your heir. Your heir shall be of your own flesh and blood. Look up to heaven and count the stars if you can. Such will be your descendants.*"

Now, the coin begins to turn a little bit, and it says: *Abraham put his faith in Yahweh, who counted this as making him justified.* That is, holy. He didn't see. He didn't understand. But he said, "Okay, You said it was going to happen. I believe." But you see that fear that was coupled with that? It wasn't despair. He could just see the reality of facts before him. He's getting older and older, he's eighty-five and his wife is in her seventies. But as soon as the Lord spoke—boom. It's okay.

Because of that, because with all the fear in his heart, the Lord counted him as justified, which means holy. You say, "Well, that's great. After all, he had a vision. The Lord spoke to him, and he believed." The Lord speaks to you. Or don't you believe the Lord spoke to you in His Son, Jesus? This vision is no different than the vision you have in faith of Jesus coming, dying, rising, sending you His Spirit. You have much more than Abraham had to give you basis for faith and belief. Much more. We have no excuse. When you see Jesus here doing this for you, how can you say Abram had more? He had little. He gave much.

You and I have much. And we give little.

So, let's ask the Lord every night before we go to bed: "Lord, give me the faith of Abraham, that I may have the love of Jesus."

SIX

Genesis Chapters 15–17

We're going to go back to Genesis. This is another episode in our Bible spirituality. Bible spirituality is extremely important. Why? Because it is the Word of God. See, the Word of God has power. We're not accustomed to words having power. You read a newspaper, it gives emotional power sometimes because it can frighten you, it can make you angry, it can do a tremendous amount of things. Most of them, not too hot. So, words can have adverse reaction, but the Word of God as given here is upbuilding. You don't get that too many places. You can be reading a spiritual book, look at a good tape, but it is always beneficial when you read the Scriptures. But the problem is you don't always understand what you read, and that's when I look at the spirituality of Scripture, rather than the exegesis of Scripture. I'm not interested in how high Mount Sinai is, but I sure want to know what happened on Mount Sinai and what does it do for me and what does it do to me.

So, I think for the common man, you and I, grassroots people, the essence of the Scriptures is the spirituality. I don't object to people learning a lot about the Scriptures and where it came from and who wrote it, and this is wonderful. I want to know, though, what it means to a six-year-old. And that is the beauty of Jesus. The children understood Jesus. The adults understood Jesus. The apostles didn't always understand Jesus and used to ask Him stuff at night. It's important that the spirituality we teach can be understood by children, the middle-aged, and the elderly equally, otherwise we have spoken to the wind. And that's why we have this series, because I want to bring out of the Scriptures what's in it for you. It's not a good phrase — "*What's in it for me?*" It sounds extremely selfish, but it's not in this instance, because we've got to know: What is He saying to me? What is the Lord God Yahweh saying to me?

We're in Genesis 15. It says: *It happened some time later* ... This is after the war and when Melchizedek comes, a great man who came from nowhere and offered bread and wine. And Abram had a vision. You learn a lot here because you and I speak to God as if, well, I can't say *as if*, because He *is* awesome, majestic, and sovereign — Lord over life and death. And so, we speak to Him sometimes as someone far away, like you're on a telephone. But see, the beauty when you look on the Old Testament is that it's always personal. Abraham spoke to God as a man speaks to a man, as a friend speaks to a friend, and you and I have to learn that, especially as Catholics. We're just not accustomed to that. We're very, *very* proper with God. Extremely proper. But God is when you can kick your shoes off and sit down and say, "I love you," and it's okay.

Now, so Abraham looked at the Lord. He's just a little bit shaky, and I don't blame him. It's okay to be shaky with your Father, but the Lord was so gentle. He says, "*Have no fear, Abram, I am your shield. Your reward will be very great.*" Why? Because of Abram's faith. Abraham believed that something would happen. It was absolutely, totally impossible that he and his wife would have many descendants. They were way beyond childbearing age. Way beyond it.

And so, the Lord looked at this man. He didn't have the graces that you have. You can be greater than Abraham. You say, "Oh, that is terrible to say that." No, because you have Jesus in this New Testament. And Jesus makes all the difference. And so, Abram said to the Lord, "My Lord Yahweh, what do You intend to give me? I really believe what You're saying, but I go childless yet." The Lord had appeared to him nine years before — poor guy is eighty-five — and he says, "Some man in my household is going to take everything I have when I die, and what would happen to my wife?" *And the Lord said, "He shall not be your heir; your heir shall be of your own flesh and blood."*

Well, I wonder if you and I would have accepted that. You know, we would have said, "Lord, maybe nine years ago." It was impossible today. It's out of the question. But Abram didn't say that.

The Lord said, "*Look up to heaven, and count the stars if you can. Such will be your descendants.*" Later on He will say: "*As many as the sand on the seashore.*"

Well, you know what Abram said? Was there an argument? No. Was there some kind of objection? No. It says he put his faith in Yahweh. He said, "Okay, okay."

All of you that are praying for someone in your family and it just seems to be going down the drain. And it looks so hopeless, and the more you pray, the worse it gets. You see your children going and living terrible lives, or some of you children look at your parents, and some of you children are so small, and yet you look at your parents on drugs, you look at them on alcohol, you're not getting the right love, you're not getting anything, and you feel so desperate. You wonder: "Is there a God at all?" Again, I believe that this is going to turn out right. Take it from me, sweetheart. You can believe that. I always think of my own struggles. I know how you feel.

I didn't think it was ever going to turn out right. But there is something about just believing that God is going to bring good out of it somehow, and you don't know. Neither did Abraham.

See, that's the mystery of faith. We don't know how. And that's why it takes humility. And what is humility? Humility is that feeling of helplessness, knowing you can't do a thing about it. You know that God has to do it all.

And you look at yourself, and there seems to be nothing to do, and that's where Abraham was. He was in the exact same place you and I are. Very often today, you and I are just in the same position of Abraham. You don't need to envy Abraham. No, you don't need to say, "I wish I were in that position where I could show God great faith." Some of you are in positions where God is demanding even greater faith. And so, as you read this, you have to say, "Oh, yeah, I understand that; I'm in the same boat. I've been praying for so-and-so for over twenty years. And last night, he got dead drunk." What do you do? Keep on trusting, loving, wanting. Trusting God. Because what you're praying for is salvation, what you're praying for is this man or this woman or this child or soul. And your faith has to go so far that even if that person died dead drunk, you would know at the moment of that death, your long years of prayer, God saw and heard even though you saw no fruit of your prayer. All of that is what happened between Abraham, whose name was Abram at the time, and the Lord Yahweh, Who pushed Abraham to the end of his faith.

Now, we're going a little bit further, and I know how this comes out. You're going to see your own life, I imagine. It's very important that you do that. The Lord said, "*I am Yahweh, who brought you out of Ur at the Chaldeans to make you heir to this land.*" But you see, the whole thing seems so impossible. You know when things seem impossible to you and to me, and we seem to express it? We get kind of confused and upset. We think: "Oh, I lack faith," or, "God is displeased with me because I questioned this." And so, you put yourself through umpteen moments of torture, saying, "Oh, God, I have sinned against You." So, now you're not only in a precarious position, now you've offended God. And so, this whole thing just goes on and on, and it's useless. There's no reason for that. You say, "Well, how do you know?" Well, if Abraham is such a great man, let's see what he says.

He says, "*My Lord Yahweh, how am I to know that I shall inherit it? I mean, I am an old man, my wife is an old woman. Forgive me, Lord, but I don't know how You're going to do this.*"

Ever been that way? I'm that way a lot of times. Well, you and I today sometimes make contracts. I don't particularly like contracts. Br. Bill Steltemeier gets me into contracts and tries to explain them to me, and they're over my head. But in those days, they didn't have contracts, and so they had covenants, which was so beautiful. Covenant, something spiritual between you and God.

So, the Lord said, "*Get me a three-year-old heifer, a three-year-old goat, a three-year-old ram, a turtle dove and a young pigeon.*" And He tells him to leave the birds whole, but cut the others in half and put one on this side and one on that side. Why do that? Well, that, in those days, was a covenant, and the parties who were making this contract, or this covenant, would walk between, which meant if any of us go back on this contract, may this happen to us. The sight wasn't too pleasant. There was a contract with two parties, so the Lord, knowing the customs of the day, always adapts Himself to the customs of the day, sometimes even to our own imagination. That's why there're so many different pictures of the Lord, different pictures of Mary. Everywhere she appears, she looked different because she adapts herself to their own imagination.

And so the Lord said, "Proceed." He put Abram in a deep sleep, but in this sleep, terror seized him. Did you ever wake up in the middle of the night? With all your problems, all your frustrations, you're scared to death, just like I'm going through that? I look at the network sometimes, and all it looks like is it's just going to go down the drain, and you wake up in the middle of the night, and that thought and the consequences of it just kind of grip you like icy hands. And you're terror-stricken. That's what happened to Abram.

Then Yahweh said to Abraham, "Know this for certain, that your descendants will be exiles in a land not their own, where they will be slaves and oppressed for four hundred years. But I will pass judgment on the nation that enslaves them, and after that they will leave with many possessions. For your part, you shall go to your fathers in peace; you shall be buried at a ripe old age. In the fourth generation, they will come back here."

Wow. Not only is He telling him he's going to have a son. That's all Abraham asked for. All he wanted was a little baby boy. He didn't ask for all this. But God always gives more than we ask. Isn't it wonderful? Isn't it terrific to know that even in our helplessness, even when we're thinking there's nothing possible anymore, God is giving to us and is going to give us more than we ask, though maybe not in this world? You say, "Well, that's where I want it." No, you don't, but you can be sure of the next world.

Well, what happens? When the sun had set and darkness had fallen, what happened to this covenant? Smoke and fire came down from Heaven. It was like a firebrand between the halves, and the whole thing went *shhew!* Why did God do that? Because the Lord wanted Abraham to know the covenant was from God Himself. It was not made of men. God came down and set it on fire and consumed it. Abraham had what he wished for. Abram had said, "Lord, how shall I know that this shall be mine? I have no contract, I have nothing." The Lord says, "You have Me."

You wonder sometimes if that's enough for us. Is God enough for you and me? You say, "Well, Mother, we live in a very practical world." I know, I know. Just bills to pay and food to put on the table. And the job you need to have, and I know, you need all those things. And God is your Father, and He will provide.

But even those of you that have all of those things have forgotten the one thing necessary. You've forgotten your covenant with God when you were baptized. That's literally what happened to you at Baptism. You say, "Well, I was just a baby." It doesn't matter that you were a baby. What does it matter that you were just a baby? Don't you want to be in God and God in you as a child? You don't begin a very serious journey with no luggage, with no food. So, when you're baptized, the Lord doesn't just want you to be born and then wait until you've had all kinds of sins and bad decisions to make before you become imbued with the Spirit. He makes a covenant with you, and a few days after you're born, the Church comes along with that marvelous Sacrament, Baptism, and pours water on your head—not fire, but water—and says that the Trinity—Father, Son, and Holy Ghost—has suddenly taken up residence in you. What a marvel of grace, what a covenant. Not just two or three animals being cut in half and burned up, not just a sign. But with Jesus, it's Someone, and that Someone is the whole Trinity which comes and lives in you. What a marvel.

Well, the Lord said, *"To your descendants, I give this land from the wadi of Egypt to the Great River."* Now, we come across a little problem, and the problem is human nature. You see, so many of you, you take for granted. I get some rather juicy letters sometimes because people say, "Mother, you always take off the apostles, you're criticizing these apostles." I don't criticize them; I look at them as they were—faulty men that God's grace did wonderful things with. And I can't get courage from someone born holy at three years old, and neither can you. God hasn't asked us to be perfect, He asked us to be holy. A big difference. You say, "Well, how do you know that?" We're going to find out right now.

Now, we've had all these marvelous promises. We've had this tremendous experience with God Yahweh. Well, Sarah—Sarai was her name at the time—had still borne him no child, but she had an Egyptian maidservant. Sarah's faith isn't like Abraham's. It's just not. She's getting tired of waiting for this promise to her. She's very realistic. I mean, here I am, I'm old. You're getting older. Nothing is happening. Let's do something about it. Does that sound familiar to you? Sounds familiar to me, because we're all in that boat. When God doesn't answer our prayer, we're going to take hold. We're going to say, "Okay, I gave You a chance. You didn't come across. Now, let me show You how to do it." And that's what's about to happen.

Sarai said, *"Since Yahweh has kept me from having children ..."* They always blame God for everything. Whatever happens, we blame God. We got a terrible pollution problem we made, we say, "Why did God allow this?" Well, you're the one who put all the pollution in the air. Why are you talking about God doing it? Why cirrhosis of the liver? You've been drinking half a quart every day.

So, Sarai is in that place as well. So, she said to him, "I give you my slave girl as your wife." Then you say, "Hey, we can't do that!" Well, you're judging in the New Testament. In those days, you didn't have the New Testament morality that we have today, or that I think we have today. The man was allowed to have three, four, five—a hundred wives.

So, Hagar conceived very quickly. She was a young girl. But once she knew that, here comes human nature in the midst of holiness in progress. Holiness in progress. Remember that. We are becoming holy a little at a time. So, she started acting kind of saucy, she kept looking at her mistress like, "What are you doing, old woman? I mean, my child is going to be your leader one day, the head of this household." Humility wasn't her virtue. I want you to think of that. See if you and I haven't been in that position a hundred times.

Human nature at its worst. I think we need to think a minute, because what happens today in your life and my life is that we think that because it's worse now, it's hopeless. In other words, my holiness has just dropped about twenty pegs, and God is very angry with us, and so as a result, we gotta give up because there's no use trying, I really have messed the whole thing up. That's the dark spot in a beautiful tapestry. It brings depth. It would be better if we weren't jealous, be better if we were not impetuous. But you know, life doesn't always deal out the situations that make those virtues easy, and we're not always at the level of holiness where we can stop and think and say, "Well, I should act this way now." But this is the holiness in progress. So, in all of this, Abram, Sarai, everybody is learning a lot of lessons, and throughout the centuries, you and I have learned a lot of lessons.

So, since the slave girl was being a little bit uppity with Sarai, Sarai said to Abraham, "*May this insult to me come home to you.*" She's the one who started this whole thing. So now the poor guy, he's looking at his wife, and it wasn't his idea. She literally pushed her slave girl on him because she wanted a child, and then when it happened, she began to realize it was never going to be her child. He was always her husband. So, she's getting angry, and she said, "*It was I who put my slave into your arms, but now that she knows she has conceived, I count for nothing in her eyes."* Sarai knows she did it, but boy, she's after Abram. And she's angry. She's getting very judgmental, she's getting very revengeful, and she says, *"Let Yahweh judge between me and you."* Oh, I bet she nagged him for days. Abraham finally said, "Okay. Okay," he says, "Do what you want. *The slave girl is at your disposal. Treat her as you think fit."* He had it.

Well, now, that's all Sarai needed. She just dug into Hagar like there was no one else around. She made her miserable.

Oh, I can see some of your eyebrows going up and saying, "Oh, that's horrible. I didn't know that was in Scripture." This book, my friend, is a book of human nature, *fallen* human nature, struggling, struggling to be holy. To listen to God, to know God. Always the struggle. Don't forget that. It's always a struggle. But it's okay, you're becoming holy slowly.

So, Sarai treated her so badly that she ran away.

Can you see the struggle in that family? It doesn't happen overnight. It may have been months that Sarai was after her and then Abram. Oh, can you imagine Abraham, he's seeing his wife whom he loved, he sees his slave girl who has a child because of him and with him, and he doesn't know what to do. I bet he went out and just hid in a tent somewhere and just hid under a tree and said, "Oh, God, what did You get me into? What kind of answer is this? I mean, is this just a way to answer Your promised good?" He had to have these thoughts. He was a human being. Instead of just getting Sarah off his back, he gets in a worse situation. See what happens when you don't wait on God's will? See what happens when you stick your two cents in God's plan? Well, God didn't forsake this woman. This was an injustice.

The angel of Yahweh met her near a spring. And he said, "Hagar, slave girl of Sarai, where have you come from and where are you going?" She said, "I'm running away from my mistress." The angel said, "Go back to you mistress and submit to her." Wow. "*I will make your descendants too numerous to be counted. Now you have conceived, and you will bear a son, and you shall name him Ishmael, for Yahweh has heard your cries of distress.*" Well, what's coming isn't too hot. "*A wild ass of a man he will be. Against every man and every man against him, setting himself to defy all his brothers.*" Wow.

You know, this girl was in a terrible, seemingly unjust situation. You see, things like this happen every time we start putting our nose in God's business. Not only did she suffer from it, Sarai suffered from it, Abram suffered from it, the child suffered from it.

It's like anything we do to our bodies that's against the law of God or the Commandments of God. We're going to have consequences. The consequences can be sanctified, but there are none the less consequences. If you commit adultery, you can't think for a moment that if your wife finds out, it's going to be, "Well, wonderful. Hope you had a good time." There are consequences to all our actions that are not according to the will of God. This was not according to the rule of God. We run ahead of God. We don't want to wait. But I know there are times you say, "Well, when do I wait, when do I hold back, and do I ever start on something?" Yes, but this situation when they said they're going to have a child, well, she's going to make up her own mind how her husband is going to have a son. And so, the consequences were not entirely good. But God would bless the child, but at the same time, he'd have a hard time. So did Sarai, and so did Abram. And you have to wonder, although the Scriptures kind of let it drop.

Hagar bore Abram a son, and Abram gave to the son that Hager bore him the name Ishmael. So, you see, my friends, life sometimes deals odds in pretty rotten deals. Sometimes, it's kind of our fault. We don't wait, or we don't pray enough, or we're just impetuous, we do things, we commit sins one after another, and we gotta pay the consequences. Is all that hopeless? No. From Ishmael has come a great nation that loves the Lord God Yahweh. From Abram's other son came a great nation that loves the Lord God Yahweh. From that nation came you and me and all Christians. So, God took the situation that was miserable at the time and unhappy at the time and built it up. See, nothing is wasted with God. That is such a marvel to me. You know, if you're making a painting and you kind of mess it up, you tear it up, you throw it away, that's the only thing we can do. We're so finite, we're so small, we're not creative enough to say, "How can I use this in some other way?" And most of the times, we can't. But God in His infinite love and mercy is going to make good out of even your sins, not because He willed them, not because He wanted them, but because you made a wrong decision. He loves you so much. He loves you so much that He will go to extremes to use the mistake you made. That big black greasy spot on the floor. That stain on your garment. He does all He can not only to wash it away, but so you'd never know it was ever, ever there.

And that's what He did when He sent Jesus, His Son. When He gave us this wondrous Church that we live in that we have the privilege to belong to, all of us who know Jesus and are caught up in Jesus and know the beauty of His redemption. And God has taken all of the misery of our human nature, and He put it on Jesus, and He said, "This is My Son, this is how you should act, this is what you should do." Think about it, will you? Think about the consequences of your life and the sin in your life. Next time you're tempted to some great sin that you know may affect yourself and your family, stop. Look at the consequences. It's just not the best motive, but at least it might put a little strength in your soul to say, "It's not worth it."

Well, if you want a lesson in patience, those of you who've been waiting so long for God to answer a prayer: When Hagar had her child, Abraham was eighty-six years old. All of a sudden, he's ninety-nine. So, this young man is almost a teenager. Ishmael is a teenager and still Sarai has no children. I mean, you talk about faith. This man waited and waited and waited, and even when he made this boo-boo, he had to wait some more. One year, two years, three years, four, five, six, seven, eight, nine, ten, eleven, twelve … Well, Yahweh appears to him again, and He says, "*I am El Shaddai. bare yourself blameless in my presence, and I will make a covenant between myself and you and increase your numbers greatly.*"

Oh, I can see Abraham saying, "Lord, not again. We've gone through this." I think that's what I would have said. "Wait a minute. It seems this is the third time we've gone through this." Really, you just can't imagine how the Lord sometimes just rams you through. Well, you know what Abram did? Unbelievable. He didn't do what I did, what I would do, rather. He bowed down to the ground. So, I think my Italian temperament would have had quite an argument with Yahweh. I would have said, "Do you realize the trouble you got me into twelve years ago?" Nothing. Abraham bowed down to the ground. That means that he had such awe of God. Abraham was a man of God.

It didn't matter what happened to him, it didn't matter what he went through, it didn't matter the frustration of the cross. When it came to the Lord God Yahweh, he bowed down in total resignation to His will. You know what is a marvel to me? The marvel to me is that this is before redemption, this is before Jesus. Wouldn't you think that after Jesus, you and I would have even more faith than Abram? Don't you think that you and I should be men and women of great faith? Today, my friends, we are so wishy-washy. Our faith is like a slot machine, we put in a quarter, and we want everything from healing cancer to Cadillacs. It's sickening. I think the kind of faith that's portrayed today is absolutely nauseous because it's not built on the cross like Abram's was. If we claim something and the Lord doesn't provide right now, in this instant, we even blame Satan the devil or a lack of faith on our part, we go on blaming people. What kind of faith is that? Read this book. Find out what Abram did.

Bow down. No argument, no excuses, nothing. He said, "*Here, now is my covenant with you.*" And God says the same thing again. "*You shall become the father of a multitude of nations. You shall no longer be called Abram. Your name shall be Abraham, for I make you the father of a multitude of nations.*" The Lord changed his name. It was no longer Abram, it was Abraham, the father of nations. The man had proved himself. And He says, "*I will make you most fruitful, and I will make you into nations, and your issue shall be kings.*"

Why has God changed names? He did it with Peter. "Amen, I say to you, Simon, you shall be known as Peter. *Rock.* I give you keys. I make you head of My Church, and the gates of Hell shall not prevail against it." Abraham had a new mission now. He had proven himself, he had kept faith in spite of the most awesome difficulties and obstacles, he was ready to be the father of nations. So, every time in Scripture that God took anyone and had a very special, special mission for them, He changed their name, and the name indicated the mission. *Abraham* meant "father of nations," *Peter* meant "rock." Nothing or anyone would ever destroy the Rock. And in this day, with so much confusion in the Church, remember you belong to a Church who has a rock at her head. No one will ever destroy her. She's gonna be here, my friend, when Gabriel blows that horn. That's the power of God in today's world and in Abram's world.

Now, there is no role that you get from God that isn't bordered with the cross. You can't get away from it. You know what I find so discouraging about today's Christianity is it's bordered with ice cream, whipped cream, with the abundant life. The abundant life is here in the Scriptures, not the Cadillac in your garage. *This* is where the abundant life is, right here, and that's the same way it was with Abraham, because you remember how he took the animals and he separated them and the big fire came? God came, and He tested this man, and He says, "*Now, this is my covenant which you are to maintain between myself and you and your descendants after you: all your males must be circumcised.*" Now, that included Abraham. Didn't have any nice surgical procedures, you know. This was one painful, bloody mess. But it was their kind of Baptism. It meant that this man and his whole household belonged to the Lord.

That was a covenant. Your Baptism is a covenant between you and God. "*You shall circumcise your foreskin, and this shall be a sign of the covenant between myself and you. When they are eight days old, all your male children must be circumcised, generation after generation. No matter whether they be born within the household or bought from a foreigner.... My covenant shall be marked on your bodies as a covenant in perpetuity.*" Forever. That's your Baptism. You are forever marked with the mark of God, the moment you are baptized in this life and forever in the next. It is an indelible sign; it shall never be erased, even in Hell. All those in Hell that had been baptized and threw away their baptismal garment, they are marked forever. Everyone knows in Hell which ones were baptized and which were not. Everyone in the Kingdom is there because they have on this wedding garment, the garment of faith that is the Father, Son, and Holy Spirit, the garment of hope and the garment of love. Your intellect has a garment of faith, covering it so that you can rise above your reason. Memory has a garment of hope so you can rise above the discouragement of this life. And your will has a garment of love, which gives you the power to say yes and no.

I love you. Remember the garment of holiness that is redeeming.

SEVEN

Genesis 17–19

We're going to continue the book of Genesis. We've gone through from Adam and Eve to Abraham. And last time, we learned that God made a covenant with Abraham, and the covenant was circumcision. And if you go down to Genesis 17:14, the Lord says: "*The uncircumcised male whose foreskin has not been circumcised, such a man shall be cut off from his people. He has violated my covenant.*" So, that was to the Israelites a form of Baptism. That was the sign that they and their families were God's children. They were very special. They were marked. And now, of course, Baptism takes that place, and we are marked for life. It is an indelible sign that you have both in life and in eternity. You can't get away from it once you've been baptized. That mark is upon you in time and eternity forever. Whether you make it to Heaven or Hell, they will all know that you were a baptized Christian.

We've been learning a lot about faith and really how negative it is sometimes. Sometimes you just don't see the forest for the trees. Sometimes you say, "Well, faith is very assured." Well, you can say that when you're talking about the Trinity and the revelations of Jesus in the Gospel, especially the Eucharist. You can say this is assured and this is a kind of faith that elevates my mind and heart to God, and it is something that I accept though my mind cannot fully understand it, no more than I can put the ocean in a thimble, because God's mysteries are so far above us many times or most of the time. And so, we learned a lot about faith. But now, we're going to see another element of faith in the life of Abraham. And we admire the man, but there was an awful lot of that struggle. He had to wait and wait and wait. But you know the difference between Abraham and you and me? Well, the difference is that we don't wait. Sometimes we just kind of intervene, and that's what Sarah did. And sometimes we just stop. We just get discouraged, and we go another direction, or we just decide God doesn't answer, He doesn't care. We get angry and frustrated. Well, Abraham could face the reality that so far nothing had happened of all the promises He's had from the Lord.

Let's see what he does.

So, look at Genesis 17:15. It says: *God said to Abraham, "As for Sarai, your wife, you shall not call her Sarai, but Sarah. I will bless her and moreover give you a son by her."* Well, now begins the questioning again. I mean, the Lord had said this before, and years have passed. Well, He goes on, and He says, *"I will bless her, and nations shall come out of her; kings of people shall descend from her."* And Abraham bowed to the ground. Well, and it says he laughed. *He laughed, thinking to himself, "Is a child to be born to a man one hundred years old, and will Sarah have a child at the age of ninety?"* Well, you have to admit, the poor guy had something to laugh about. You wonder, though, why the Lord didn't get angry with him. You wonder if it was just a laugh that says, "Oh, golly. What a promise." But Abraham is a little bit leery about it. He says to God, *"Oh, let Ishmael live in your presence."* In other words, "Look, it's too late. I'm almost one hundred, my wife is ninety." *But God replied, "No, but your wife Sarah shall bear you a son whom you are to name Isaac."* Names are very important to the Lord. "*With him, I will establish my covenant, a covenant in perpetuity.*" In perpetuity. Forever. Never-ending.

Well, the Lord looked upon Ishmael, and He loved him, and He gave him a great promise. He said, "*I will grant you your request: I bless him and I will make him fruitful and greatly increased in numbers. He shall be the father of twelve princes, and I will make him into a great nation. But my covenant*" — oh, now we got something different — "*I will establish with Isaac.*" Now, you look at that and say, "No, wait a minute. Ishmael was first. And he should have had it all. This was an unjust situation." But no. What you and I forget is that the Lord God is sovereign. He has a right to do as He pleases, and if we were to understand that today, we wouldn't have as many problems as we have. We have forgotten not only that there is a God, but that He has to have sovereign rights over us, and He can give to one and take from another and do no injustice. And until you understand that, you're going to be at least tempted to bitterness sometimes. Because here we're not talking about love. We're talking about mission. Isaac was the son of Sarah and Abraham. And from those two, from this man of faith and his wife — not his servant — came the blessing, came the covenant. So, we look at this, and we have to admire Abraham, and yet we know that every great act of faith that God called Abraham to, there was pain, doubt, questions, and tremendous long periods of time elapsing between.

Now, examine your life. I've had this same thing in my life I can't tell you how many times. There was that assurance that this is really what God wants me to do. And then comes darkness, and then comes doubt, and then come questions, and then it looks like everything is falling apart and the whole thing is never going to become a reality — and then it suddenly comes up again but only as another assurance that it's going to be. It's going to be. Not here yet. I guess that's why I never want to trouble with people who have the kind of faith that says, "Here it is, right now. Right now, I see it, I see it." And there's nothing there. Why does it take us so long to understand real faith? It goes through this process, and Abraham went through this process at least three times so far.

Well, we're looking at Abraham with kind of new eyes. I hope it gives you courage, I really do. I really feel that so many of you out there, including myself, just agonize ourselves and go through all kinds of spiritual guilt when people or ministers or friends or relatives or family, or my own or your own conscience, your own head, your own mind, keeps saying to you, "You don't have enough faith. If you had faith, you wouldn't question. If you had a lot of faith, you wouldn't doubt." Well, you have only to look at Abraham, this great man of faith. There is no question that Abraham is a great man of faith, but it's a workable faith, it isn't a perfect faith. We work at it and work and work, and we struggle, and like Abraham, sometimes we laugh when we think God is going to do this or that because it looks so absolutely impossible.

You know, I think if Our Lord were here, He would say, "Be of good heart." Know that in the struggle, faith grows. It's okay, as long as you keep your eyes on the Lord, as long you keep your eyes on Jesus. These are purely natural feelings that just come to us. Why? Because we have a mind about *that* big, and God is *so* big, and it is hard to squeeze knowledge and wisdom and all these things into this little tiny area.

Well, let's go on with Abraham in Genesis 17:23–37. He has all the male servants, everybody circumcised, and he wants to do God's will. So, when you start chapter eighteen, you learn there he is. Scripture said it was the hottest time of day, so we're figuring it must have been sometime between noon and three o'clock in the afternoon. And he's sitting at his tent, and they didn't have air conditioning in those days, so he's sitting there, and it's so hot, he is sweating. And it says here: *He looked up, and there he saw three men standing near him. As soon as he saw them, he ran from the entrance of this tent to meet them and bowed to the ground.* You say, "Oh, he knew it was Yahweh." No, not yet. He didn't quite know that it was Yahweh.

Was it the Trinity? Who knows? But he didn't know it was anything supernatural yet. You say, "Well, why did he run out and bow to the ground?" And then he said, "*My lord . . .*" You say "Oh, now he knew." No, they used to call anybody that who came for a visit. Hospitality in the East is something just unreal. We don't understand that kind of hospitality. When friends come to our door, we see them far away, and, "Oh, are they here again?" Or, "Why are they always coming at supper time?" Or, "Why do they bring friends with them?" Our hospitality has gone down to nothing. But this was normal Eastern hospitality. He ran. "*I beg you,*" *he said,* "*if I find favor with you, kindly do not pass your servant by.*" You also have to realize how many people pass you by in the desert. He was so happy to see somebody he could talk to besides his wife and servants. So, he brought a little water. He said, "*You shall wash your feet and lie down under the tree. Let me fetch a little bread, and you shall refresh yourself before going further. That is why you have come in your servant's direction.*"

So, he says, "Please let me serve you." What a lesson in hospitality. You know, St. Paul says in Hebrews that some men have served angels. He alluded to this. A beggar comes to your door, and you say, "Why don't you go get a job?" All he wants is a sandwich. The Lord said, "If you give it to the least, you give it to Me." You know what's wrong with us? We get so practical, so human, that we kind of have a really good reason to knock everybody out of our box of charity and love and compassion, and we use this as a kind of excuse to say, "Well, I don't need this problem, I have a legitimate reason for not giving a couple of quarts of milk or a sandwich." But we would never go out to somebody rapping on our door and say, "Hello, can I help you?" He says, "Yes, I want a sandwich." You say, "Oh, please, let me give you more. Let me give you a cup of coffee with your sandwich. Or is there anything else I can do for you?" You say, "Are you kidding?" This is *before* Jesus, my friends. This is before Jesus. Can you imagine what God expects of us *after* Jesus? We've got to know, when we read this beautiful book, that we fall far short even of Old Testament demands, let alone New Testament demands. We fall short. You wouldn't think of saying, "Oh, come on, let me wash your feet." Your guest would probably say, "What are you, a wacko?" We don't need to say, "We wanna wash your feet," but we have to make them feel like it's such a privilege for us to have them come in.

Well, *Abraham hastened to his tent to find Sarah, "Hurry," he said, "knead three bushels of flour and make loaves."* I don't know what in the world they would do with that much bread. And then he ran, and he got a tender calf, got the very best. And that's another thing. Do you ever have some guests come in, and you've just baked some fresh cookies or some kind of raisin bread, and it looks so good and fresh, and you've got it all planned for somebody else? And so you look up on the shelf and you get one of the boxes. You open them up and it's got some stale cookies, and that's what you give them? I'm pricking your conscience. That's not what Abraham did. Because he went and got a fine tender calf, and he told his servant, "Prepare it." That means they had to slaughter it, get all the blood out, and put it on a spit, and turn it and turn it and turn it until they had enough.

He didn't give them leftovers. He didn't say, "Sarah, what's left over from lunch?" Well, he took cream and milk and the calf, and I can't imagine what they did with cream, milk, and a calf, but he prepared it, and they ate, and he stood there under a tree.

So, now we're beginning to understand who the visitors were, but only after all of this hospitality. You say, "Well, Mother, if I thought it was the Lord, I'd be gracious too." Oh, but you see, Abraham didn't know it was the Lord. He just suddenly looked up from his tent that had nothing but desert for miles around, and he looked, and there were three men standing there. He had no idea it was the Lord. Now, while they were eating, they asked him, "*Where is your wife, Sarah?*" He said, "*She's in the tent.*" Then his guest said, "*I shall visit you again next year without fail, and your wife will then have a son.*" At ninety years old. Well, guess what? Sarah was listening at the entrance of the tent, eavesdropping, her ear glued to that tent, trying to figure out what they were saying. Well, maybe you can't blame her because I think she was surprised as anyone else to know there's company. But the women didn't visit, you see, that was a man's job.

And so, she wanted to know what in the world these men wanted, so she is just listening. And when she hears that, she starts to giggle. And now Abraham and Sarah were old and well on their years. Poor Sarah was past menopause, and I mean, as far as the possibility of having a son, it was *zilcho*. So, she giggled, she laughed. And why was her laugh wrong and Abraham's laugh right? He wasn't reprimanded for his laugh. Well, I think her laugh was a kind of "I can't believe this is going to happen." And she thought within herself: "*Now that I'm past the age of childbearing and my husband is an old man . . .*" Now, you see, this is that crucial point of faith. Abraham didn't question it could be done. It was hysterical to him that it would. She questioned it could at all be done. She's very much like Zechariah in St. Luke's Gospel, when the angel appeared to him and said, "Look, your wife is going to have a son, and he's going to be great," and he said, "How can this be done? My wife is old. Forget it. You're too late."

Do you see the difference? Abraham is very much like Mary. He was chuckling to see how would this be done. And Mary said, "How will this be done?" Now you're beginning to see, I hope you are, that fine line. The questions may be there, the doubts, because we're just puny minds, and we just can't comprehend how God is going to do things or why. The difference, and I want you to understand this about faith, is as long as you know He *can* and have the humility to wait until He does, your faith is growing in the midst of doubt, in confusion.

But Yahweh said, "Is anything too wonderful for Yahweh? At the same time next year, I will visit you again, and Sarah will have a son." Sarah came out, and she said, *"I did not laugh."* She lied because she was afraid. You find here two people that are extremely earthy and extremely human. Think about that. Think about yourself.

I think we learned something very important, and I hope it's encouraging for you, because we just torment ourselves over and over and over and over when we don't get a quick answer to prayer. When things just don't come our way as fast as we would like them. You know, it took a long time to convince Sarah. She was always questioning, and I bet she nagged that poor Abraham to death.

And so, now we have a different scene coming along. From there, the men set out, and Abraham, being the beautiful host that he was, he goes with them. And this is really something beautiful. When you see that personal relationship between Abraham and Yahweh. And now Yahweh is kind of thinking.

And He says, "*Shall I conceal from Abraham what I'm going to do, seeing that Abraham will become a great nation with all the nations of the earth blessing themselves by him? For I have singled him out to command his sons and his household after him to maintain the way of Yahweh by just and upright living. In this way, Yahweh will carry out for Abraham what he has promised.*" So, He's thinking to himself: "I don't know if I can hide this from him or not." What a beautiful relationship between God and Abraham. And it came about through faith in the darkness, and it came about through waiting, waiting on God's time. Believing every time He promised, and nothing happened. Promised, and nothing happened.

And He says, "*How great an outcry there is against Sodom and Gomorrah! How grievous is their sin! I propose to go down and see whether or not they have done all that is alleged in the outcry against them. I am determined to know.*" Now God is all knowledgeable, so it was not that He didn't know. It was that kind of putting Himself behind, putting His power and His knowledge behind Him, so He could speak to Abraham as a friend. And you know, I wonder if we understand that relationship. And you and I should understand that relationship now that Jesus has come. It's just like: "I've got this marvelous friend, and I just can't keep anything away from them. And if I keep this away, how will they feel? What are they going to do if I keep this away from them?" That kind of relationship would be a grace indeed. And to have that kind of relationship with God. And so, Abraham remained standing before Yahweh, and the two angels left. And Abraham can't believe it. He speaks to God like, "*Are you really going to destroy the just man with the sinner?*" It just didn't seem right. I mean, if Sodom and Gomorrah were so evil, well, just pick out the evil ones. You and I do that today.

He said, "Look, if there're fifty men there, would You really overwhelm them? I mean, if I can find fifty just, holy men in that city, will You save the whole city?" And he said, "You wouldn't treat the just man and the sinner alike?" And God says, "Well, if I can find fifty men, I will save the whole city." But Abraham's pretty smart. He has probably heard a few rumors about Sodom and Gomorrah too. And he says, "Well, perhaps fifty less five." And the Lord looks at him, and He says, "Okay." And he says, "Well, how about forty? Can we come down just a little bit?" And the Lord looks at him, and He says, "Okay, if I can find forty." Can you imagine just talking to God like that? It's a fantastic example of intercessory prayer. You say, "Well, God answers *him*." But He answers you.

And Abraham, he's getting a little scared now. He says, "*I trust My Lord will not be angry, but give me leave to speak. Perhaps there will be only thirty there.*" "Okay." Well, he goes down finally to ten. He said, "If there are only ten men, will You save that city?" He couldn't even find ten. That says something for each one of us. You know when Our Lady of Fátima said to the children, "Pray and do penance"? Our Lady of Medjugorje, "Pray and do penance"? Prayer and penance are such important aspects of today's life. Our Lady has asked us to pray and do penance so that we, too, may become just. Well, what is *just*? It means holy. The just man lives by faith, the holy man lives by faith. And you and I are called by God today to intercede for mankind.

Now, we're not too sure how many hundreds or thousands of people may have been in Sodom and Gomorrah. One thing we can be pretty sure of, there were a lot of people there. And they were wicked. Unbelievably wicked. Unbelievably defiant, proud, arrogant. The concept being, "I will not serve." I will give in to every pleasure, to anything that pleases me. Immorality, thievery, robbery—every kind of evil was in Sodom and Gomorrah. There was not a possibility of finding ten people who prayed to Lord Yahweh for deliverance or prayed for the salvation of that city.

I don't know how many people are in your city. Maybe eleven million, maybe eleven thousand, maybe eleven hundred. Do you realize that ten of you, maybe your family and relatives, could save that whole city with intercessory prayer and by being holy and just? Oh, it doesn't mean you have all kinds of ecstasies and everything that goes with it. It means that you accomplish the will of God, that you practice faith and hope and love in the midst of darkness and doubt and tension and anxiety and frustration and everything that the world, the flesh, and the enemy pour around us. But you keep going through like light, a light in the darkness, a light that darkness cannot overcome as St. John says in his prologue, so that you and I, with great faith and great hope and great love, persevere.

Ten people. So many of you say, "Oh, I can't do anything, I'm only one person." Well, ten of you could save your whole city, obviously, and if it could be done at this time without the Precious Blood of Jesus, can you imagine what can be done *with* the Precious Blood of Jesus? Imagine ten holy people in Birmingham, ten holy people in New York, in Chicago, in New Orleans, in San Diego, in Los Angeles. Big cities, little cities all over this world. Ten people, one holy people offering the Precious Blood of Jesus to the mercy of God the Father, day in and day out.

Yeah, you can save the world. You can. Otherwise, Our Lady wouldn't be asking peasants and people like you and me and all the rest of us to pray so that the Father will have mercy on the world. You say, "That's an awesome responsibility." You're right. You're absolutely right. We are all called by God to be holy, not just for ourselves, but for the whole world. You say, "Well, I don't wanna respond." Well, then that's unfortunate if you don't want to respond because you're not an island, you're not by yourself. You are your brother's keeper, you are responsible. I don't mean that the whole world can go down the drain because you didn't pray, but you may be one of many that creates that swell. That's why we have the Rosary on every night. For me, to think that the Rosary is being said, coast to coast, and people are joined together in this country, saying the Rosary on the air, is a fantastic gift from God. It's a fantastic grace for the whole country. And those of you that are not Catholic, it doesn't matter if you don't say the Rosary; you can respond with any other kind of prayer. You know, you can't listen to the news or read a newspaper or read a magazine without realizing this whole world—it's not just a nation—needs the faith of Abraham.

And sometimes I think a lot of the world is another Sodom and Gomorrah. There are many parts of the world that *are* Sodoms and Gomorrahs. We must pray for them. We must ask the Lord God to have mercy. That's your role, that's my role—intercessory prayer. And in the act of interceding for others, we ourselves become holy because our prayer is unselfish. It is God-centered, it is Kingdom-centered. Think about that for a minute.

Well, we're going to find out what happens. It's kind of sad.

The two angels reached Sodom in the evening, and Lot was sitting at the gate. Now, you have to realize that Lot was Abraham's nephew. Remember, he was the one that looked out, and Abraham said, "You choose what you want, and I'll take what's left." Unselfish man, humble man. Well, Lot took the best. Green grass, lush, water, everything. Well, what he got was Sodom and Gomorrah.

As soon as Lot saw the angels, he rose to meet them and bowed to the ground. He said, "I beg you, my lords, please come to your servant's house and stay the night and wash your feet. Then in the morning, you can continue your journey." So, you see this as a part of hospitality, it was an honor.

"No," they replied, *"We can spend the night in the open street." But he pressed them so much that they went home with him and entered his house. He prepared a meal, baking unleavened bread, and they ate. They had not gone to bed when the house was surrounded by the men of the town, the men of Sodom both young and old, all the people without exception. Calling to Lot, they said, "Where are the men who came to you tonight? Send them out to us so we may abuse them."* Now, we come up against something that's kind of hard for all of us in this day and age to understand. *Lot went out to them at the door, and having closed the door behind him said, "I beg you, my brothers, do no such wicked thing."* What were they talking about? Homosexuality, without question. He said, *"I have two daughters who are virgins. I am ready to send them out to you."* Now, that is absolutely obnoxious to us. But you see, hospitality, to him, took the place of his daughters, and you have to realize that women were like nothing in those days. He said, *"But as for the men, do nothing to them. For they have come under the shadow of my roof.* I am responsible for them."

But they replied, "Out of the way! Here is one who came as a foreigner, and would set himself up as a judge. Now, we will treat you worse than them." Then they forced Lot back and moved forward to break down the door. That looks like a movie! But the angels reached in and pulled Lot back and slammed the door. *And they struck the men who were at the door of the house with blindness, from the youngest to the oldest, and they never found the doorway.* You know, I told you this before. We were talking about Zechariah in St. Luke's Gospel. Don't fuss around with angels. They're toughies.

We look at this, and we just are appalled, but now you begin to realize why they couldn't find ten people that wanted to live a holy life. It was foreign to them, holiness and morality and commandments and goodness and virtue and gentleness and love and compassion. I mean, what are those? And so, you have here a city who had lost all concept of God, goodness — anything. They had degraded themselves to a point where they couldn't see a stranger walk down the street without abusing them.

And so, the whole city, Sodom and Gomorrah, is a city of such permissiveness, of such evil, that it had to be totally destroyed by God. And the angel said to Lot, "The Lord Yahweh has sent us to destroy the city."

You know, I don't like to scare you, but what do you think the Lord will do today? Do you think He'll straighten us out? Do you think He will let us go on and on the way we are? Do you think we'll change? Do you think fire will come from Heaven and consume just the evil? Do you think the earth will quake and the stars fall before we wake up? Wouldn't it be a shame if you and I, who know Jesus and know God and know the Bible, if we force the Lord to that point by refusing to pray for all mankind? And I don't mean you've got to spend all day at it. I'm just saying throughout the day, say, "Lord Jesus, I love You. Save souls." Is that too hard? Say the Divine Mercy Chaplet. Those of you that are Catholic, say your Rosary once a day. We're not asking that you dedicate five, six, seven hours in prayer, but that you pray for mankind whenever you pray. Pray for mankind over the world, not just your own country, your own neighborhood, your own family. Let your prayers be universal.

When you read all these terrible things that are happening, do you just say, "Oh, what an awful thing," or do you kneel down or just close your eyes and quiet your soul long enough to say a prayer? "Lord, have mercy on the hijackers, have mercy on those who are so petrified on those planes and being murdered, all the violence in the world." Do you love enough to do that? Well, if you don't, and nobody else does, are we any different than Sodom and Gomorrah? You say, "Oh, Jesus came and died for our sins and saved us." Oh, I'll buy that. But people are still going to Hell, and they go because they don't take advantage of the Blood of Jesus. They really don't.

And poor Lot. He gets really excited, and he goes to get his future sons-in-law, but they think he's joking. "What are you talking about it? There's gonna be a destruction of this city? Come on, now!" But I hear people say that today. I hear them say, "Oh, come on. What do we have to pray for? It's not that bad. It has always been like this."

It doesn't matter what it always was. It's that souls are being lost every day. "Why would I put that burden on my shoulders?" I'm not asking you to put the whole burden on your shoulders, and neither is God. I'm only saying that when you pray, pray for the whole world. Pray that our dear Lord will have mercy on the world, that our dear Lord will have mercy on sinners, especially hardened sinners. Sinners are so hard in prison in different parts of the world. Sinners who do nothing but plot evil against others and violence. You see, prayer works.

When dawn broke, the angels urged Lot, "Come, take your wife and these two daughters of yours, or you will be overwhelmed in the punishment of this town." And as he hesitated, they took him by the hand because of the pity Yahweh felt for him. And why? Because of Abraham. *They led him and left him outside the town and said, "Run for your life, and neither look behind you nor stop anywhere on the plain. Make for the hills if you would not be overwhelmed."*

So, I hate to end on such a serious note, but I think we've read enough to know that we need to pray, and pray with faith and pray with hope, and know that we have the Lord Jesus with us.

We have the Lord Jesus in our hearts and our minds and our souls. We have the Lord Jesus' Precious Blood to call upon the Father to send down upon all mankind and pray for His mercy upon us. Whatever way He must straighten out the situation that we have messed up so badly in this world, we can, with His love, pray with confidence and ask Him to bless us, to bless the world and save souls.

Jesus and Mary, I love you. Save souls. And may the Precious Blood of Jesus rest upon all of us, have mercy on us, and give us the peace that no one can take away.

EIGHT

Genesis Chapters 19–21

This evening, we are going to continue in Genesis, and you're going to look at Genesis 19:23. It says here: *As the sun rose over the land, Yahweh rained over Sodom and Gomorrah brimstone and fire.* Well, you have to wonder what that means. It's a very unstable section of the country. Even today. At one time, they had an earthquake and it was all flooded, so they built a little bit higher, but it was always an unstable area. And you say, "Well, what is the brimstone and fire?" It may have been a meteorite, who knows? May have been some kind of volcanic ash or something that fell upon them, but it was taken as a kind of clean house from God. You know things have gotten so bad that He decides, "Well, I've gotta clean house. There's no way of getting this thing straight, and I'm gonna really clean it up." And you look at it and say, "Gee, I didn't know God would do that." Well, when something He has made for such high things, such great things, deteriorates more and more, and it's going to get even worse, I think it's an active mercy on God's part to clean it up, because these people obviously are not going to repent. God knows that.

He doesn't want other people getting more and more involved into something, and I think there comes a time when His mercy brings out His justice. We're not always too sure of that, you see. We have to think to ourselves: "Well, I didn't know justice and mercy went together." But they do. They really do go together. The Lord Jesus, when He chastises us—*corrects* us is maybe a better word—but when He chastises us, or He corrects us, it is done out of love because we're absolutely running and rushing in the wrong direction. And so, what happens? His mercy, I think, activates His justice. Because He says, "Now, if I keep letting you go, it's going to get worse and worse and worse." And so, we can't look at this as something very cruel God did. Just imagine how long He waited. He may have waited for 1,500 years before He decided, "Well, it's just no good, they're not gonna change." And then, you see, you don't know what happened to a lot of those people when they saw the fire and the brimstone. They may have all repented. It doesn't take much for us to see God. It doesn't take much for us to repent.

It doesn't take much for God to look down and say, "Oh, you're wonderful." It just doesn't take a lot of repentance. It just takes, "Lord, I'm so sorry." And how do we know that all those people in Sodom and Gomorrah looking at the fire and the brimstone didn't say, "Oh God, Yahweh, help us. We're very sorry"? And I'm sure that many of those may have been saved by that fire and brimstone that would have never been saved, had they continued to go on and on and on and on and on, and we've got to understand that aspect of chastisement. Because if you don't understand that act of chastisement, that act of love and mercy coupled with justice, then you're going to be extremely bitter over everything that happens. So, I am convinced, because I know a little bit about God, that at a time of this sort of chastisement, many souls were saved because of the fire and brimstone that would not have been saved otherwise. So, you have to see in this, not anger, the kind of anger that you and I have that says, "Just wipe them out," but the kind of love and mercy that is coupled with justice and says, "I want to save these souls. I'm gonna have to do something. I'm gonna have to clean up. But in the effort, in the process of cleaning house, I will save their souls. They will repent out of fear." Do you see how important that sentence is? And please keep this in mind. But you know, I think we're living in a time of correction, of warning. Lots of little things happen. We live in serious times.

Well, it says here: *He overthrew these towns and the whole plain and everything that grew there. But the wife of Lot looked back and was turned into a pillar of salt.* Now, she may have strayed back also, and the very fact of salt and brimstone and everything fiery coming down from the heavens may have just covered her and she died. There are kind of weird formations of rock salt in that place. And so, the woman looked back. And this is a lesson for all of us. I don't know whether the salt is a lesson, but I think the real lesson here is that you and I should never look back.

You can always look back and pick out something positive from something very negative. You can just say, "Oh, I made that mistake before, I don't wanna do it again," and those kinds of looking back are good. Those are a good time to look back, to make the present moment and what you're doing in this moment more beneficial and more God-like. But you can't always look back and sit there and get more and more guilty and more and more angry or more and more resentful or revengeful. All the things that we just sit in, some time for years and days and whatever.

And so, I think the idea here is not the fact that she turned into salt. The idea is that looking back out of curiosity, perhaps to see what's going to happen to these other people. But how do we know if she didn't look back, wishing she were there? You know, it's hard to visualize the Israelites wanting to go back to Egypt just for a bunch of onions and garlic. Now, I like onions and garlic, but boy, I wouldn't trek through a desert for them, and I wouldn't want to offend God for some smelly garlic. And I like the stuff—it doesn't always like me—but I like the stuff. But you see, we do have a tendency to give up so much for such a little pleasure, and then some of you that are having affairs and committing adultery, I mean, you could be giving up your entire future—never-ending happiness for a little bit of pleasure. Now, that's just as ridiculous as Lot's wife turning back. Because so often when you turn back, where are you going? Nobody advances going backward. You gotta look forward. Now, if she would have just said, "Well, I trust You Lord, I don't want to go back." You see, when you say she looked back, do you ever look back at your past and think, "Well, I wish I were where I was five years ago, I would do a much better job"? No, you didn't know what you know today, and you would have done the same thing. So, we gotta look at this looking back and say, "Well, I can turn to a pillar of salt too." Well, not literally, it's not like a whole bunch of salt is going to fall on top of you and you're going to freeze, but you're just gonna be stiff and hardened and unapproachable because you keep looking back and you think, "Oh, this is what I had too"—you get bitter. Bitter that all these things happened to us. That could be very salty.

So, sometimes people have a salty tongue when they start living in the past. They say, "Boy you have a salty tongue. It is kind of sharp, cynical, and critical." And so, it's very important that we look at this little paragraph. There is a lot to learn for our lives. Your life and my life. The first is that we shouldn't keep turning back. In fact, St. Paul says somewhere, "I forgot the past, I strained forward ahead to what is to come."

Well, let's go on to the next paragraph. Isn't this fun? I enjoy these lessons.

Rising early in the morning, Abraham went to the place where he had stood before Yahweh and looking towards Sodom and Gomorrah, and across the plain, he saw smoke rising from the land, like smoke from a furnace. So whatever meteorite or fire or brimstone fell, it consumed everything, even the trees on the land. It was just like a blazing fire. *And thus it was that when God destroyed the towns of the plain, he kept Abraham in mind and rescued Lot out of disaster when he overwhelmed the towns where Lot lived.* What a powerful intercessory prayer.

What a beautiful power you and I have before God, that even when a whole town is totally destroyed, one person survives because of intercessory prayer, and that one person was saved by one other person. It wasn't like Abraham's tribe prayed with him, and his wife, and Ishmael. Nothing. It was just a prayer of one man arguing with God. See, the Lord had promised He would save the city if He could find ten. Well, He didn't. But for the sake of Abraham, He saved Lot and his wife. Well, his wife turned around, so she was gone. So, his daughters. So, no matter how bad things are — and believe me, you can't imagine anything getting worse than Sodom and Gomorrah — you have to realize that the Lord God can save your son, your daughter, your husband, wife, mother, father, friends, whoever, they can be saved through your intercessory prayer. Just keep ding-donging at the door of the Lord's heart and say, "Please save Johnny," or Lucy or whoever.

Now, after leaving, Lot settled in the hill country with his two daughters, for he dared not stay in Zoar. He made his home in a cave, himself and his two daughters.

Now, we come along and we find the originality or origin of the Moabites and Amorites, and it's kind of tacky because we find our first account of incest in the Scriptures. And you have to understand here a terrific influence, and I think we're going to look at it because I think it's a great lesson today. You see, Lot's two daughters never had any children because, if you remember, their husbands decided to stay, so they went up in smoke. Well, wherever they were, they were quite alone, so these two daughters got what they thought was a bright idea, and each one slept with their father and became pregnant with a son. One they called Moab, and the other one Ami. And so, this is wrong. The point I think it makes here is that these women, they were so immoral and were influenced by that immorality even after the chastisement was over and they were saved. You would think their gratitude to God would be so overwhelming that they would have taken the fact that they had no children and there was no one around to marry, that they would have taken that with a lighter heart and said, "Well, Lord, we're just so grateful, Lord Yahweh, that we're here. We're living, that we're alive." But they both decided that they'd get their father real drunk, and each one of them in turn became pregnant so they could have what they wanted. They wanted something God obviously didn't want them to have in that way.

So, with all of this as embarrassing as it is even to read, there are two fantastic lessons here. Number one: You can be influenced by evil if you stay in that evil position, even if the Lord God takes you off and puts you in another place. That aura of evil, that permissive spirit, that spirit that no longer sees what's wrong, that spirit that gives you a reason to do unreasonable things, and sometimes even under the guise of righteousness. That's pretty bad. But we do it today over and over and over and over. It's an amazing phenomenon to me. But it shows to stay away from bad companions, bad situations, and occasions of sin, because it grows on you like a fungus, and even if you're taken out of that situation and put somewhere else, if you don't be careful, you're going to kind of backtrack. Because you've allowed this to become a part of you, and this is so very, very important for us to realize. Stay away from occasions, and especially those of you who've had pretty bad lives, and you suddenly come out of it, and now you know Jesus, and you know the Lord—you have to be very careful. Don't think now because you know Jesus, you can just put yourself in occasions of sin, because here is another place where wrong was made to look right. And you find this today—wrong things, evil things, adulterous things, murderous things are looked upon as right.

Drug addiction that blows people's minds and takes away their wills and makes them literally vegetables suddenly becomes legal. You see, we live in a society that's not unlike Sodom and Gomorrah, and the effects are almost the same. We think we've reasoned out something, but it is just a deceptive move toward greater evil, so these two women basically didn't do any better than the people in Sodom and Gomorrah that were slaughtered. Think about that.

So, now we have the origin of the Moabites and Amorites. Unbelievable, isn't it? That people could reason out evil and make it good, or try to think it is.

So, Abraham left there for the land of Negev and settled between Kadesh and Shur, saying once again that his wife Sarah was his sister. You've got to realize that Sarah was about ninety years old. *And Abimelech the king of Gerar had her brought to him. But the Lord appeared to Abimelech in a dream at night: "You are to die because of the woman you have taken, for she is a married woman."* To hear that! All you who think that God doesn't care that you go out on your wife or you go out on your husband and have an affair, well, you've got to look at the Scripture here.

There's so much theology today that seems to give you the right to do that, but it's not true. And you say, "What right does the Church have to say I can't do that?" This book—the Bible. Now, if you don't believe in this book, then you're not a Christian. You're going to pick out some things you like and some things you don't.

Now, Abraham lied again. Seems to me he had kind of a problem. When it came to losing his skin, he was always saying, "She's my sister, she's my sister." So, the Lord God spoke to Abimelech. And you know, the poor king, he said, *"Did he not tell me himself 'She is my sister,' and did not she herself say, 'He is my brother'?" I did this with a clear conscience and clean hands."* And he said, "I didn't touch her." And the Lord said, "Yeah, *because I prevented you from sinning against me. Now send the man's wife back, for he is a prophet and can intercede on your behalf for your life."* Now, that's hard to understand, isn't it? Because after all, Abraham did fib in a way.

I think they were sister and brother in a way; she was his half sister. As you go along, you find that out. But still, Abraham did intercede for the king, because the king, too, should never have just picked her up. There was fault on both sides. When you read the Scriptures, you have to see exactly what it says and what it really says to you and me, that God is always pursuing us, always looking at our sinful condition, but in spite of it, always trying to make us rise above and do something great. Always.

So, Abimelech rose early the next morning and summoning all his servants, told them the story, and they were afraid. Then summoning Abraham, Abimelech said, "What have you done to us? What wrong have I done that you bring a great sin on me and my kingdom? What possessed you to do this?" Abraham said, "*Because I thought there would be no fear of God here and the people would kill me because of my wife. Besides, she is indeed my sister, my father's daughter, though not my mother's; and she became my wife.*" So, there was that element of truth, but the bad part was that Abraham feared himself. He didn't trust God at that point. "I didn't think they were of God," he said. "*So when God made me wander far from my father's home, I said to her, 'Everywhere we go, say of me that I am your brother.'*" So Sarah was his father's daughter, but not his mother's, a kind of half sister.

Abimelech took sheep and cattle, men and women slaves, and presented them to Abraham and gave him back his wife Sarah. And he said, "See, my land lies before you. Settle wherever you please." To Sarah he said, "I am giving one thousand pieces of silver to your brother. For you, this will be compensation in the eyes of all those with you." So, life was different in those days. As God taught us how to be good and how to strive for holiness, you can see a development of spirituality, a development of the pursuit of goodness, virtue. You can see how God revealed Himself to very, very, very primitive people, who had long lost sight of God. And sometimes today, when you talk to people, you realize that, well, how much do we know about God? How much do you and I really comprehend of the Lord God after almost two thousand years of Christianity? Of the Son of God coming down and living in our midst, having such a wonderful Church, and wonderful sacraments, especially the Eucharist? The real Body and Blood, Soul and Divinity of Jesus? Having such a pure creature that we call Mary, having the Spirit within our hearts to bear fruit in plenty, all the wonderous things that God has given us? You have to kind of wonder sometimes how much have we advanced.

Now, I think it's a good question because I would encourage all of you to go on a retreat every once in a while. And even if you just go out in the woods for a couple hours just by yourself or with your husband or wife or children or family—go out and commune with God and go in the back of the church and just sit there and talk to Jesus. You need that relationship.

So, it says that through Abraham's prayer, God healed Abimelech, his wife, and his slave girls so they could have children, because the Lord made them all barren on account of Sarah. Kind of harsh, wasn't it? But Abimelech should have never looked at another woman since he was married. They just kind of collected women like you collect anything else. And the Lord was beginning to reveal to us the sacredness of married life. And the beautiful thing about God is He went according to their ability and their comprehension and their light. So, you can't say today, "Well, I can do the same because that's what they did here in the Scriptures." No, you're talking about development. It's like saying as an adult of fifty that you can go back and say what a book on a three-year-old says, what three-year-olds do. They have books on everything today. In my grandma's day, they had children, they fed them, they raised them, that was it. Now, you gotta do one thing at one year old, another at two, another at three, another at four—it's complicated to have children today. But you get one of these books that tell you what you should do with your child at five. Just because it's true and just because it's written in a book, it doesn't mean that at fifty-five you can go back and do it.

And so it is with the Scriptures. There is a development in Scriptures, so you can't say if it's written in the Scripture, I can do that too. The Scriptures give you courage and strength, talk about reconciliation a lot, because they deal with sinners, and then talk about how God chooses sometimes the very weakest to do the greatest things. You've got to understand this aspect of the Scriptures.

Now, Yahweh dealt kindly with Sarah. So Sarah conceived and bore a son to Abraham in his old age, at the time God promised. Abraham named the son born to him Isaac. Abraham circumcised his son Isaac when he was eight days old, as God commanded him. Abraham was one hundred years old. Then Sarah said, "God has given me cause to laugh, and all those who hear of it will laugh with me. Who would have told Abraham that Sarah would nurse children? Yet I have born him a child in his old age." What a miracle it was. She was ninety-one when he was one hundred. You can't imagine it today. It would sure make news. And it made news then. Because she said, "Everyone is gonna say, 'Wow.'"

Well, if it says anything to us, it says what was said through the angel Gabriel about the birth of John the Baptist: "Nothing is impossible to God." Nothing.

We're not too sure how old Elizabeth was when John the Baptist was born, but that was also another miracle, very similar to this. And there is a similarity because Isaac was the son through whom the promise would be fulfilled. He had Jacob in turn. And from Jacob came the twelve tribes of Israel. Will you look at John the Baptist? John was a forerunner who proclaimed Jesus the Son of God, the Messiah, and from whom and through whose side on the Cross you and I have come. And so even here, God is constantly, always giving us little hints, little tiny hints of the New Testament that is to come. Because these people had no idea that they were being used by God for such a great work. Do you think Abraham knew one day he would be in a book called Scripture, the Bible? And all men would look upon him as a man of faith? That never crossed his mind. He just thought: "Well, here I am, an old man. God promised me a son, and I got it." He had no idea. There he is alone in the desert with his wife, and now a son, and just living a humdrum life. And yet God was using him in a mighty powerful way. And it's the same with you. I know you keep saying, "Well, I'm not doing anything. I'm just trying to be good. I'm just a housewife. I'm just a working man. I'm just a child. I'm just this, or just that." You're not *just*. You're an individual God is using to build up the Body of Christ, to build up the whole Kingdom. That's not just this or just that. That's very important for you to understand.

Now, so after this, he finally gets his son. *The child grew and was weaned, and Abraham gave a great banquet on the day Isaac was weaned. Now Sarah watched the son that Hagar the Egyptian had borne to Abraham, playing with her son, Isaac. And she said, "Drive away that slave girl and her son. This slave girl's son is not to have a share in the inheritance with my son, Isaac."* It's kind of sad. You know, it was the second time it happened. But God said to Abraham, *"Do not distress yourself on account of the boy and your slave girl. Grant Sarah all that she asks of you, for it is through Isaac that your name shall be carried on. But the slave girl's son I will also make into a great nation, for he is your child, too."* I wonder so often these days if we realize that one truth. That the son of the Egyptian girl is Abraham's son also. I wonder if there would be as much quarreling and fighting in the East if they realized they were brothers that go way back to Abraham. I wonder it would be like if we all would understand that one truth.

I think sometimes the saints had that gift of hanging onto one truth and just zeroing in on it and zeroing in on it and just keeping at it until they became great saints because they never lost sight of that one truth. Some of us may call it a motto. There was one truth that just seemed to be in their mind constantly. Well, if we were to ever think of this one truth, that we are all brothers and sisters, we all share the same Father, I wonder if we would really quarrel and fight and build bigger bombs and bigger guns; I wonder if we would even need them. Well, no use wondering. You've got to live with the way things are.

So, *rising early the next morning, Abraham took bread and a skin of water and, giving them to Hagar, he put the child on her shoulder and sent her away. She wandered off into the wilderness of Beersheba.* And you have to feel sorry. She puts her child under a bush, and she went and sat in the distance, and said, "*I cannot see the child die.*" So, she wailed and wept, and you have to feel for her. But God heard the boy and the angel of God called to Hagar from Heaven, "*What's wrong, Hagar? Don't be afraid. God has heard the boy's cry. Come pick up the boy and hold him safe, for I will make him into a great nation.*" *Then God opened Hagar's eyes, and she saw a well. So she went and filled the skin and gave the boy to drink. And God was with the boy.*

So often when you think of Hagar, we just want to kind of push her aside and push her son aside and just say, "Now that was a big boo-boo, and that was a great mistake as far as Abraham is concerned," and it was. Really, this slave girl was a victim of Sarah's bad judgment, bad decisions, and jealousy, there's no question of that. And you can't put sugar coating on that, it's just the way it was. But God permitted it and gave Hagar's son Ishmael a great blessing. He performed a miracle so the boy could drink. *He grew up and made his home in the wilderness, and he became a bowman. His mother chose him a wife from the land of Egypt.* Today, there is still that antagonism. And I think to myself, if we were to read the Scripture sometimes and say, "We're both blessed by God and both protected by God." One was not the chosen one from whom will come the Messiah, from whom would come God's own people. But still, they were blessed by God.

When you look at the neighbor that you despise or hate— and I hope there isn't anybody, but if there is, or a race or a color—then learn something from this. You also must understand that God is good to them, God loves them, God brought them into being, and God has blessed them. Then who are you and who am I to hate them or to do harm to them? Remember, both have been blessed by God. Will you think about that?

Well, I think we've learned a lot. We're going to take a little bit more here. *At that time,* it says in Genesis 21:22, *Abimelech came with the commander of his army to speak to Abraham, saying, "God is with you and all you are doing. Swear by God to me here and now that you will not trick myself nor my descendants nor any of mine, and that you will show the same kindness to me as I have shown you."* They never forgot what happened to them.

Then Abraham said, "I swear it." But he reproached him, Abimelech, about a well that Abimelech's servants had seized. Boy, the king wanted him to know—"*I do not know who has done this. I've only heard of it today.*" They made a covenant between them. Abraham put seven lambs of the flock on one side, and Abimelech said, "How come seven lambs?" Abraham said, "*You must accept these seven lambs from me as evidence that I have dug this well.*" *This is why they called that place Beersheba, because there the two of them swore an oath.*

You see, in those days they didn't have written contracts, so human nature being what it is, somebody went up and said, "That's my well." But Abimelech was afraid of Abraham. He knew God was with him. He wasn't about to get in trouble for something his servants were doing. He'd had trouble with Abraham before. So, what lesson does it teach us? Well, I think honesty, for one. And don't covet. Covetousness is a great sin today. I think it is. We covet other people's goods, other people's talents, other people's possessions. We either envy them and wish we had them, or we try to destroy them or try to get them ourselves or try to humiliate them, or act like what they have doesn't seem to be that good.

So, we spend a tremendous amount of time in our lives coveting, trying to get something that really doesn't belong to us, but getting it for ourselves. There again, you learn, what is the way of God? Now, when the Church speaks to us about moral issues and faith issues, all the other issues, they are all in the Bible. The Church is just the voice of God that is saying, "Instead of you having to plow through this thing"—and it's a beautiful thing, this is the Word of God, it's a holy Word of God—but you can't possibly get all of it together, looking at one thing and having to take other things into consideration, knowing that they all go together. When you begin to take things out of context, then that's where you get in trouble. So, look at the Scriptures and look at the Church, and you'll find the same thing. If you don't like what the Church is saying, then you don't like what the Scriptures are saying. Because the Church interprets and tells you exactly what the Lord God wants. And we've learned a lot here. We've learned an awful lot. Maybe you learned things you didn't want to learn.

I hope not. I hope you realize that God's mercy is also within and sometimes pushes forth His justice, and then He turns around and brings so much good that He will save the souls that brought down His justice. Maybe that's the only way to get them into the Kingdom. We've learned we can trust God's promises, certainly. We've learned that we must be honest, we learned that we must trust. And that's what I want you to do. Trust God with your life. Just as I have to trust God with mine—my sisters, all our staff, and crew employees on this network—we're all on the journey of trust.

NINE

Genesis Chapter 22

We have been taking a look at Genesis. Well, we saw that the Lord finally fulfilled His promise. And that was that Sarah and Abraham would have a child, and that child was named Isaac. Well, the child grew up. Everything looks great. I mean, Abraham got his wish, God's promise has been fulfilled. His faith has been rewarded, I guess we could say. So, life seems to be going on very well, and then something happened. And I want you to understand that your life and my life are very much the same. You just think, "Oh, I've got it made, I'm healthy, my kids are healthy, everybody's doing fine, we got our house paid off, and I've got a good job," and suddenly it just either blows apart or something happens that makes whatever we had that made us happy seem suddenly not there. Well, if it's any comfort to you, this happened to Abraham, the man of faith. So, if you think your faith is weak, well, don't get disheartened because this great man of faith had quite a trial.

Let's look at it. So, you want to turn to Genesis 22. Now, you have to remember in these lessons we're giving, we're not looking at the exegesis of Scripture, we're not going to tell you the exact height of Mount Sinai or all the geographical information that's possible. We're looking at what I call devotional Scripture. What does it mean to you in your present life right now? I think, today, this is the most important aspect of Scripture. So, let's look at it.

Okay, it says: *It happened some time later that God put Abraham to the test.* That brings up quite a few questions, doesn't it? You say, "Well, is my test from God, or did I bring it on myself? Or is it from the enemy, or is the world crowding in around me?" Oh, that's what you need discernment for, that's why you need to pray to the Holy Spirit, so you know whether something in front of you is a real test or it just happened and you've got to handle it. We'll go into that a little deeper later on.

Now, He called, and Abraham said, "Here I am." In Latin, "Here I am" is Hic sum. And in religious life, in our order when I was a young sister, if your superior called your name, you said, "Hic sum," which means "Here I am." The reason being that you were imitating the voice of Samuel when he tried to say, "Here I am," when the Lord said, "Samuel, Samuel." Now, here is the Lord saying to Abraham, before Samuel, "Abraham, Abraham." And he gets the same reply, "Here I am." And you know, wouldn't it be wonderful if we could say that to God every day? Isn't that what Mary said when the angel Gabriel said to her, "The Spirit will overshadow you and you shall bear a son and call Him Jesus." Well, Mary said, "*fiat*," which means: "Be it done to me according to Your will." *Fiat.* Basically, this is the same "Here I am." But the *fiat* to me was deeper. It says, "Whatever You want, Lord." Here, it's a little different because Abraham is merely saying, "Well, I'm here." He didn't know what He wanted yet. And sometimes, Our Lord treats us that way. There are times He says, "Mary," and He just wants to know you're there.

He wants you to be present to Him, and I wonder during the day how much we're present to His presence. If He called our name, would you say, "Here I am"? Or would you even hear it? Would you hear the voice of God if He called you like He did Abraham? Maybe we're too busy. And we have so many things that happen to us. So many things that are important things, that are part of life. But you know, I think we need some time to sit down and say, "Well, what is important in my life? And I'll put it down on a piece of paper." So, if the Lord ever said, "Abraham, Abraham," you could say, "Here I am." You wouldn't say, "Well, now wait a minute, Lord, I gotta go to a football game. You understand it's the game of the year." Or, "I've gotta do this, or I'm gonna do that, or this is so important, that's so important." And you just keep yourself all revved up for nothing. And many things are important. That's okay. But, there's a certain amount of superfluity in our life that I think we could just blow away. So, if the Lord ever said to us, "Abraham," or "John," or "Jim," or anything, "Carol," you could say, "Here I am," kind of willing to drop it all. That's what Abraham said.

"*Take your son,*" God said, "*your only child, Isaac, whom you love.*" The Lord is kind of putting it on him. "*And go to the land of Moriah. There, you shall offer him as a burnt offering on the mountain I will point out to you.*" Oh, that's unbelievable. You have to go back a little bit to see how many promises and how long Abraham and Sarah waited. The boy may have been nine, ten, eleven years old. Who knows? And maybe older — fifteen, sixteen, who knows? And He says, "I want you to take the one you love, the one you've waited for, and I want him as a burnt offering." Do you realize what it would mean to be killed, slaughtered, and burned? I mean, it's hard to do that with a pet. All you animal lovers, what if the Lord said, "I want you to take your pet now and slit its throat"? I mean, how far do we love God? You say, "I don't understand." But that isn't the point. You see, here understanding was not the point at all.

How much do you love God? How far are you willing to go if He should ask? Not some little idea you got in your head, "I'm gonna do this and that." If He should ask, and you were *sure* He was asking you, how far would you and I be willing to go?

Well, rising early the next morning, Abraham saddled his ass and took with him two of his servants and his son Isaac. You know, can you imagine that evening when Isaac went to bed? Abraham must have asked himself a thousand times during the night, "Why does God want this?" Well, you have to remember that right in the middle, right in the very beginning, it said, "God put Abraham" — what? "To the test." It was a test. "I just want to see how much this man loves Me." I mean, how far are you willing to go? Well, sometimes you and I have a hard time with tests, let alone knowing whether it is from God or not. I think you could have talked yourself out of this real well.

I think I would have tried it. You know, I think I would have said, "Well, that's not the Lord. I mean, why would the Lord give me something and then ask me to offer it up? I mean, we're talking about a human being, we're not talking about a cow or a pigeon. Why would He do that? So, it must not be the Lord." I think in those days, Abraham was sure, because he'd heard the same voice, he saw the Lord. I think he was sure, because he had this experience before. You and I may not be too sure, and God would never ask us to sacrifice any individual today as a test. But He does ask things within reason within our own realm, and some of them sometimes don't seem reasonable, but they are if God asks them.

You know, I think a lot us have had this experience. I have. Sometimes, the Lord pushes us just to see if we're willing to give up something, and then when He see that we are, He doesn't even take it. Ever had that happen to you? "Are you willing to do this?" And you really start to give this thing up, and the Lord says, "It's okay." These are tests. And yet in the Our Father, the Lord said, "Do not put us to the test." In the Agony in the Garden, He said to the apostles, "Pray, lest you are put to the test." Well, we know that the test was going to come, so what was He really praying about? You say "Well, is God playing some kind of game with me?" No. Your soul must grow in faith, hope, and love. And it is in darkness or offering and sacrifice that I say, "Lord, I believe, even though You've taken everything away from me, I believe in Your love. Lord, I hope even though I see nothing ahead of me, I hope in Your Word, I hope in Your promise, I put my hope in eternity." And when it's so difficult to love, not only some people, but just to love at all, that's when we continue making that effort, making those decisions. In marriage, to stay together. In family life, to stick together. We just have to do that. We must do that.

And these sometimes are tests, and as I said before, they're sometimes things that are thrown upon us by other people's evil intent, though God does not will them. And as Our Lord said, "It's better for them that they drown in the ocean." Still, we are sometimes victims of other people's ill will, but even if those seemingly unreasonable, unfair, unjust times are in our life, faith says, as it did to Abraham, "God is with me, and I will accomplish His will." You say, "I don't understand." You don't need to understand why something has happened to have great faith in God. The greater the faith, most of the time, the less you understand. I hope that's a comfort to you. It should be.

So, Abraham rose up early, chopped wood for the burnt offering, and started on his journey to the place God had pointed out to him. On the third day—oh, do you realize the agony of this man? The night before he started the journey, three solid days of looking at his son, thinking it's all over, thinking of the heartache, the frustration, wondering how in the world he could get up the gumption to do that.

But nevertheless, this is an important lesson. Remember, this *is* a lesson. As he proceeded on the journey to accomplish the will of God, at that moment his faith was growing every single day, higher and higher. He felt worse and worse and worse. I know the concepts you get today of people having great faith and great joy, and they claim everything, and everything just kind of pops up like flowers in spring. I don't see that here. I see a man whom we look back at and admire, whom Paul says was a man of faith, the greatest man of faith in all of the Old Testament, by whom men are cursed or blessed. And yet the greater his faith was and the greater it grew, the more agony he had. Three days is no short time, it must have seemed like eternity. His feet must have gotten heavier and heavier and heavier.

Well, you know, that's similar to things that are happening today. A lot of parents have children on drugs and alcohol and prostitution, and tough love is just as agonizing when you are forced to say for the good of the rest of your family, "Son, you've got to go. You can no longer act like this and live under this roof." Isn't that the same kind of agony? You say, "Is it a test?" I don't know if it is or not. It's an effect of a bad cause, it's an effect of other people's bad decisions, but perhaps the test is whether or not you're willing to protect your own soul and your wife's soul and your other children's souls and try to help this son in another way. See, Abraham never ceased to love his son. In fact, it was his great love that made this so difficult. Although you and I are not called to sacrifice those we love as burnt offerings, is not the pain similar and just as difficult? When you have an alcoholic husband that is causing a rampage in the house night after night, and the children are getting nervous, and they can't study, and they're being abused. Maybe you still love him or her, and yet you're put to the test, aren't you? You've got to make a choice, a greater good instead of a lesser good—most the time, instead of an evil.

So, don't look at this incident in the Scriptures as something that only happened to Abraham. You have to look at Abraham and say, "What did it do to Abraham?" And I feel sorry for the son, I really do, because he doesn't know yet that he's the sacrifice. It took a while for him to catch on. So, it's just one of those things that's so delicate and yet, oh wow, it's so important for you and I to understand.

Well, here we are. It says here: *On the third day, Abraham looked up and saw the place in the distance.* Oh, can you imagine Abraham's heart skipping about fifty beats? He's been traveling with his son three days, knowing that the Lord has said this: "I want you to offer him up as a burnt offering." Now, he's hoping he can't find the mountain, and all of a sudden, he's traveling three solid days, and he looks up … there it is. It's really going to happen.

Well, *then Abraham said to his servants, "Stay here with the donkey. The boy and I will go over there; we will worship and come back to you."* Can you imagine his heavy heart? He didn't have the heart to tell the servants what he was going to do or what he was asked to do. See, it's very similar to if you've got to tell your son or your daughter to leave the house because it's just creating such an uproar constantly. You've got to be having the same feelings as Abraham, that heaviness of heart that you just don't want to tell anybody. It just has to be a horrendous effect emotionally, spiritually, physically, mentally. Your whole being paralyzed. Well, don't forget now we're talking about the man of faith feeling all these things. It's so contradictory to what you hear so much about faith: faith is joy, faith is this, and faith is that. I get so angry when I hear that because this is *real* faith, and you don't need to take a backseat because you feel the same way. You also have faith, and if you didn't, you wouldn't be making a hard decision. You have to understand that.

Now, *Abraham took the wood for the burnt offering and loaded it on Isaac.* You're talking about an old man; he may have been 110, 112, maybe 116 by this time. He loaded the wood on Isaac *and carried in his own hands the fire and the knife.* He had a torch in his hand and a knife. You don't need much imagination at this point to understand that this man of faith wasn't even thinking of faith, he was only saying, "Oh, I've only got to do what God has asked me: an awesome sacrifice." When the two set out together, Isaac, he's beginning to catch on. *He said, "Father," and Abraham said, "Yes, my son?"* I mean, we're getting close to that moment of moments. *"Look," he said, "here are the fire and the wood, but where is the lamb?"* He's beginning to wonder. "What kind of sacrifice are we going to have?" *Abraham answered, "My son, God himself will provide the lamb for a burnt offering." Then the two went on together.* I would imagine, extremely silent, because Isaac must have been looking around and seeing that there are no lambs on this mountain.

Now, you begin to see two men struggling. They're not thinking, "Oh, I have faith." Now, Abraham said, "God Himself will provide," but at that moment, you have to understand that was just a way of not telling his son: "You're *it*."

When they arrived at the place God pointed out to him, Abraham built an altar there and arranged the wood. Then he bound his son Isaac and put him on the altar on top of the wood. You have to admire Isaac for letting him do it. I mean, I think he had every legitimate reason for saying, "Hey, wait a minute. You remember, I'm your son! I'm the one you waited for all those years." The remarkable thing to me also is that Isaac laid on the wood and permitted his father to bind him up. And Abraham stretched out his hand and seized the knife to kill his son. I mean, this is what you call the twelfth hour.

Now you say, "Well, does God push you that far?" Yes, He does. Sometimes, we don't understand, but He does. So, why don't we just rest on that a minute and think about it. Try to put it in the context of your own life. And understand that in many instances, not as serious as this one, and of course never to take another person's life, but the Lord was giving us all throughout the centuries a prefiguration of His own Son and a test of faith. Remember, the terrible thing that you're going through right now is also a test to faith, not something always designed by God, but something permitted by God to make you grow, even though you feel absolutely, totally miserable.

So as soon as Abraham raised the knife and was about to fulfill what the Lord had asked him to do, he heard the same voice that said, "Abraham, Abraham."

And Abraham said, "I am here." Well, I would probably say, "Well, it's about time." I would have said something like that. I don't have that kind of faith, I guess. But you know, you find in Abraham two foundation stones for faith: obedience and humility. Only an obedient, humble man would have said, "I am here." Before he said, "Here I am," meaning, "I'm ready to do what You want." When He said, "Abraham, Abraham," he said, "I am here." In other words, "I'm doing what You told me to do. I don't understand, but I'm here." Well, you see, he said that with a heavy heart, and he said it with a clouded mind. He didn't understand. He said it with lead feet. But he said it. That is faith. "I am here."

Okay. Now, the Lord said, "*Do not raise your hand against the boy. Do not harm him, for now I know you fear God. You have not refused me your son, your only son.*" Now, here we have to stop because this prefigures the sacrifice of Jesus. The Father gave us Jesus out of love, willingly. And Jesus consented willingly. We have a difference here. A little difference. Abraham obeyed, and so did Isaac. Their fear of God. They wanted to please God, and their faith led them to make any sacrifice rather than to displease the Lord, and it was love.

Fear of the Lord is not a bad thing. It's one of the gifts of the Spirit. I can be afraid of you, and so I cringe at your presence. Or I'm afraid the way people are afraid of bullies, so they just do what they want just to keep them quiet and peaceful. But this isn't the fear Abraham had. I don't think the fear of God that he had was that type of fear. It was the fear that comes from love. He didn't want to displease the Lord, he knew He was Yahweh of Heaven and earth, the God of all creation. His humility told him that He has absolute sovereign rights over me and everyone and everything that belongs to me. You and I have forgotten that, oh, we have forgotten so bad. Women say, "God has no right over my body, I have rights over my body to abortion." So, you see how bad it is that she's just not only having an abortion, which is killing a child, but is also that awesome rebellion that says: "I will not serve."

And there is no fear of God at all. Afterward, there is guilt. But there is no fear of God. You see, fear is a good thing. It has to be the right kind of fear. But fear is not a bad thing. Fear is a good thing. But see, what Jesus and the Father did was so much more exalted than what Abraham did. Jesus came down, looking forward to His sacrifice. The Father sent Him, looking forward to His Son's sacrifice so we could be redeemed. That's the extent of Their love for you. There was no one around to say, "Well, we're going to stop it at this point. We just want to see if Jesus is willing to do this." The Father at no place said, "It's okay, Son." In the Agony in the Garden when Jesus said,

"Father, let this chalice pass from Me if it's possible," at no time did the Father say, "Okay. You've gone this far, I know You love Me." So, what God does not ask of us, He did Himself.

You see, and both the Father and Son did it willingly. Not only willingly, They did it with infinite love. He said, "I have a baptism—He called all of his passion a baptism—with which I am to be baptized, and how straightened I am, how anxious I am, to accomplish this for You."

You see, there is a difference. But it prefigures, so that we mentally would begin to understand love, we would begin to understand love when we look at Abraham. *Well, looking up, Abraham saw a ram caught by its horns in a bush. He took the ram and offered it as a burnt offering in place of his son. He called that place "Yahweh Provides."* We've all been pushed seemingly to the end of our faith, that we did not realize what we thought was the end of our faith was merely expanding it beyond our sight. Beyond our wildest dreams. And God somehow provides.

You know, my life and my sisters, since we've been here in Birmingham, and especially with this network, many a time the Lord has pushed us through other people or through circumstances, lack of funds, whatever, pushed us to that point of seemingly no return. The edge of the top of the hill or the mountain where there's nothing but a straight drop all the way down. And yet when you got to that point, when you got to that point where you were totally helpless and had to admit it and knew that only God was your Defender and your Protector and your Provider, when you really got to the point where you believe it, not only with your heart but with your mind and your soul and every fiber of your being, you could say to God, "O Lord, only You can provide."

At that point, He always provided whatever it was. And so, we see in this marvelous incident a test. "How much do you love Me?" The Lord says this today in other ways. I think it's just as difficult for many of us because there's so much confusion. Theological and spiritual confusion in the churches, the doctrines and dogmas. You get confused, and so you want to just give it up and give in and say, "Oh, I'm not going to church anymore because it's all confusing, and I don't like the music." And how much do you love the Eucharist? How much do you love Jesus? That even in the midst of sour notes, you're willing to be there for His sake? So, it is hard. So, it is difficult. So, it's different than it was in the past. So, you don't have incense. And they're not carrying candles. How much do you love God? So, some priest or nun did hurt you. So, you found one drunk. So, they weren't what you thought they were, they're imperfect human beings. So, somehow it didn't ring true. But how much do you love Jesus? How much? Is that what keeps you back, that little test? That you don't love Him enough to just push all of these things aside and say, "Jesus, no matter what, You are still in the Eucharist."

When He says, "This is My Body and this is My Blood"—it is the Real Presence of Jesus. Don't you know that your faith will grow and is growing when you keep going to Mass? "Well, I don't get anything out of it." What do you go for? To tickle your gizzard? You get out what you put in. If you're going there to be some kind of a family with some kind of social group, stay out. The Mass is a sacrifice. You've got to put your sacrifice in that chalice, and maybe the only sacrifice is getting out of bed or having to give up the incense and all the rest, but nothing has changed. Jesus is coming into our midst. So, why do you stay away? Why can't you take that little test, when God has asked this man and other people even around you for greater things, to prove your love? Or you succumb to temptations? Adultery, sex, drunkenness, drugs. How much do you love God? Abortion. All those things. Disobedience. Rudeness to your parents. Gossiping about your neighbor. You say, "Well, you can't compare that with Abraham's son." Look, my friends, it doesn't take a big thing to do you in all the time, just a lot of little things that pile up, and suddenly, *boom!* Something happened very drastically.

Let's look and see what the Father said to Abraham. He said, *"I swear by my own self—it is Yahweh who speaks—because you have done this, because you have not refused me your son, your only son, I will shower blessings on you. I will make your descendants like the stars of heaven and the grains of sand on the seashore. Your descendants shall gain possession of the gates of their enemies. All nations of the earth will bless themselves by your descendants, as a reward for your obedience."* The next time you're tempted to do something very big, whether it's embezzling money, stealing five bucks from your dad, or going out and goofing off, drinking more than you can handle and all the other stuff that you seem to be tempted to all the days and during the nights ... Know that though the pain of sacrifice may be long, the reward is forever. Are you willing to give up this much? Are you willing to give up treasures for a nickel? Are you willing to give up your soul forever for five minutes of pleasure, for a night where you're dead drunk, and you have no idea what you're doing?

Does that make any sense to you? Does it make any sense that you say, "I wanna live in a shack," when you could live in a three-hundred-room mansion? That makes sense to you? Obedience and humility are absolute necessities for faith, otherwise, your faith is just one of these emotional types of things that make you feel better, kind of builds you up.

I think we've learned a lot about Abraham. I think we learned a lot about our own life and how similar we are to Abraham and how all the other things that happen to us are very similar to what happened to Abraham. Maybe the intensity isn't as great, but we did learn a lot of things, didn't we? We learned that in the midst of the greatest act of faith, there is a certain amount of, well, pain, darkness, problems. So, I hope that you and I got a lot more courage to trust God, not to ask why, but just say at some times, "Here I am," and other times, "I am here," and know that whatever sacrifice you make to follow the Lord, He will reward you a millionfold.

God bless you.

TEN

Genesis Chapters 23 & 24

We went through that marvelous opportunity that Abraham had, to sacrifice his son to the Lord. And we learned how God pushes us. He really does. He pushes and pushes us. Right now, I feel pushed. And that said, sometimes that rat race that you and I seem to live in today, you've got to apply the Scriptures to where you are. If they're just a historical fact that existed thousands of years ago, or if it's only something that you go to for inspiration when you're in a crisis. But when you're in a crisis, inspiration comes hard. Unless it comes directly from the Lord by some infused thought, it comes hard to be inspired when you're just hanging on, huh? That's just where you and I are many times in our life, and I want you to know it's okay. The Lord tests us. Oh, not because He don't have anything else to do. He wants you to know that He matters to us more than anything else, and I think sometimes that's what He meant by, "Unless you're willing to leave your mother, father, brothers, land, possessions for My sake." They're hard words.

And before we go to Genesis, I would do a disservice to my guardian angel if I didn't talk a little bit about the guardian angels, and some of you don't even know you have one, and that's a shame, because you do. You know what I marvel about God? So many things I marvel about God. And that is

His extravagance. He's absolutely extravagant. To think that each one of us has a companion close to Him, I mean, I've got my own supernatural being that knows God so well. The beauty of this morning's Gospel is that it says, "Be careful that you don't offend him because he always sees the face of My Father." You and I, most of us, are very busy. Especially if you have children. You're bringing one here and one there, and one has basketball, and one has football, and it's a thousand things you're going to, and you just run from one thing to another, so obviously your angel is busy, but he never takes his face away from God. What does that mean? It means that in the midst of it all, you make right choices. If I have a choice of being rude because I feel like being rude or of being kind and imitating Jesus in my life, if I make that choice, I have kept my face toward God. I don't think it means that I'm in a state of prayer all the time, though I try to be. Just things get you here, they get you here, that get you all around. You try hard, it just doesn't seem to come easy. But if we're making right choices, we're always then facing God. So, you see, it's really not hard to be holy by just doing what you're doing—providing it's good, of course—being faithful to the duties of your state in life and keeping your face, your mind, your heart toward God.

This way, when you have these choices—and sometimes there're sudden choices—you'll almost automatically choose God over yourself or anyone else. And this is so important today because we are just so rude, so selfish, we almost compete with one another on who can be the most selfish. And so, when you look at virtue, it's almost: "*What?*" Virtue is that ability to choose God over oneself. And so today, the great feast of the guardian angels, pray to him, pray and ask him every day to guide you and guard you and protect you. But most of all, if you have problems praying, especially meditating, when you want to see God in the present moment, ask your angel to help you. He was there. He was there when the Lord was born, and he was there when He walked the earth, and he was there when He had to argue with the Pharisees and Sadducees. He was there when He was hurt and saddened. And when He laughed, he also had to laugh. And he was there when He was crucified and rose from the dead. He was there the whole time and waited probably, if we can measure time, and you can't measure time really in relationship to eternity, but it took a lot, it took millions of years for you to be born. Yet he waited all that time. To know and love you. To be such a friend. There's no friend on earth you could ever have like your angel—your guardian. So, I suggest you give him a name, so you don't just say, "Hey, you." Give him a name. And talk to him. I'm talking to mine quite a bit these days because who else is as interested in my heartaches and frustrations as he is?

So, okay, we're going to go back to Genesis 23. And we learned here that Sarah died at 127 years. So, she lived quite a few years after Isaac was born. She had the joy, the pleasure of seeing her son grow up.

Sometimes, I wonder if Abraham ever told her what he was almost going to do. Can you see her having just one big fit? I don't think she understood the Lord God Yahweh that Abraham loved so much and had so much faith in and was willing to give everything. Well, I bet he didn't tell her. I bet he didn't even tell her when it was over. Whatever. She does die. And of course, Abraham goes to a lot of trouble trying to find a burial place. And we're not going to go through that, but if you turn to chapter twenty-four, you'll find that Isaac is old enough now to marry. And we find here the same problems you have. That's amazing how everything in here is just very much like everything, everything in your home. You all worry about your sons and your daughters, you all worry what's going to happen to them, you all worry that they're on the wrong track. You worry especially if they're on drugs or all of you who have children that have run away or been kidnapped or whatever. What a terrible, terrible heartache. So today, one of the main problems of parents is that constant concern about your children, what's going to happen to them when you're gone. What's going to happen? See, everything looks so bleak. So, what's going to happen to them now?

Well, Abraham had the same problem. We're going to talk about that in just a minute. We're going to learn something here about Providence, and it's very providential that today is the feast of the guardian angels because we're going to hear something about them in this very chapter. *By now*, it says, *Abraham was an old man, well on in years. He said to the elder servant of his household, "Place your hand under my thigh."* This was a way of swearing an oath to the Lord. And he said, *"You will not choose a wife for my son from the daughters of the Canaanites."* He wanted to be sure that his son would always be knowledgeable in the ways of Yahweh. To Abraham, that was so important. Sometimes at the thought of death, we wonder how much we're going to leave our children. Are you going to leave them a house? Are you going to leave them money? And all these things are good, and if you have them, you've got to dispose of them, certainly. That's what wills are for. I wonder, though, if we shouldn't also be concerned about their spirituality. And Abraham's only concerned with that. He said, *"Go to my own land and my own kinfolk to choose a wife for my son."* Aren't you glad somebody didn't choose a wife or a husband for you? Of course, maybe they would have done a little better.

So, the servant is getting a little bit uneasy. These oaths were very, very binding. *And the servant asked him, "What if the* woman does not want to come with me to this country? Must I take your son back to the country from which you came?" And right away, we see Abraham's faith.

You know, sometimes we have to examine ourselves. When we're in a very bad situation or heartache, or we lose someone we love, does God come to our mind first? Does the Lord Yahweh come to our mind? Does Jesus and His suffering and all He did for us—does that come to your mind first? Or do we just wander off in bitterness and wondering what happened or why, and getting angry and frustrated? See, that's what it means to turn your face away from God. It means that you have turned your face away from God because you're angry. It's like a child pouting because you didn't give them what they wanted. And so, for a moment, you just turn your head. Well, you see, Abraham says, "*On no account take my son back there! Yahweh, God of heaven and God of earth, took me from my father's home and from the land of my kinfolk, and he swore to me that he would give this country to my descendants. He will now send his angel ahead of you, so that you may choose a wife for my son there.*"

Can you see the depths of Abraham's faith? You know what really gets me? This man was the father of the faith of all the Israelites. He is our father also. So, the faith he had, as great as it was, should be nothing—absolutely nothing—compared to the faith you and I should have because of Jesus. We are children of the promise. They waited for something. They didn't even know what they were waiting for. But you and I are children of the promise. We know Jesus. You and I are living in the time of Jesus. We know Him, we love Him. As St. John says, "We have seen Him." And our daily life in our faith should be ever so much higher than Abraham's because we have more. We have so much more than Abraham had.

So, let's go on and see what this man did and then compare it with what God must expect from you and me.

"*If the woman does not want to come back with you, then you will be free from this oath.*" What a gentle, kind man.

You and I might have said, "Look here, buddy, if you don't find her, you just better stay there till you do." But you see, Abraham saw God in everything. What he's saying is that if you leave this land and you go here and you don't find exactly what it is, it is the Lord. You know, you and I don't say that. You say, "Oh, it's rotten luck. It's circumstances. It's so and so. It's unfair. It's unjust." Well, you say, "God doesn't send bad things." He permits them. When He gave you and I free will, well, then He permits some people to make wrong decisions, and you and I, as we've mentioned many times before, are oftentimes victims of other people's bad decisions. And our own too. We make our own bad decisions. You can't blame everything that happens to us on everybody else. Sometimes, it's us. Let's look and see what happened.

The servant took ten of his master's camels and something of the best of all his master owned, and set out. In the evening, at the time when women go down to draw water, he made the camels kneel outside the town near the well.

And then here comes even the servant. They talk to God all the time. The servant didn't say, "Well, now see, I better get smart here, or I'm in trouble. That girl looks kind of nice. Or that one?" *He said, "Yahweh, God of my master Abraham, be with me today.*" He didn't even understand the God of Abraham. He just said, "You're the God of my master. *Show your kindness to my master, Abraham. Here I stand by the spring as the young women from the town come out to draw water. To one of the girls I will say, 'Please tilt your pitcher and let me drink.' If she answers, 'Drink, and I will water to your camels too,' may she be the one you have chosen for your servant Isaac. By this, I shall know you have shown your kindness to my master."*

Now, you say, "Well, am I supposed to go around asking for signs for everything?" No, that's not the point here. The point here is that God was in every moment of their lives. The poor man didn't know what to do, and so he just made up a kind of sign. He said, "Look, I'm gonna tell one of these girls to give me something to drink and choose the one who does it and says, 'I'll also give some water to your camels.'" And you say, "Well, gee, it seems like in the old days, God was more active." Now, I don't think He was more active. He's got to be more active *now* because of Jesus. What did Abraham have to work on? He had his problems, he had his troubles, he lived in a desert. You could look around, and there was nothing for miles but dust. They keep traveling to find enough grass for their cattle and sheep, and life was so difficult, and yet with all of the struggle, with all their frustration, they talked to God. I mean, here's Abraham, who takes a servant he trusts. He says, "Look." He was getting old. "Go find a wife for my son." Now, obviously love didn't mean that much in those days, but now we have to leave that aside because much that you read here in this beginning of Scripture, we have to remember they're products of a very crude, primitive people who didn't know what you know, didn't have the standards that you have, and yet today we see all these beautiful standards just being crushed and dissolved into nothingness, where right is wrong and wrong is right.

God has given us so much. We polluted the air. We have messed up His doctrines and the deposit of faith, so people don't know what to believe. Where rebellion, defiance, disobedience, dissent seem to be the brave thing instead of all those beautiful virtues that we used to imitate in the lives of the saints, and that's why I urge you, especially your teenagers, I urge everyone: go to your bookstore, go to the library, and get the lives of the saints. Get somebody that you can imitate or at least give you courage. Courage to keep your face toward God. That's what's so important.

Now, let's see what happens. *He had not finished speaking when Rebekah came out, and she was the daughter of Bethuel*, the son of Abraham's brother. And we have to remember, they married cousins because they wanted to keep everything in the tribe. *She had a pitcher on her shoulder. The girl was very beautiful and a virgin; no man had touched her.* Isn't that strange? That was so important. Is it important today? When they give birth control pills to high school students? Doesn't that tell something about the mentality of the age? Instead of saying that this is sinful and that your soul is in danger, they give you pills so you don't get pregnant. Do you realize how far we've gone down? They say, "Well, that's better than having an unwed mother."

Do you realize that you add evil to evil? It's in the Scripture here. It was a point of honor. Nowadays, to be a virgin is almost a point of which to be discreet. They say, "What's wrong with you?" If you are a virgin, male or female, hang on to it until God chooses that partner for you that He wants. It's so important that we begin to raise up a chaste generation. Where values become important again. Where it's important to give yourself to God. Think about it. I think it's extremely necessary for us because we have so diluted and so brushed aside all the grace and beauty and faith and hope and love and everything that God has literally poured down upon us in His magnificent extravagance. Now we have to almost go back to Abraham to learn some very fundamental virtues like virginity and obedience and Providence.

Well, it says here that Rebekah was very beautiful. She was a virgin. And the servant ran to meet her. She went down to the spring and filled her pitcher. *The servant said, "Please give me a little water to drink from your pitcher."* And the girl said, "Drink, my lord." She gave him to drink. *And when she had finished letting him drink, she said, "I will draw water for your camels also until they've had enough."* So, she quickly emptied her pitcher into the trough and ran to the well again to draw water and drew water for all of the camels while the man watched in silence, wondering whether Yahweh had made his journey successful or not.

Isn't this a great example of how to live with God? With your face turned towards God, as the Lord has asked us in this morning's Gospel, saying, "Do not scandalize him—your angel—for he always sees the face of My Father in Heaven."

Well, when the camels had finished drinking, the man took a gold ring weighing half a shekel and put it through her nostrils and put on her arm two bracelets weighing ten gold shekels. You say "I don't particularly like that idea." But that was the custom of the day. *He said, "Whose daughter are you? Please tell me. Is there room at your father's house for us to spend the night?" And she answered, "I am the daughter of Bethuel."* She went on, *"We have plenty of straw and fodder and room to lodge."*

Now, there's another lesson here that you and I have to learn, and we've learned it before from Abraham, and that's hospitality. God only knows how many trips she made from that well to the trough in order to give drink to those camels. She didn't say, "Well, look, you're a man, why don't you go in and get this water?" She didn't have any trouble with her identity as a woman, and that was the custom of the day. That's what women did. And not only that, but she found no problem with them staying the night. So, we're not saying you should open your door to every Tom, Dick, and Harry, we are saying that there is that element of kindness and love and hospitality that you have to give even your friends. Sometimes, we're so rude. You make people feel, "Well, are you here again?" Somebody calls, it's like, "I'm in a hurry." Well, maybe you are, but you see, there are times you can say it nicely. If you have to, say, "Oh, can I call you back? There's somebody at the door," or whatever, there is that thing you need to run to, it can be done in such a way that you're just sorry that this interruption came along. And that's just a tiny thing, but each one of us can do so many little things to keep our face toward God.

Well, the servant bowed down and said, "*Blessed be Yahweh, God of my master Abraham, for He has not stopped showing kindness and goodness to my master. Yahweh has guided my steps to the house of my master's brother.*" That's something.

Well, we can just imagine that Rebecca was shocked. She certainly didn't expect that to happen. That's so typical of God's Providence. Just out of the blue. Sometimes, He'll do something that's astonishing. But she runs to her brother, Laban, and she shows him. She says, "Look what I got. These are gold bracelets and a gold ring." And he's astounded too. And a little thing, he was kind of a crafty man, his wheels must've started working. It's like your daughter comes home with this boyfriend, and he drives up in this big Cadillac, and you say, "Oh, wow. Not bad." That's what Laban said. So, he runs out to meet the servant, and he says, "What are you doing standing here with your camels? I've made a place for you. Come on." So, he gives him food.

But the servant had a job to do. He wasn't about to do anything but that. And so, he goes on, and he tells Laban the whole story. About the oath, about the request of Abraham, that he find his son Isaac a wife, and that it should be from Laban's house, how Rebecca came up. And he tells him the whole thing. And then he mentions what Abraham said, "God will send His angel to make your journey successful to help you choose a wife for my son." And so he goes on, and he says, "Everything happened exactly the way my master desired it." And he says, "*I blessed Yahweh, God of my master Abraham, who had so graciously led me to choose the daughter of my master's brother for his son. Now tell me whether you are prepared to show kindness and goodness to my master. If not, say so, and I shall know what to do.*" No fuss. He had a job to do from his master. He gave glory to Yahweh, and there we see something rather interesting. It's maybe a help to you and me. You know, everything happened here the way Abraham wanted it. Abraham asked for a sign, and he got it, and the servant asked for a sign, and he got it. Everything worked together. And the hitch here is the servant, who knows human nature a little bit, said, "Now, all this has been done, this is the way the Lord Yahweh has prepared everything."

Now, what do you say? You see how dependent we are sometimes even though God prepares a lot of things for us. It's still dependent sometimes upon somebody else's will. As to whether or not he would say yes. Would Yahweh be known to Laban enough that Laban would say yes? You see, God works through human nature. He can perform miracles, and He certainly did here. And we learn that Laban and Bethuel say, "*This is from Yahweh. It is not in our power to say yes or no to you. Rebecca is there before you. Take her and go; and let her become the wife of your master's son.*" *On hearing this, Abraham's servant prostrated himself on the ground before Yahweh. He brought out silver and gold which he gave them to Rebecca; he also gave rich presents to her brother and her mother.* We really don't know too much about Laban, but there's a beautiful sentence here that it would pay for each one of us to meditate on and make it a motto. Listen to it again. "*This is from Yahweh. It is not in our power to say yes or no to you.*" Do you realize what that says? This man also realized, as Abraham did, God's sovereign rights. Today, oh, we have pushed those sovereign rights aside, so everything and anything goes, and when it comes from those in the Church, it really is astounding.

When immorality is approved of. When independence to the point of disobedience is praised. When the body belongs to the individual and not to God. When the person makes all the decisions. God is just supposed to look down like some doting old man and say, "Oh, well … okay, go ahead." We have forgotten God's sovereign rights. It is not in our power to say yes or no. It is in our power to let God do what He wills to do. Why? You say, "Well, He gave me free will." Of course, when I'm talking about all the decisions we have to make. But when it's so evident that something is God's will, why can't we just do it? You can't excuse immorality. You know what's in the Scriptures, you've got the Church to tell you. Well, the bad thing is that we have forgotten, we no longer desire to accomplish only the will of God.

This is a beautiful reply from Rebecca's father and her brother Laban. "It is Yahweh. It's not in our power to say yes or no. Take her." You know, when sometimes we lose a child — it's so difficult to accept the child that has leukemia at five and all of these terrible diseases — and it's so hard, and yet we have to know that these children belong to God. And if He calls, wouldn't it be wonderful if we said, if I could say, "It is not in our power to say yes or no. It is the Lord." Meaning that I could say yes or no, but it wouldn't do any good if the Lord's going to call them, but to just say: "The Lord is here. Blessed be the name of the Lord. So be it." To have that kind of total confidence, to be able to see God in the present moment to that extent. And it puzzles me. It really does. It puzzles me to think that these men had these special gifts. And we, after Jesus, seem to squander our talents. That's what bothers me.

Well, let's go on. They ate and drank, he and his companions, and spent the night there. *The next morning when they were up, he said, "Let me go back to my master."* Well, they wanted Rebecca to stay a few days, perhaps ten. Her brother said, "And then she can go too." *But the servant replied, "Do not delay me. It is Yahweh who has made my journey successful. Let me leave and go back to my master." They replied, "Let us call the girl and find out what she has to say."* So, the brother and mother wanted to just keep her ten days, just hang in there, and let's just have a family gathering for the last time.

And the servant said, "Hey, I've got to get going." *So, they called Rebekah and asked her, "Do you want to leave with this man?" "I do," she replied. Accordingly, they let her go, with her nurse and Abraham's servant. And they blessed Rebecca: "Sister of ours, increase to thousands and tens of thousands! May your descendants gain possession of the gates of their enemies!"* There, again, you see the influence of the human will. She had to say, "I do. I want to go." And you see our human nature. Some of you, your daughter, your son is about to get married or leave home and go to college, and you just wish the whole thing wouldn't be. But you know, that's what they really want to do. That's a good thing. And so, you've got to say, "Okay, I do. Go." There's so much to learn here. And so much to learn about God's sovereign rights. About that ability they had in those days to always keep their face toward the face of God, the ability to seek out and want to please Him all the time. We've grown cold and independent to the point of indifference, and we don't have that kind of loving father image to face.

We look at ourselves most of the time, it's like looking in a mirror, and we look at ourselves all day long, all day long, we look at ourselves instead of having our face toward God. We turn around and look at ourselves, and all we keep seeing is what we want and what we would like and what would please us, what's going to make us better off. We don't turn our face toward God. And if there's anything we learn today from this book — I mean, there's so much in it — is that there's something very similar here.

Do you remember the time Jesus said, "He who puts his hand to the plow and looks back is not worthy of the Kingdom"? The time He gave us a parable where the king went and had this big banquet, and the men said, "Well, let me go and tend my ox," and "I've just gotten married," and so forth? They all had excuses. Like Laban and his mother, they come up with an excuse. They said, "Look, let's keep her for ten days, and then you can have her." But the Lord said, "No, it's now." There is a sense of urgency almost, isn't there, in accomplishing the will of God in the present moment? So much hangs on Him.

ELEVEN

Genesis Chapters 25 & 26

We're going to go to Genesis 25, and before we go to verse nineteen where our lesson begins, we're going to kind of go back a little bit and find out that Abraham remarried and had six more sons. Only one son, though, was of the promise, and that was Isaac. Ishmael was from the slave girl, and we know from St. Paul that the slave girl was not in line for that great promise or inheritance. The promise was given to Sarah through Isaac. Well, life was almost as normal as yours and mine. There was that tent experience in the desert and all the inconveniences. They didn't have washing machines and didn't even have rivers sometimes to wash clothes in. It was probably unheard of that you took a bath. And so, in those days, things were extremely primitive.

Well, it was how many cows you had, how many sheep you had, how much gold and silver, but even when you had, it was more of an accumulation. They didn't have that kind of methodology of spending money on the luxuries that you and I have. So, their recreation was just sitting in the cool of the nights in the front of their tent, talking. And the women cooked all day because it took so long to get anything accomplished. You could say, "Oh, what a horrible way to live." Well, you kind of wonder, though, they had a simplicity about them that all the gadgets have kind of taken away. We've got so many gadgets and so much time for leisure that we're out of breath. You know, in the old days, in my grandma's day—I think I've said this before—but I think it comes in here very well. I came home from work one day, and I said to my grandmother, "Boy, I was nervous today, uptight." She said to me, "What are nerves?" Here's a woman that was in her seventies, bore eleven children. My grandpa owned a saloon, so that wasn't the easiest life in the world, and life in those days was very, very tough.

They came to this country. They couldn't read or write. So, with all the difficulties they had though, there seemed to be a more contented attitude or spirit than we have today. They were content with their lot. We're never content with our lot. No matter what you buy, no matter what you get, no matter what you strive for, you only want more tomorrow or want something else tomorrow. Today, you buy one car, but your goal is to buy another one next year. As a result, we're never happy. That's an important lesson.

We're going to change the scene and go to the story of Isaac and Jacob. I think the son of Abraham was forty years old when he married Rebecca. And Isaac prayed to Yahweh on behalf of his wife, for she was barren. Isn't that a strange coincidence, huh? His mother, Sarah, was barren for a long, long, long, long time, and he waits till he's forty years old before he gets married, and his wife Rebecca is barren. So, he does very much what his father Abraham did. He prayed to Yahweh, and his wife conceived. Now, we see here something very human and yet something very strange. It says: *The children struggled with one another inside of her, and she said, "If this is the way of it, why go on living?"* So, she went to consult Yahweh.

Today, we consult doctors. But they didn't have doctors then. The Lord was so much a part of their life that she said,

"I'm gonna talk to Yahweh." Here again, you see that thread of God being in everything in their lives. You see, you and I have relegated God to specific incidences, specific problems in our lives. And the rest, we take to other people, which is all right for advice, or we try to solve it ourselves, which is all right too. But you see, these people had no other place to go. There was nothing else for them to do. Who was going to explain to her what was going on? So, she said, "Well, I will consult Yahweh."

It just is a beautiful picture. I think if they did this without knowing Jesus, without the Messiah being in their midst as you and I have, just imagine what God expects of you and me. He certainly has a right to expect much more. Much more confidence, much more adherence to His will, and a camaraderie almost with God. "I will consult God." What a beautiful thing to say. In regards to prayer, what are you going to do? "I'm going to consult the Lord." Wouldn't that be a beautiful way of saying, "I'm going to pray"? But you say, "Well, they would really think I flipped my rocker if I said, 'I'm gonna consult the Lord.'" But isn't that what prayer is all about? Isn't that what it means to pray? To consult Yahweh? Or to praise Him, or to give Him glory, or thanksgiving, or to say you're sorry? Or to adore Him as sovereign Lord? Isn't that what prayer is all about? But instead of saying, "I want to pray for a petition," or, "I want you to intercede for me," or, "I want this favor, Lord," consult the Lord in your prayer. Say, "Lord, what is Your will for me?" What a fantastic way of praying. We usually go before the Lord, and we clunk down on His lap all the million things we want, and we don't want to take no for an answer. So, we run around claiming everything. We say, "Look, this is here, I put it in Your lap. I want it, I got it." What kind of prayer is that? Where's the humility? The word *to consult* means to ask for advice, favor, love—whatever it is you need.

But in today's world, we don't consult Yahweh. We demand from God, and it was very difficult for me to think that these people had more humility and confidence than we do. But they didn't have anything that you have. They didn't have Jesus, they didn't have the Gospels, they didn't have all these years of accumulated knowledge. And why is it that we seem to be so further back spiritually than they were? In just a few lines here, we've already learned a lot. That when we are in trouble, we pray. We say, "Lord, I don't know what to do."

So, Rebecca prayed, and the Lord answered her, and He said this: "*There are two nations in your womb. Your issue will be two rival peoples. One nation shall have the mastery of the other, and the elder shall serve the younger.*" Now, these chapters here kind of create a lot of problems for us, because as we see it unfold, you begin to realize it's a little bit of, well, conniving. Let's go on, and we'll see.

It says, *When the time came for her confinement, there were indeed twins in her womb. The first to be born was red.* It means he had red hair. I mean, it says he had a lot of it: *as though he were completely wrapped in a hairy cloak.* I hate to think what that poor kid looked like. Can you imagine a little baby that big, full of red hair? Bet they called him Red. I know a lot of people named Red; they all had red hair. But they called him Esau, which means red. His brother was born with his hand grasping Esau's heel. And because to grasp the heel of another was to supplant him, the word *Jacob* means to supplant. Because even though Esau was born first, Jacob held on to his heel as if to say, "I also am first." So, way back in their mother's womb, they began to be two separate people.

Now, you say, "Why was that?" Don't ask me. It's one of the things you and I will learn in the Kingdom. It's one of the things that we can conjecture, we can come up with all kinds of stuff, but it's a mystery. We shouldn't feel bad about accepting mysteries in our life, we shouldn't feel stupid either because God used it, and yet He punished all the conniving that went along to make it happen.

But God foresaw that the temperaments of these two children are so different. And you know what? You have temperaments in your house. Your children have entirely different temperaments, entirely different. And, well, it makes a problem. Let's go in and see what a problem this was.

It says: *When the boys grew up, Esau became a skilled hunter, a man of the open country.* Isaac was sixty years old at the time of their birth. You have to realize he waited twenty years for children. I mean, the Lord made him wait a long time, just like his father, Abraham. *Jacob, on the other hand, was a quiet man.* He stayed at home. And here's the hitch: *Isaac preferred Esau, for he had a taste for wild game* — and Esau kept bringing in wild game — *but Rebecca preferred Jacob.*

It didn't work then, and it doesn't work now. I suppose it's inevitable that when you have three, four, or five children, some temperaments appeal to you even as a parent more than the others. Maybe this one is very quiet and gentle, and you don't have any trouble out of him, so you love him. And there's another one that's always in trouble. Or maybe the father prefers that one, it looks like he's got some life in him. Now, you can't help how you feel about a child, even your own. No more than you can help how you feel about anyone. There's personality chemistry that just kind of goes together. Now, there may be other children you find more difficult, and they find you more difficult. It doesn't really make any difference that you're a mother or a father, and they're your children. They are cut from the same loaf. It just happens that their personalities are so different that it kind of rubs against yours. But you see, that causes a lot of problems if you don't overcome it. Because you can't help how you feel, but you can help how you treat them. If one comes in and always gets the bread and butter, and you come in and you don't have any left, or if something is going around, that one is the one you think of first, and then the others take the leftovers. If when you go to buy gifts, if that one gets the trousers or the best dress, and the others get second best because you suddenly ran out of money.

You see, all of these things show in a family — preferences. And it's difficult, very difficult not to. You just have to understand, there's nothing wrong with feeling more love for another, but you have to make a tremendous amount of effort to treat everyone equally, and although you may want to hug the one you love the most more often, you've got to hug them all. You have to say, "I love you" to all of them, even the one with whom you have perhaps the most trouble. Because, you see, that preference is not of God. Jesus, apparently, loved John more than the others, or at least John loved Jesus more than the others. And as a result, it was noticeable that John had a special love for Jesus and vice versa. But Jesus never allowed that to interfere with His duty or His mission, and so He treated every single one individually. He didn't make John the first apostle, the first pope, and I know that's going to make some of you angry, but He didn't make him the leader; He made Peter. He didn't give the keys to the Kingdom to John; He gave them to Peter. He didn't say, "Thou art John, I give you the keys because I love you more." He said, "Thou art Peter." And so, Jesus never permitted His love for John, or vice versa, to interfere with what He was supposed to do at that moment. And so, neither can you. You can't have a Jacob and Esau in your family. So, when you begin to think of this, you say, "Oh, I'll never do that" — yes, you will. Human nature

Genesis Chapters 25 & 26

being what it is, you're going to be tempted. But you're going to do all in your power to treat everybody as an individual with their own particular love that they have and they need for their personality, and then you go on.

So, let's go on and see some of the terrible things that happened with this situation. *Once Jacob had made a soup* — really a lentil soup, a kind of porridge, I guess — *and Esau returned from the countryside, exhausted. And Esau said to Jacob, "Let me eat the red soup,"* probably a bean soup, *"that red soup over there. I want to eat some. I'm exhausted."* Hence the name given to him was Edom. And Jacob was cunning. He thought: "Here's my chance. He's hungry. There's no food around but mine." He was cunning, and he said, *"First sell me your birthright."* So, he knew that Esau was first, and all the blessing and all the inheritance was going to go to Esau. *And Esau said, "Here I am at death's door."* He must have been really hungry, or he exaggerated. *"What use would my birthright be to me?"* Now, he either hadn't eaten for three, four days, but he apparently thought that death was imminent. Jacob says, *"First give me your oath." So, he gave him his oath and sold his birthright to Jacob.* And here it is — I was right: *Jacob gave him bread and lentil soup. After eating and drinking, he got up and went. That was all that Esau cared for his birthright.* A bowl of soup. See, in those days, the firstborn got everything. He kind of took the father's place when the father died. He was head of the family. Well, he felt, "Here I'm dying of starvation, what do I care about a birthright? I mean, I'm on my own, I'm a hunter, what do I care about that old tent they're going to leave me? A few heads of cattle? I can get my own cattle."

You know, this is a kind of arrogant way of thinking. Some of you kids out there that are listening to me, you may have an idea, you want to be so independent, you're going to do it

165

on your own, you're going to get your own apartment when you're sixteen, you're going to get a job, you're going to conquer the world, or you're going to do a better job than your parents did, you're going to do all these things. And your parents say, "Well, I'm going to dis-inherit you, or I'm going to give your brother your inheritance." "Eh, who wants it?" So, you see, in those kinds of situations when you are at a point where you're willing to give it all up for some emotional experience or some anger or passion or whatever, you're going to end up pretty much like Esau. And so, you have to see in this account of what happened here, acting at the wrong moment, making a big decision when you're weak. He was weak. Physically weak. Mentally tired, fatigued. Exhausted. If there's one thing this teaches you, that is when you're in that condition, especially if you're burned out, don't make big decisions, because those decisions may stay with you the rest of your life.

Well, this gets more interesting as we go along. *There was a famine in the land—a second one after the famine that took place in the time of Abraham—and Isaac went to Abimelech. But Yahweh appeared to him and said, "Do not go down into Egypt; stay in the land I shall tell you of. Remain for the present here in this land, and I will be with you and bless you. For it is to you and your descendants that I will give all these lands. I will make your descendants as many as the stars of heaven. And all the nations of the world shall bless themselves by your descendants in return for Abraham's obedience."* So, here is Isaac being blessed because of his father, Abraham. It says that Isaac went to Abimelech, and God said, "Look, don't go any further." *So, Isaac stayed at Gerar. When the people of the place asked him about his wife, he said, "She is my sister," for he was afraid to say, "She is my wife," in case they killed him on Rebecca's account, for she was beautiful.* You know, it's almost amazing to me that son followed father in so many things.

Abimelech happened to look out the window and saw Isaac and his wife Rebecca. *And Abimelech said, "Surely, she must be your wife. How could you say she's your sister?"* Isaac answered him, "Because I thought you'd kill me." You know, it's amazing how we're willing to lie, but you can excuse him because he didn't have the light you and I have. Because they didn't have the light, they didn't have the conscience. But you know, we kind of act today that it's whatever suits me the best, whether it's lying or whatever it is, whatever suits you the best. This is what the world tells you to do. So, kids in school will look over someone else's paper and take their solutions to problems that they should figure out themselves, and that's cheating. And people will take change, take more change, or make the wrong kind of change. And they don't think anything about it. So, there're all kinds of little, tiny things that we do all day long that're just as bad as this. The only trouble is that you and I have the light to know it's wrong. And Isaac was saying here, "Look, I'm afraid of you." *And Abimelech said, "What is this you have done to us? One of my subjects may easily have slept with your wife, and then you would have made us incur guilt."* So, Isaac sowed his crops in that land, and that year reaped one hundredfold, because Yahweh blessed him. But Yahweh blessed him because of his father. His father's obedience.

You know, it's amazing, and so important for fathers today to understand their obligation under God because your children are going to be blessed by your faithfulness to the Lord God. And if you're an unfaithful husband and an unfaithful father — and that is so prevalent today. I don't think there's been a time when there's been so much incest, using your children for your own pleasure, what a horrible crime that is. Do you think your children are going to be blessed by you? They incur so many problems, guilt, shame, psychological problems, mental problems.

You've got to ask yourself, what has happened to the world? That children are not blessed very often by their parents. They aren't blessed because of their parents' obedience in love and desire for holiness. They're almost cursed by the lying and the cheating and embezzling and all the things that parents sometimes do as a normal way of life. Do you see? When you become a parent, you take on yourself an awesome obligation, and the obligation is good example. Because it says here, very explicitly: "*All the nations will bless themselves by your descendants in return for Abraham's obedience, for he kept my charge, my commandments, my statutes, and my laws.*"

Well, it says: *He had flocks and herds and many servants, and the Philistines began to envy him.* See, human nature hasn't changed, has it? Hasn't changed a bit. Because in our human nature, poor as it is, we are constantly envious of other people. We somehow don't believe they deserve all of this. And someone happens to make good and had to struggle from the very bottom, we inevitably look at them and say, "Oh, I knew them when..." What does that mean? You see, human nature hasn't changed a bit, and yet again, I have to say it should have.

With Christianity here, it should have changed. Are we going back to the beginning? Are we a people who are so ignorant of God's laws, have we so twisted them and watered them down, that we can no longer see the truth and the light? Are we content in living in darkness? Are our eyes so weak they cannot look at the light? These are some very serious questions that we must ask ourselves as we go through the Scriptures, when we see, oh my Lord, we haven't changed much. And we say that is human nature, and I grant you that. But the grace of God, through His Son Jesus—isn't that greater than anything they had? Don't we have something greater than Abraham and Isaac, and Esau and Jacob? Don't we have all this divine indwelling? Are we throwing away this great gift that God has given us? Well, I think those questions may be hard, but we've got to answer them in our own individual lives.

Let's go on. Now, *the Philistines had sealed all the wells dug by his father's servants, filling them with earth.* These had existed from the time of Abraham. So, the king of Gerar goes to Isaac, and he says, *"Leave us, for you have become more powerful than we are."* *So, he left. And Isaac dug again the wells made by the servants of his father Abraham and sealed by the Philistines, and he gave them the same names his father had given them.* But there again, we have the same old problem of human nature. Servants quarreling with servants. One said, "No, this water is ours," and one said, "No, no, we dug the well, the water is ours." Well, so he went to Beersheba, and Yahweh appeared to him that night. And it's strange. God pushes you sometime to the nth degree of your endurance. Do you ever feel that way? Do you ever feel like, "Lord, I can't take another thing, I can't take another hour, I can't take another minute"? Well, sometimes He pushes us in that direction or allows us to be pushed in that direction because He wants to speak to us, He wants to fill our hearts. But they have to be empty first; we have to empty ourselves of all of our self-sufficiency and independence, the rebellion that's in our hearts. We have to be sometimes so down in the ground, so helpless, and though we fight that situation and we fight those times, I think you have to admit, if you look back in your life, that those times were the times when the Lord suddenly at some point began to feel very close to you. And maybe it took all that. Maybe it took all of that to get to you to a point where you could say, "Lord, You are all. I am nothing. You can do everything. I can't do anything by myself."

Well, Yahweh spoke to Isaac. He said, *"I am the God of your father Abraham. Do not be afraid, for I am with you. I will bless you and make your descendants many in number on account of my servant, Abraham.*" I think the Lord wanted to remind Isaac that what he was being blessed for was not so much on account of what he was doing, although he was trying very hard, but because of his father. God is faithful to His promises. He is faithful, and you and I have to be faithful, because belonging to the Mystical Body — and by Mystical Body, I mean *everybody* affects everyone else — we are all under the headship of Christ. Jesus is our head.

The whole world is like a ship going through the sea. It just moves. The whole sea is different because a ship went through it, nothing is the same. Once you throw a pebble in the ocean, and the ocean begins to ripple, the ocean is different, and so everything you would do with it, good or bad, the whole world is affected. And we call that the Mystical Body because it's a mystery. We're all bound together under the same Father. And so, we all benefit, we all suffer from each other's goodness or evil.

There he built an altar and invoked the name of Yahweh. And there he pitched his tent, and there Isaac's servants sank a well. Well, life went on, and Abimelech went to Beersheba to see him with his adviser and commander of his army. *And Isaac said to them, "Why do you come to me since you hate me and have made me leave you?" He said, "It became clear to us that Yahweh was with you. Let there be a sworn treaty between ourselves and you, and let us make a covenant with you. Swear not to do us any harm since we've never molested you but were unfailingly kind to you and let you go away in peace. Now, you have Yahweh's blessing."* He made them a feast, and they ate and drank.

Well, this says a lot for Isaac. I want you to think of that for a minute. That's a big step forward. To forgive your enemies. See if you don't think of something Jesus said.

Do you recall what Jesus said about loving your enemies, doing good to those who hate you and abuse you? Here are people forgiving each other, asking God to bless them and making a feast. *He then made them a feast, and they ate and drank. Rising early in the morning, they exchanged oaths. Then Isaac bade them farewell, and they went from him in peace.* The servants came that very day and said, *"We have found water."* So, *he called the well Sheba, and hence the town was called Beersheba.* It looks almost as if the Lord was waiting for that reconciliation between Abimelech and Isaac before water came to him. Although the Lord was blessing Isaac because of his father Abraham, there was still the necessity of personal involvement and personal fidelity to the will of God in the present moment. Let's look at a very wealthy man, and he leaves all his wealth to his children. Obviously, the children benefit by the father's blessing, but if the children are not faithful also, then the blessing becomes a curse.

That's what happened to a lot of our youth today. They've been given too much, too soon. They have benefited by their father's blessing before they had the head to handle it, or the knowledge of the struggle. They never had to struggle. Your children need to struggle. I don't care how wealthy you are, your children need to struggle. Don't give them everything they want. They don't need a brand-new car when they're sixteen. Let him work for it. This is not going to be appealing to all the youth I'm speaking to, but sweetheart, I'm not trying to be appealing. I'm trying to keep you from going down into the pit. And you see, it happens very often that you are striving for holiness, even though you benefit by your father's goodness, you're striving for holiness. It will uphold the whole thing; it would make it pleasing to God also.

The servants didn't find water until this reconciliation occurred, and what does water symbolize except life? Water has been used to symbolize life. You can do without food a long time, but you can't do without water a long time. It was water that the Lord used for Baptism. It was the water He sanctified. He said Himself, "I am living water, I will give you living water."

And sometimes, all the problems in your life are not going to be solved until there is a reconciliation with the one that you hate or dislike, or who has done you in. There was a terrible injustice done to Isaac. All he did was succeed, and they threw him out. They had put mud and earth in his wells so he had no water. He had to leave this place and started digging new wells. You know, that was a hard thing. You didn't have these great, big well-diggers come down with such force. You had to dig it by hand, let people down with the rope, and they kept on digging and putting dirt in a bucket, and then they rolled it back up. I mean, they would have to go down one hundred feet. They didn't find any water. So, although Isaac was blessed by his father, Isaac himself had to imitate his father in order to retain that blessing.

Some of you parents think that all you need to do is to give your children everything you didn't have. Well, maybe you haven't given them the thing you had that they need most of all: God. Maybe you haven't given them the Lord, and if you're Catholic, maybe you haven't made them understand the sacraments and Holy Communion and all the rest. You say, "Well, I've done all this, and they have strayed." I'm not blaming you. I don't intend to put guilt on anybody. I'm only saying and talking to the children, I'm talking to parents. Don't give them everything they need or want because it's not always good for them. What they need is good for them, but all the superfluities—is it going to make them really happy?

And you youth out there. You think hard. Your father and mother worked very hard for what they're giving you, they've had sleepless nights, they've had near tragedies and catastrophes, and although it seems like they have lots of money and lots of everything else, the blood and sweat that went into it that they themselves may have long forgotten deserves your attention and appreciation and your love. The only way we can build family is for everyone to understand each other's weaknesses and be able to know that it's okay. That we can live together under the Lord God Yahweh, and we can do so in peace. It's only when we become isolated individuals living in a house, instead of family living in a home — only then will we understand. But what Jesus gave us by His life and His death, and the Spirit gave us at Pentecost, and the two thousand years of great men and women that we call saints today have given us — it's light, living water, but we've got to take it and work with it ourselves. It's not going to come that easy. When things have come too easy to me, I'm a little bit suspicious. I just wonder if God is within it when there's not that struggle.

Well, Esau was forty years old, and he married Judith, the daughter of Beeri the Hittite. It was a bitter disappointment to Isaac and Rebecca. A bitter disappointment. Well, many of the parents listening to me tonight have had that same disappointment. Your son or your daughter married someone that doesn't even know God. Married a drug addict, married someone whom you know is going to bring him or her to ruin. And "bitter disappointment" is a good phrase because your heart gets heavy, you see them going headlong in the wrong direction, but you can't talk to them. There's just nothing you can do. Isn't it amazing how similar our daily life is to the book of Genesis? But there again, I get this big question mark in my heart and mind: Why isn't there more difference between us since we have Jesus? Since we have the sacraments in the Eucharist and Reconciliation? Because we have all these marvelous things at our fingertips?

Are we like the rich man, who only looked at today and not tomorrow? Are we like Esau, who's willing to sacrifice his entire heritage for a bowl of lentil soup? Are we willing to throw our souls away for a momentary pleasure? Are we willing to sacrifice all of eternity and never, never, never, never-ending joy for a tiny bit of time? Is that what we're doing? Is that what you're doing? Doesn't make sense, does it? Doesn't make sense that we are willing to sacrifice our whole life and eternity and never-ending joy for a few moments of illicit pleasure or money or anything else.

I think we've learned a lot about our own human nature, about the problems that these people had in their lifetime, very similar to our own. And what they did about it—consult the Lord.

So, before you go to bed tonight, consult the Lord. Just say, "Lord, I don't know what to do with Jim or John or Mary or Sue. I've done my best. Lead me. Guide me." Give your troubles to Yahweh. Most of all, give Him your joys. Tell Him all the good things that happened today. Thank Him that you found that parking place, that Johnny won the game, and so many things.

TWELVE

Genesis Chapters 27 & 28

So now, turn to Genesis 27. And again, we're going to see human nature—not always at its best—in Scripture. You know, I get kind of criticized by a lot of people when I kind of take down the apostles or the saints. I'm not taking them down. I'm just trying to make you understand they were human and they had the same struggles you have. And so, when you look at the Old Testament, there is just no way you can cover up some of the stuff that they did. I mean, we consider them very holy people, but they grew into holiness, they had to struggle like you struggle, they made mistakes, they committed sins. They were very and beautifully repentant, and then it would go downhill again. But you and I have got to know that. Otherwise, we stand back in awe at these so-called saints who seem to have it made, that had never lost their baptismal innocence. I don't think there are that many saints up there that didn't, that never lost their baptismal innocence. I think they were like you and me, who rise and fall and struggle. And we're going to see Jacob appear with his good, old mom, Rebecca.

Isaac was growing old, probably had cataracts, couldn't see. So, he summoned Esau. Although Esau and Jacob were twins, you remember when they were born that Jacob had a hold of Esau's heel. It's purely symbolic that Jacob was one day to supplant his brother. And they were so different. Esau was very hairy, and Jacob very smooth. Disposition is different. Esau was a strong, violent, emotional man who sold his birthright for a pot of lentils. So, you've got this quiet, smooth, shrewd Jacob. Well, now we're going to see what happened.

It's interesting because you and I are constantly discouraged over the fact that we're not too hot. And because we're not too hot, we think, "Well, we don't have a chance, Lord. We just don't have a chance." And we're going to see.

So, Isaac said to Esau, "*My son, see, I am old and I do not know when I may die. Now, take your weapons, your quiver and bow; go out in the country and hunt me some game. Make me the kind of savory food I like and bring it to me, so that I may eat and give you my blessing before I die.*"

You say, "Well, what's so big about that?" Well, the blessing of the father was the will. You understand a will. So, you had two of you, you were twins, and your father was dying. He hadn't made a will yet. I think you'd get pretty hot and bothered. And if you were the son to whom he said, "Go out and get me a great, big meal, and I'm going to eat it, and then I'm going to sign my will," it would be the same thing. They didn't have wills in those days. If you got the father's first blessing, and the firstborn did that, then you got everything. And the other one got something, but he wasn't lord of the mansion. That belonged to the firstborn. Besides, Isaac liked Esau better than he liked Jacob.

But now we've got a woman. Rebecca liked Jacob more than she liked Esau. And you know, it's unfortunate, but in families that happens. The father prefers one, the mother prefers the other. This is so bad, and I'm going to show you it didn't work then, and it doesn't work now. If you're doing that, you're being terribly unfair to your children.

So, anyway, Esau goes out, and he's a great hunter. *Well, Rebecca happened*, it says, *to be listening.* But I think probably she always listened. See, women were not allowed in the tent when men were speaking even to their own sons. Well, they listened. You can see Sarah listening when Abraham is talking to the Lord. Now, you find Rebecca listening. They didn't have anything to do after they made their meal, and they just weren't in with all the secrets that the men always had. So, they listened at the tent. I don't suppose it was very hard to hear because those tents were not that thick.

So, while Isaac was still talking to his son Esau, Rebecca takes off. She didn't even let him finish. She took off. And she goes to Jacob, and she says, *"I've just heard your father saying to your brother, Esau, 'Bring me game, and make savory food for me. Then I shall eat and bless you in the presence of Yahweh before I die.' Now my son, listen to me."* Can't you just see this? You don't need much imagination.

 Can't you just see this woman saying, "Look," speaking in a low voice and saying, "Look, you go out to the flock, get me two kids." Well, you see, he's already ahead of his brother because his brother has to go into the field, he has to look for game, he's got to kill it, he's going to hit and miss a few times, he's got to dress it, bring it back. She said, *"Go out to the flock, get me two kids*—just lambs, little lambs—*so that I can make the kind of savory food your father likes."* She knew how he liked it. *"And then you can take it to your father for him to eat so that he may bless you before he dies."*

Kind of sneaky. And you know, some people excuse this and say, "Oh, well, that was God's will." It's never God's will if you're sneaky. God may have had an entirely different plan to get Jacob head of the clan. Well, the problem with Rebecca, and the problem with all of us is about the same problem, is we don't want to wait for God's plan. God does not want you to lie to accomplish what He wants. Now, He will use your lie for a greater good, but He never says, "Now, I want you to lie," because lying is a sin. It was a sin then, and it is a sin now — to cheat. So, I'd like to look at this thing as it really is: Jacob lied and cheated. You say, "Oh, well, God had a plan." God's plan does not include evil. He permits evil because we cheat. Please don't blame God in this incident. We're the ones that cheat and lie. God used that. Now, I want you to look into your own life for a few minutes, see whether you've done something like this.

Look at Genesis 27:11. Well, we see Rebecca telling her son Jacob, "Now, go out and get a couple of kids, and I'll dress them up for your dad. I know what he likes, and he'll bless you instead of your brother." *Jacob said to his mother Rebecca, "Look,"* — he's getting kind of practical about this thing — "*my brother Esau is hairy, while I'm smooth-skinned. If my father happens to touch me, he will see I'm cheating him, and I shall bring down a curse on myself instead of a blessing.*"

So, he knew this was cheating. He said, "He'll know I'm cheating him." He didn't seem to mind he was going to cheat. He just didn't want his father to *know* he was going to cheat. Well, listen, this Rebecca is one smart cookie. She says, "*On me be the curse, my son! Just listen to me; go and fetch me the kids.*" *So he went to fetch them, and he brought them to his mother, and she made the kind of savory food his father liked. Rebecca took her elder son Esau's best clothes and dressed her younger son Jacob in them, covering his arms and the smooth part of his neck with the skins of the kids.* Now, that is clever. She knew her husband would touch his hand, take hold of his hand, that's natural. She also knew that he would hug him, and what would he touch? The back of his neck. So, she takes the skins of the kids and she covers him, covers his arms and covers his neck. Takes the clothes of Esau. Why would she take the clothes? Well, a man, he didn't have Brut in those days. They didn't have any kind of deodorants. And naturally, his clothes must have had a specific odor, especially since he was a hunter.

And she knew, first of all, that Jacob wouldn't even wear the kind of clothes that Esau would wear. So, she had this whole thing figured out, though it's a scheme, to cheat to obtain what she felt was a greater good. However, you can never lie for a greater good. You have to depend on the Lord to attain that greater good. The fact that it happened again — I want to repeat this because it's very important — the fact that it happened, you say, "Well, God was protecting her." But God didn't need a lie to protect her. Esau may have gone out and just disappeared. God could have done a thousand things to protect her. Once you begin to take things on your own, you can be assured you're going to mess them up because we don't want to wait. So, she handed the food and the bread to her son Jacob, and I bet he was shaking in his boots. But he went. He went with full knowledge that he was cheating and that it was wrong. *He said, "Father, I am here."* I don't know how he disguised his voice. That must have been a little bit harder.

He said, *"Who are you, my son?"* He didn't recognize. I bet his heart was going *boom, boom, boom, boom.* Because he thought: "I'm gonna get caught!" He says, *"I am Esau, your firstborn."* Lie number one. *"I have done as you told me. Please get up and take your place, and eat the game I have brought, and then give me your blessing."* Well, Isaac isn't as dumb as he looks. So, he says, *"How quickly you found it!"* We mentioned that before: it wasn't as easy to find game in those days. Now here's another lie: *"It was Yahweh, your God, who put it in my path."* You know what's wrong about lying? Very evident right here. Once you start, the next one comes. You have to lie because there was something in your first lie that wasn't quite right, so now you've got to lie again. Then there's going to be something wrong with your second lie, so you lie again. So, you keep on lying. Isn't that amazing? The bad part of it is that eventually it is possible for you to believe your own lie. Because it's so strong in your mind.

Well, now Isaac said to the Jacob, "*Come here, then, and let me touch you, my son, to know if you are my son Esau or not.*" He is beginning to suspect. He may not see, but he's not stupid. And Jacob came close to his father and touched him. And you know, he just questioned a moment ago, "What about his voice?" The father says, "*The voice is Jacob's voice, but the arms are the arms of Esau.*" He recognized there was something wrong. *He did not recognize him — but he suspected — for his arms were hairy arms like Esau, so he blessed him. He said, "Are you really my son Esau?" And he replied, "I am."* You see what he just said? Lie number three. Isn't that amazing to see this in action? *And Isaac said, "Bring it here that I may eat the game my son has brought so that I may give you my blessing." He brought it to him and he ate; he offered him wine, and he drank. And his father Isaac said to him, "Come closer and kiss me, my son."* Here's how clever Rebecca was. *He went closer and kissed his father, who smelled the smell of his clothes. He blessed him saying, "Yes, the smell of my son is like the smell of a fertile field blessed by Yahweh."*

"*May God give you dew from heaven and the riches of the earth, abundance of grain and wine! May nations serve you and peoples bow down before you! Be master of your brothers; may the sons of your mother bow down before you! Cursed be who curses you; blessed be he who blesses you!*" He got the whole bit.

Now comes the sixty-four-dollar question. Why would God allow Jacob to get all of this blessing from deceit? Well, let's go back and see what happened to Sarah and the slave girl. Sarah refused to wait for God's time, and so she said to Abraham, "Go on and have a child with my slave girl. At least I will have someone." This caused a lot of trouble. She wasn't willing to wait on God's time. It wasn't God's will. But you see, here is not a question of what was God's will. It *was* God's will that Jacob be blessed and Esau not, because of their dispositions, their love for Yahweh. One didn't love Yahweh; he could care less. Very much like Cain and Abel. Jacob was like Abel. Esau was like Cain. And so, what happened here is God's will. Just like it was God's will that Isaac be born to Sarah and Abram. But they just couldn't wait.

So, they anticipated. They tried to make a prophecy work in their time instead of waiting on God's time. And so, this is the same thing here. Rebecca took it out of the hands of God and tried to accomplish it herself. You say, "Well, Esau was about to get the blessing." We don't know what God had in mind for Esau. And Jacob would have been next in line, so we don't know what God's plan would have been. But they took it all into their own hands and ruined it. We'll see later on that Jacob had to pay for this dearly.

You know, what's interesting about these incidences in the Scripture is the Providence of God. He uses everything for our greater good. Everything. He uses even our mistakes, even when we disobey Him, even when, well, when we make decisions, when we anticipate His will. And you wonder what even greater good it would have been had we waited. For example, where would we all be today and what would the world or history be if Adam and Eve hadn't sinned? If they said no, and never ate that apple? Never yielded to pride? Isn't that amazing? What would have happened if Sarah had not insisted that the accomplishment of what she thought was the will of God would be done in her way and in her time?

Maybe in Heaven we'll know the greater good that might have happened had we waited.

Well, as you can suspect, it's amazing to me that Jacob wasn't shaking in his boots because it took time to dress the kids, and it took time to cook them, and it took time to do all of these things. So, he just barely made it. Because as soon as Isaac had finished the blessing, and just when Jacob was leaving the presence of his father, Isaac — his brother, Esau, returned from hunting. And he had prepared and brought the savory food to his father. Isn't that strange that he prepared his own food? He didn't go to his mother and say, "Mother, will you prepare this for Dad?" Kind of shows his disposition and his temperament a little bit. He went and got his own game, he cooked it, wasn't going to wait for anybody. Independent. Probably a violent kind of man. Emotional, hot tempered. Cooked it himself.

He said, "*Father, get up and eat the game your son has brought you and then give me your blessing.*" His father, Isaac, said to him, "*Who are you?*" "*I'm your firstborn, Esau,*" he replied. At this, Isaac was seized with great trembling and said, "*Who was it, then, that went hunting and brought me game? Unsuspecting, I ate before you came; I blessed him, and blessed he will remain!*" When Esau heard his father's words, he cried out loudly and bitterly, and he said, "*Father, bless me too!*" But Isaac said, "*Your brother came by fraud and took your blessing.*" Esau said, "*Is it because his name is Jacob that he has now supplanted me twice? First, he took my birthright, and now he has taken my blessing.*"

Well, that was clever on Jacob's part to take advantage of a hungry man and say, "Okay, I've got a big dish of lentils here. I'll give it to you. Give me your birthright." At that time, the young man was starving and hungry, what's he worried about? Something that may happen one hundred years from now, ninety years, seventy years, or whatever? And some of you think that's stupid, but are you not doing that? Have you sold your birthright to the Kingdom because of drugs, because of alcohol, for a life of debauchery, sex, permissiveness? All Esau sold is a birthright with a lot of territory and servants and slaves and gold and silver and cattle and sheep. But that's nothing compared to what you sell your eternity for. A pot of lentils. A shot of heroin, crack, pills that dull your mind. Puts you in some kind of euphoria that makes you unconscious of reality, going around acting like a wild person, doing as you please, when you please, how you please.

You're selling your birthright. But it isn't just a birthright, you're selling an eternal right to the Kingdom. You're selling your place in eternal joy, eternal happiness for a moment of pleasure. Think about it. If you think Esau was not alert, well, I'm not too sure you're very alert either if you're doing these things. We look here, we say, "Oh, wasn't it a shame that Isaac was blind?" Maybe you're blind though you see, maybe you're blind to what's around you, to the things that are happening around you, or the things that you ought to see, to the correction you should have made of your children, the things you must change or should change. Are you blind? You know these lessons in here are given to us for a reason. Are you going to be at the last day saying, "Well, they stole my birthright"? No, you gave it away—for a pot of lentils.

And so, Isaac said to Esau, "*See, I have made him your master. I have given him all his brothers as servants. I have provided him with grain and wine. What can I do for you?*" And Esau said, "*Was that your only blessing, father? Father, give me a blessing too.*" Isaac remained silent, and Esau burst into tears. And Isaac said, "*Far from the riches of the earth shall be your dwelling place. Far from the dew that falls from heaven. You shall live by your sword, and you shall serve your brother.*" There's nothing left. "*But when you win your freedom, you shall shake his yoke from your neck.*"

Well, you look at it, and you say, "Well, I feel sorry for Esau." But you see, Esau was not a man who cared for the afterlife, for integrity or honesty or anything. And certainly, Jacob was not an honest man. But God couldn't work with Esau. He wasn't attuned to loving or listening or fulfilling the will of God. So, Jacob got the blessing, but he had to run. He became a fugitive. His first punishment was he couldn't enjoy the blessing at this point. Not at home. And we're going to learn something, that the Lord punished Jacob for that deceit because he became later on a victim of deceit. What you sow, you reap. And don't let anybody tell you that God's going to forget the whole thing. Because when you've got a deceitful heart, there's somebody who's going to come along more deceitful than yourself to cheat you to death.

Well, Esau hated Jacob because of the blessing his father had given him, and thought thus to himself: "The time to mourn for my father will soon be here, then I will kill my brother, Jacob."

And when the words of Esau, her elder son, were repeated to Rebecca, she sent for Jacob her younger son and said to him, "Look, your brother, Esau, means to take revenge and kill you. Now, my son, listen to me." Boy, she's always ruling the roost here. "*Take refuge with my brother Laban. Stay with them a while until your brother's fury cools, until your brother's anger against you cools, and he forgets what you have done to him. Then I will send someone to bring you back. Why should I lose you both on the same day?*" So, she had love for Esau, but she remembered the prophecy: "*There are two men in your womb. One will supplant the other.*" You say, "Oh, God destined it that way." No, He didn't. God knows all things, and all things are before Him. He knows you and me. He saw us at conception and at death, all in the same look, in the same gaze. And He permitted a lot of things in your life, in my life, and brought great good out of it, as He did with Adam and Eve. The Church says on Holy Saturday: "O happy fault that has merited us such a Redeemer." But then we still don't know what would have happened had we not fallen, what great good would have come.

Well, all this is kind of enlightening, isn't it? *Rebecca said to Isaac, "I am tired to death because of the daughters of Heth. If Jacob marries one of the daughters of Heth like these, one of the women of the country, what meaning is there left in life for me?"* Boy, I tell you, in those days people could swing the words around. They wanted what they wanted and the way they wanted it. "If this is gonna happen, why should I live?" Hot tempered.

So, Isaac summoned Jacob and blessed him; and he gave him this order (and I bet Esau wasn't around): "*You are not to choose a wife from the Canaanite women. Away now, go to your mother's father, and there choose a wife for yourself among the daughters of Laban, your mother's brother."* So, it would be a cousin. Those days, they married cousins. *"May El Shaddai bless you. May he make you fruitful and make you multiply so that you become a group of nations. May he grant you the blessing of Abraham, and your descendants after you, so that you may take possession of the land in which you live now, which God gave to Abraham."* So, Isaac realized that although this was wrong—the way it was accomplished—God did want His initial will, and that was for Jacob's inheritance to be used by God to establish the religion among the small tribe of Israelites. They weren't known as Israelites yet, that name was given to Jacob later, but the plan was there, and although men from Adam and Eve to Sarah to Rebecca constantly stuck their nose in God's plan and messed it up badly, God's will was still accomplished. Amazing. I mean, we've got our stubbornness, self-will, pride. Now you really have to watch yourself. You say, "Well, it really doesn't matter what I do, I mean, God will use it." Yes, it does. Because you run the risk of presumption, and that, my friend, is not worth it. You may die in a state of sin. A state of disobedience or pride. Then what?

Isaac then sent Jacob away, and Jacob went there. And we know that the same thing began to happen to him. *And Esau saw that Isaac had blessed Jacob and sent him to Paddan-aram to choose a wife there, and that in blessing him he had given him this order: "You are not to choose a wife from the Canaanite women," and then in obedience to his father and mother, Jacob had gone. Esau saw from this that the women of Canaan were not held in favor by his father. So he went to Ishmael and chose for a wife, in addition to the wives he had, a daughter of Abraham's son Ishmael.* So, you see this contest between Jacob and Esau, and Isaac and Rebecca, and you can see the consequences of Original Sin here. It's so strong.

The moment Adam and Eve's pride reared its head and said, "I want to be like God, I want to know good, I want to feel evil"—from that moment, we became a rebellious people. But through Jesus, through Jesus's redemption, through His death, His Precious Blood, and given to us at Baptism—and that's why Baptism is so important to us: that mark takes away that terrible adherence we have to evil and gives us the grace to overcome and be humble like Jesus, compassionate like the Father, merciful like the Father, filled with faith and hope and love. Amazing. That's why, please, if you're not baptized—get baptized. It's necessary for this stigma of Original Sin. And although you and I are still cursed by this pride that clings to us, like the odor on Esau's clothes, we must realize that God's grace through the power of His Spirit and the Precious Blood of Jesus is much more powerful and gives us the grace not to be deceitful.

Are we meditating enough on the wonders of God and the beauty of His wisdom, not ours? His will, not ours? Maybe we'll meditate more and think more as we go along. We really haven't covered much, but in what we've covered, we've learned a lot. And if you were to ask what is a common denominator between everything you've learned, it's, first of all, God's infinite mercy and love. That even when we bungled up His will, He keeps after us and never lets us down. He will bring good out of all our bungles and sins and wrong choices and the whole mess that we are. And how beautifully He does it! He just keeps on. God's awesome wisdom and Providence, so far above us and beyond us. I want you to look at your particular life. Watch out when deceit comes your way. Be careful when the opportunity looks so logical to lie and cheat for a so-called greater good. God may use it, but it is still a sin, it is still wrong.

You cannot read this and say it was right, and if you do, you're trying to cover up truth. It was a rotten thing, and we can put a lot of great excuses on it. We know God used it, and we know God wanted to bless Jacob. But He would have done it in another way had they not interfered.

THIRTEEN

Genesis Chapter 28 & 29

Let's turn to Genesis 28:10. I think we left off where Jacob was sent by Isaac to look for a wife.

It says: *Jacob left for Beersheba. When he reached a certain place, he passed the night there. Taking one of the stones he found at that place, he made it his pillow and lay down.* You know, the people there were kind of primitive, and you and I would have probably grumbled over the fact that there wasn't a pillow and we weren't in our bed. And he looked around, very nonchalant, and he said, "Well, this is a nice-looking rock. I'll put my head on this." Laid down and intended to go to sleep, and he did. He had a dream.

It's amazing how God speaks to many people in dreams. I'm not one of these people who think that every dream has some kind of meaning. But the Lord has used dreams, no doubt. Joseph, for example. The Lord spoke to Joseph about Mary in a dream and told him when to go to Egypt in a dream, told him when to come back in a dream. Don Bosco — if you ever want to read the life of Don Bosco — a great man, always had dreams. Or Mother Cabrini, who had fantastic prophetic dreams. And I remember the time she wanted to buy some property in New York that was owned by the Jesuits, I think, at the time, and they were willing to sell it real cheap because there was no water on the property. I mean, *no* water. And so, they practically gave it to Mother Cabrini. But she was a smart cookie. The Lord told her in a vision in a dream where the water was. And so, she bought the property, and she said to the men, "Dig here." And they said, "Mother, there is no water here." And she said, "Dig here." And they protested, and she said, "Dig here." And they dug, and they've had water ever since.

Now, some of you are wondering, "Well, how come she didn't tell the Jesuits that, and then they could have water and keep the property? I mean, if you know where the water is, why don't you tell them?" Well, she did. She said, "There is water on this property." And they said, "No, there isn't." She said, "Yes, there is." And they said, "Well, if you can find it, go ahead." Who's going to believe a little, old immigrant nun? I tell you, you got to watch those saints. God speaks to them. So, they found water.

And now, we're looking at Jacob. So, you see, the Lord doesn't always change in His economy of holiness, He just repeats it in many centuries in many people's beautiful lives. Well, anyway, *he had a dream: a ladder was there, standing on the ground with its top reaching to heaven.* I mean, that's some kind of ladder — way up. *And there were angels of God on the ground, going up it and coming down.* So, here were these angels, this huge ladder, and the angels coming up and some coming down, and he looked at it. *And Yahweh was there, standing over him.*

You know, there's something so awesome in the word *Yahweh* — God. I think that's why I like mountains and the ocean, and a storm, because it depicts to me the power of the Father.

And so, the Lord Yahweh, with these angels going up and coming down, said, "*I am Yahweh, the God of Abraham your father, and the God of Isaac.*" Well, now Jacob's father was Isaac. So was Abraham. He said, "*I will give to you and to your descendants the land on which you are lying. Your descendants shall be like the specks of dust on the ground; you shall spread to the west and the east, to the north and the south."*

You have to wonder, when you look at this, what was the meaning of those angels going up and down this ladder? Well, that's the intercession of the angels. They bring your message from you to God and from God to you. One of the saddest things in today's life, one of the worst heresies in today's life, is the negation of the power of the angels. I have a hard time with this new kind of theology and exegesis of Scripture, when they say, "Well, there were no angels, there was just God, and they were afraid to say *God,* so they said *angel.*" Why do we always want to destroy God's gifts? What is it? We're so proud, we can't stand it, that there is another kind of creature that is smarter than we are, and greater and more beautiful and more powerful—is that it? I think it's terrible, terrible, terrible pride. Because if we had any common sense, you can start way back at the beginning of Genesis, and you find these magnificent creatures so like God.

And you have one. Jesus says you have a guardian angel. And He said, "Don't scandalize one of these little ones." Why? "Because their angel always sees the face of My Father in Heaven." And when you try to talk to any of these human-ists who destroy God and destroy His gifts to us, they look at you like, "What is it? You're not intelligent. You haven't got the news that there are no angels." Well, let me tell you some-thing. There are angels, and you have one, and I wouldn't let anybody rob you of that truth. The worst they can do is think you're stupid, but you'll have the last laugh. Because one day, they'll know. Unfortunately for them, it may be too late. And so, we see God telling us something here about the power of this angelic spiritual nature. They have a work to do. That work is to guard us, to guide us, to protect us, to have charge over us. Lest we dash our foot against the stone. And that, my friends, is a truth that I hope you remember.

If you don't remember anything else I say here, I want you to remember that, and tell your children about these magnificent creatures, teach them how to live a spiritual life even when they're five and six years old. Don't make God someone up there that is only there to punish you. Look at God as a Father, Who has given you a powerful friend that we call a guardian angel, who does exactly what Jacob saw these angels do: bring your needs and your love and your prayers to God, and bring God's grace and answers back to you. What more do you want? And why are we so ungrateful? You know, it's going to be sad for some of us, that we will never know the love of God except at the point of death. Isn't that the saddest thing that could ever be?

Well, let's go on. And He said to Jacob, *"All the tribes of the earth shall bless themselves by you and your descendants. Be sure that I am with you."* You know, in our daily life, and in the crisis we've had for a couple of months and it almost seems years, we've had to remind ourselves that God is with us. And the Lord God Yahweh knew what was in store for Jacob. And He said, "Look, remember, I'm with you." He said, *"I will keep you safe wherever you go."* Do you think God would say this to Jacob and not say it to you? Do you think that He would say it then and not say it to you now, after Jesus His Son came? How could that be? How could it be, when He sent His Son and became a man, when that Son took on your flesh and your blood, so that He could suffer what you suffer, and then put Himself in a little host that we call Eucharist? What kind of humility is that? What kind of love is that? When He can do all that, do you think He's not with you? So, don't look at this book and say, "Oh, He was with Jacob," or, "He was with David," or, "He was with Peter." If He was with any of them, He is with you. But if you don't remember that, if you don't bring it to your mind, if this Word doesn't register in your memory so that when things are bad and things are going wrong and nothing is turning out right, you can remember: "He's with me."

You know, I think there's no other time that you can seek out God as well as in pain and suffering. It's hard to see God in a lot of that. I don't want to say it's hard to see God when you're happy, because God is a God of joy, and He wants us to be joyful. But if you're happy about something, it's so hard to keep your mind on God unless you realize that that moment of happiness comes from God and give Him honor and glory and thanksgiving. And so, as a result, we start taking things for granted, and it's so easy to take things for granted when you've got everything going well. Most of all, we attribute to ourselves or "How great I am that all of this turned out so well." We're not the humblest people in the world. But in suffering and pain, you never attribute that to yourself, and so you have no other place to go but to God. And my friends, that's why I believe firmly in my heart that if we don't repent to change our lives, all nature will rebel against us. God is going to make His people holy. And so, He is saying to you and to me, "*I will keep you safe wherever you go and bring you back to this land, for I will not desert you before I have done all that I have promised you.*"

I've had to recall this during these weeks of crisis. "Lord, you promised that this was Your network and it would glorify Your Son. You promised, Lord." God never goes back on His promise. We do constantly. He never does.

Well, it says: *Jacob awoke up from his sleep and said, "Truly, Yahweh is in this place, and I never knew it!"* I want you to look at that sentence for a minute. "Yahweh, God, is in this place, and I never knew it." What kept him from knowing it? The desert was bleak. He could only lie down and sleep on the hot sand, or cold sand in the evening. He had a rock for a pillow. How would you see God in that desolate place? But you know, you and I have desolate times in our life, and sometimes they last more than a night, they last for weeks and months and years. And whether that desolation is brought on by ourselves or other people's wickedness or our own dryness within our own hearts and minds, our own sinner condition, when there seems to be nothing around but desert and hard rock, where there's not anything that's beautiful or green or lush that would remind you of the Creator and His love for us—when everything is tragedy and heartache and suffering and everything goes wrong, when everything is desert, when everything is bleak—I think we could all say when it's over: "Truly, God was in this place, and I knew it not." Well, I want you to think about all the times in your life and all the places and all the tragedies when He just didn't seem there but He was.

And it says here in Genesis 28:17 that Jacob was afraid. Isn't it strange? So many times in our life we find God's awesome presence fearful. We get so afraid. And it's amazing to me because we were created by love, for love, to love. We're not afraid of human love, ordinarily. We covet it, we try to get as much as we can. And yet that awesome silent, loving presence of God—we're afraid. So afraid. Well, Jacob says, "*How awe-inspiring this place is! This is nothing less than a house of God.*" Isn't that strange to you that he calls this desert a house of God? He didn't say, "This is the place of God," or, "God appears to come down here. Now He's gone." He said, "This is the house of God." So, he realized that God was around him, and he was in that presence. What is a house? Well, a house is a structure in which people live, but he said, *"This is the house of God and the gate of heaven. And I didn't know it."*

You see, you are constantly living in the house of God because the whole universe is His house—the earth, the stars, the planets. Isn't that some kind of big house? But that's what Jacob was talking about. The whole world is the house of God, but he didn't know that. Do you know that this universe is the house of God? Well, if you do, why do we defile the house of God? Why do we sell and buy? And cheat and lie? Why do we make God's house a den of thieves and robbers? Why do we take His creation and destroy it with smog and smoke? Why do we look at the ground and defile it with insecticides and pesticides? Would you do that in anyone else's house? Would you go in anyone else's house and just tear it up? Would you go on anyone else's yard and just say, "I don't like these flowers," and begin to pull them out and say, "I want it bare"? Would you do that? Well, if you did, I think they'd either come and take you in a paddy wagon or put you in jail. Well, if you don't expect to get away with it there, why do you expect to get away with it when you do the same thing to God's house? When you split atoms and make fire that destroys and puts everybody in the state of ashes, when you take life and pull it apart and kill it?

If you ever knew you were in God's house, do you think you'd do that? You see, we don't read the Scriptures. We don't take time because we're so busy. "I've got so much to do." Because we have said to God: "This is my house, and I am the master of my house." And that's a lie. You live in God's house. You're not its master. He's got the whole thing in the palm of His hand.

Well, *rising early in the morning, Jacob took the stone he used for a pillow, and set it up as a monument, pouring oil over the top of it. And he named the place Bethel. And he made this vow: "If God goes with* me and keeps me safe on this journey I am making, if he gives me bread to eat and clothes to wear, and if I return home safely to my father one day, then Yahweh shall be my God. And this stone I have set up as a monument shall be a house of God, and I will surely pay you, Lord Yahweh, a tenth part of all you give me." Well, I wonder if we've come any further than Jacob was. You say, "Well, what does that mean?" You have to realize at this point here that the Lord God, the true God, was just beginning to make Himself known and loved and feared. We're like way back at the beginning.

And so, the only way they could judge that they were pleasing to God is what Jacob said: "If you keep me safe, if you give me bread to eat and clothes to wear, then when I return safely to my father, then you shall be my God forever." I wonder if we have changed since then, to love God for God alone. House and home and riches and possessions are not the criteria by which we judge His blessing. Because in the fifth chapter of Matthew, the Lord says that the poor are blessed and the sick are blessed. You see how much higher the New Testament is than the Old? And those that are persecuted should dance for joy. So, we have come a long way, from judging the abundant life of material things as God's blessing, to that other blessing of detachment, poverty of spirit. But then I have to wonder: Have we crossed that bridge or not?

Moving on, Jacob went to the land of the sons of the East. He looked and there in the fields was a well with three flocks of sheep lying there, for this well was used for watering the flocks. The stone there was really pretty big. So, he sees some shepherds coming, and he said, "Brothers, where are you from?" And they said, "We're from Haran."

He said, "Well, do you know Laban?" They said, "Yeah. He is well." They said, "In fact, there's his daughter Rachel coming." And he said, "See, it is still broad daylight out, is it not yet time to bring the animals in. Water the sheep and go and take *them back to pasture." But they answered, "We cannot do that until all of the flocks are gathered and they roll the stone off the mouth of the well."* So, you're talking about a kind of communal effort to move the stone.

So, Rachel came with the sheep. And it's amazing, way back there, how many people were shepherds or shepherdesses. That symbol of taking care of sheep. And then sheep aren't those nice, gentle sheep you think they are. We've got sheep, and I can tell you a lot about sheep. They're stubborn. I mean *stubborn*. And they go where they want to go. And they're dumb. They're not very bright. They don't know when to stop eating. If you put corn in front of them, they'll eat buckets at a time. So, sheep are a symbol of people, of all the people, because we are sheep. We love to think we're very intelligent, and God has given many of you great IQs. But I don't think that makes you bright. What makes you bright is the love of God in your heart. It really doesn't matter how much you know *about* God. It's only important that you know God, and the difference in that is the difference between looking at a piece of pie in a magazine and eating a piece. Oh, there's a big difference. You have to experience God. I'm not talking about effervescent feelings, but that deep awareness in faith: God is with us.

And so, *as soon as Jacob saw Rachel, he came up and, rolling the stone off the mouth of the well, he watered the sheep. Jacob kissed Rachel and burst into tears. He told her he was her father's kinsman and Rebecca's son and she ran to tell her father.*

So, we have a kind of distant nephew suddenly showing up in the desert. You can imagine what a tremendous event this was because how many people show up in the desert, especially one of your own. So, they have a great celebration. And he says, *"Truly, you are my bone and flesh,"* and Jacob stayed with him about a month.

You know, it's amazing to me that people are accustomed to being nomads, living alone in tents in the desert, that they would get very independent, kind of, "Who are you, and what do you want, and get out of here as soon as possible." That kind of attitude. But it's amazing how these people had such a concept of family life. There's a nephew that he had never seen. But it was such an occasion of joy, such an occasion of celebration, and you know, we've missed that. There doesn't seem to be family gatherings anymore, where all—even distant—relatives come. When I go back up north and I'm around my own town of Canton, I go to see my uncle and my aunt. It's a wonderful experience because my uncle is the only one I have left of my own immediate family, but my cousins will come there, and my other aunts and their children and neighbors come with their children. And you feel family, and they're glad to see you, and you're glad to see them. And you sit down at table, you reach over, and you eat out of the same pot, and you share the same fork once in a while, and somebody else takes off a piece of bread and puts it on your plate, and it's family. And so often in today's world, we miss that.

You see, let me tell you what happens to us. When you get away from our Father in Heaven, when you get away from our Family in Heaven—the Father, the Son, and Spirit—when you get further and further away from that Family, then you get further and further away from the fire. You get further and further away from love. But then your immediate family and your neighbor's family, your community family, your state family, your country's family, your church family doesn't mean anything. If you stop the source of love, then all these things dry up. It's really very simple. It's very simple. You say, "Oh, I'm having so many problems in my family." How is your family's relationship with the one Family in Heaven? If you drop the

Father, Son, and the Spirit, if you drop the Lord Yahweh from your life, what do you think? It's like a beautiful fruit mixer, or whatever they use to mix things with, and you've got this gorgeous thing. It's made out of gold. It's all beautiful, and it'll do a fantastic job. But if you never plugged it in to a receptacle, it's never going to work. I mean, there is no way it can work.

Or if you don't ever go to the gasoline station and put in that little dollar for a gallon of gasoline, you're not going anywhere with your Rolls-Royce. And that little motorbike runs with the same power as your Rolls-Royce, and neither one is going anywhere without that power.

Now, if you understand that, why is it so complicated to understand that when you begin to get away from the one Love and one Fire that there is, you're going to get cold, and you're going to die out? In the winter time, I like to stand over the register, especially if my leg is bad. And that heat kind of warms it up. But there's one bad thing about standing over a register and feeling that warm heat. As fast as you get away off of that register, it gets colder and colder and colder. Try it. All of you that live up north and it's snowing already. Stand on your register, and then move away from it. You'll know the difference real quick. It's no different with God. Once you leave God out of your life, you're out in the cold. You say, "Well, I'm having a good time." No, you're not. You're just fooling yourself. You're just kidding yourself. You can't have a good time. You have guilt. You feel far away from God. There's that gnawing feeling of weakness in your heart where you lose control. You can't have joy without God, no more than you can have heat when you move off the register and you get further and further away from the heat, or take that gallon of gasoline out of your car.

Laban said to Jacob, "Because you are my kinsman, are you to work for me without payment? Tell me what wages you want." Now

Laban had two daughters, the elder named Leah and the younger Rachel. There was no sparkle in Leah's eyes, but Rachel was beautiful and Jacob had fallen in love with Rachel. So his answer was, "Well, I tell you what. *I will work for you seven years to win your younger daughter, Rachel.*" Well, Laban looked, and he said, "That's not bad. It's better you marry her than some stranger."

We're going to keep the rest of this for the next chapter because it's extremely interesting to see what happens to Jacob. And what he did to his father turned around and happened to him rather quickly.

You know, you can't read this book fast. Because if you do, I think you miss the point of your daily life. And this book is so great that you could read maybe a paragraph a day and apply it to your life. Put yourself in Jacob's shoes, and remember the world you live in is the house of God. Don't be on your death bed and have to say, "I never knew it." Know it now. Understand it now. Stay close to your Family, the Trinity, and let the love of God — the Father, the Son, and the Spirit — so fill your heart that you will be able to warm your brother's cold, selfish, proud heart. Because the further away you get from God, the further away you get from love.

FOURTEEN

Genesis 29–31

Well, we're going to continue on with Genesis chapter twenty-nine. We realize that Jacob had some problems, and I think some of you were kind of just a little bit surprised at my interpretation, but it really wasn't my interpretation. This is the reality.

We have to see that in those days, as in our day, there was, well, kind of taking the line of least resistance. If we can do something more easily or maybe not quite as honestly as it should be done, seems like many people will take that course. And it's amazing to me how we rationalize all of this, and then if we see something like this in the Gospel and the Scriptures, especially Old Testament, we get all excited, and we say, "Oh, you're downgrading the prophets." Well, it's written this way. Sometimes, they lied and cheated. But you have to realize, in those days, they didn't have even what you have. Do you realize that you have more life than a lot of the great men of the Old Testament had? Like Jacob, Abraham.

You say, "Well, these were men of great faith." And, well, I think there were times that they had great faith, and they were great men. I didn't say you were greater than they are. I'm saying the little they had, they used so well that they became great. But they have less light, and you have more light, by the very fact that they were the beginning, the very beginnings of love and relationship with the one true God, Yahweh. And so, as you read the Bible, whether it's Genesis or Kings through all the rest, you've got to admit that with Jesus, as children of the New Testament, you have much more. You have seen the Messiah. You know the Messiah. He has lived, He has died, and He rose. You've got all that knowledge. If you're Catholic, you have the Eucharist. Oh, God with us.

And so, you begin to realize as you go along that you do have much more, and I think we need to see what did they do with the little they had. What do we do with the 100 percent we have? Now, if they became greater, it isn't because they had more light or more gifts; it's because they used what little they had *more*. If I only have bread and water, but I eat it three times a day, it may be a little food, but if I do that consistently, I can survive. But if there's a man who has all kinds of food in his refrigerator but never touches it, then he could starve to death in the midst of plenty. So, I think as you go along here, you need to understand that you don't need to envy anybody in the Old Testament. In fact, you've got a lot more light than some of the apostles had because you've got two thousand years of development of the gospel, development of doctrine.

And there's no question they had lots of light, they died for the Faith, they were the ones that God used to begin the whole thing. But you see the progression of light and faith and revelation, and the fruits of sanctity and the fruits of the Spirit, all together. You've got a lot of light. Like the man who was given ten talents and made ten more. Well, you and I have been given ten talents, and it's up to us to make ten more. Keep that little thing in mind.

I think we need to go and see what Jacob's doing. And how the dear Lord permitted that what he did to his brother happen to him. It's amazing. So, *Laban said to Jacob, "Because you're my* kinsman, *are you to work for me without payment? Tell me what wage you want.*" He knew the young man was there and said, "It is not fair just because you are one of my relatives that you should work for me for nothing. Tell me what you want, and I will pay you." So, Jacob is a smart young man, and he looked at the two daughters that Laban had. One was named Leah—that was the elder—and one named Rachel—she was the younger. There was no sparkle in Leah's eyes, and I think some of the exegesis thinks she was a little bit either cross-eyed or had something wrong with her eye, just not very beautiful. And young Rachel was very beautiful. *So, he said, "I will work for you seven years to win your younger daughter, Rachel."* I think that's a pretty heavy payment to work seven long years, and right where you really see someone you love every day, and he loved Rachel. Well, *Laban said, "It's better for me to give her to you than a stranger."*

So, it says: *To win Rachel, Jacob worked seven years, and they seemed to him like a few days.* Why was that? Why is it that some things we do are so laborious? Oh, we fuss and fume and gripe. It's just so hard. It's so hard to get up and go to Mass. It's so hard to have to go to Confession. It's so hard to do this or do that, but if you love, it isn't hard at all. So, *he worked seven years for Rachel and they seemed to him like a few days because he loved her so much,* just looking forward to having this beautiful woman as his wife. So, for seven years, he worked up a real love for this girl.

Then Jacob said to Laban, "Give me my wife, for my time is finished, and I would love to marry her." So, they have a great banquet. *But when night came, Laban took his daughter Leah and brought her to Jacob.* Oh, boy. You say, "Well, how in the world could they get them mixed up?" Well, they got mixed up because they wore veils. The bad thing here is that when Jacob woke up the next morning, he looked at his wife Rachel. But it wasn't Rachel, it was Leah. Can you imagine that kind of shock? I mean, to work seven years so you can marry someone's daughter, and you wake up the next morning, and it's the elder daughter. They had such a gross way of doing things. Well, nobody's saying it wasn't gross, but you've got to realize this is a primitive people. You can't judge this day by your day. Because you're a child of the New Testament, a lot of things that they did are so, so wrong today. It doesn't mean they were ever right in their day. It only means that when you're developing, you do things that you wouldn't do as an adult. You can realize that when you're children, as you grow, you're doing more and more things on your own, you develop. Nobody is feeding you at this point. When you were a child, your mother had to feed you a couple years. There is a sense of development here.

So, Jacob went to Laban, and he said, "What is this you have done to me? Did I not work for you to win Rachel? Why then have you tricked me?" Laban answered, "It is not the custom in our country to give the younger before the elder." Why didn't he explain that to Jacob ahead of time? Well, I guess the logical reason is he wanted to marry off Leah. Who was going to marry her?

But doesn't that sound kind of familiar to you? Isn't it basically what Jacob did to his brother, Esau? Putting all that hairy skin on him and then getting his father, instead of venison, a young lamb and cooking it for him, and pretending he was his brother? That sounds kind of familiar. You say, "Would God do that?" No, God didn't do it, but He permitted it to happen because it seemed to be a family trait, this conniving. So, the conniver is the one who is connived against. It just seems that whatever you give somehow comes back to you.

So, Laban says, "Finish this marriage week." They celebrated for a week. "And then I'll give you the other one too in return for *working with me another seven years."* So, Jacob didn't have to wait seven years this time. It says that after a week, Rachel also became his wife. So, in those days, they had a kind of dowry. And so, Laban gave both daughters, Leah and Rachel, a slave girl each to be their own individual servant. So, you see a kind of family picture here of people who we were not only crude but sometimes dishonest. And it's amazing, isn't it? How God used all of these unjust, cheating things that people do. He doesn't want them, He does not ordain them, and they're not His fault. That's amazing to me that God can use garbage to make something beautiful or to accomplish His end.

Well, so Jacob loved Rachel, but he loved her more than Leah, and I would imagine that caused problems. He had to work another seven years. This man, Laban, was a smart cookie. He got free labor for fourteen years. Sometimes, when you lie and cheat, all it looks like is you seem to draw down upon yourself a hundredfold punishment or correction or something. Because when Jacob cheated his brother, Esau, it looks to me like he's paying fourteen years for something that only took him about a half-hour at the most. Just unbelievable kind of correction from God. I wonder if he ever thought about that. I wonder if he ever thought, "Oh, I did the same thing. The Lord Yahweh is telling me something."

You wonder why would the Lord permit that to happen to him. But you know, sometimes we are not conscious of something we did wrong or how much we hurt somebody or how much we destroyed them or how much harm we did unless and until that very same thing happens to us. And then when we begin to feel inside, we begin to understand exactly what we did. Isn't that amazing? Because we do things to people kind of, well, "It's for my benefit," and we're so bound up in what is for "my good" that we don't ever put ourselves in somebody else's shoes and wonder how are they going to feel, how hurt are they going to be. Of course, if we did that, we wouldn't do the things we do sometimes. Maybe that's a remedy before you get some bright idea on what you're going to do for your own self. It might be good to think, "How is this going to relate, how is it going to affect somebody else? And if I do affect them adversely, how are they going to feel?" But that spirit of empathy, it is more than sympathy. See, sympathy is for someone that something has happened to already, that's already happening. But if you have empathy, you kind of project what might happen, and you put yourself in that person's shoes, and you feel what they feel. How about if we did that? We probably wouldn't hurt as many people as we do right now.

Well, let's come back and see exactly what happens. And it states that Yahweh saw that Leah was neglected. Jacob didn't love Leah, and she was just a woman that occasionally he slept with. You say, "That sounds gross." That was life. He married two women, they were both sisters, and before Leviticus came along, that's something that was permitted. So, Leah gave birth to a son, and she named him Reuben.

Now, you're going to notice as we go along here the tribes of Israel are beginning to form. So, the first is Reuben. And you know why she called him Reuben? It says: *Leah conceived and gave birth to a son whom she named Reuben, because, she said, "Yahweh has seen my misery; Now my husband will love me."* So, I have always felt sorry for Leah. She couldn't help she wasn't born beautiful.

And obviously, I would imagine it pretty hard for a man to hide the fact that he didn't love her. Especially when he loved the other one more. I mean, there had to be pronounced signs of affection and pronounced signs of rejection because Leah would constantly be a reminder to Jacob, first, that he cheated his own brother and, second, that he was cheated by her father.

So, that constant reminder to a man's ego must have been a phenomenal cross to him. And not knowing about virtue and all the things that you and I know, and having no one to imitate like we have—Jesus—I feel so sorry for her.

Let's see what happened to her. It says: *Again she conceived and gave birth to a son, saying, "Yahweh has heard that I was neglected, so he gave me this one too." And she named him Simeon.* Now we have Reuben, and we have Simeon. And she birthed another son, and named this one Levi. And if you remember, it was the tribe of Levi that was ordained by God to become priests. And only that tribe. It was the tribe of Levi. Again, she conceived and gave birth to a son, and named him Judah. Well, she has more and more children—for a while, anyway.

Now you've got this family problem. Here's Rachel, who is loved by Jacob, and here's Leah, who is not loved by Jacob. But Leah gives him four sons, and Rachel gives him nothing. *Rachel said to Jacob, "Give me children, or I shall die."* You see, these women didn't understand. This is real primitive living. And Jacob got angry with her, and he retorts, "Am I God?" Well, now here another similar thing happens. She does exactly what Sarah did to Abraham. It was the custom of the day. So, she says, "Here is my slave girl, Bilhah. Sleep with her, and her son will be my son." Well, she bore him a son, and his name was Dan. Now, we've got five names of five men who were going to be heads of, each one, a different tribe. And then she brought forth another son, Naphtali. Can you put yourself in that family? The competition must have been fierce, just fierce. Because, you see, the sign of loving God and being loved by God was many riches and many children. So, you have to understand that, in those days, life was not easy.

Well, I bet you look at this, and you think you have troubles. They really had troubles. Because Leah looks at Rachel's slave girl. They didn't remain slaves, they became Jacob's wives. Then Leah gets the same idea. And she said, "Well, if you can do it, I can do it." So, she gives her slave girl to Jacob as a wife, and she bears him a son, and his name was Gad. She has another son, and his name is Asher. So, we had this trading off. All the time, though, Rachel does not have a son, and this creates more and more problems because she's got to bear the humiliation now of two slave girls who have become his wives and her sister, Leah. And although she found some kind of happiness, in as much as her slave girl was hers and the children were hers, it was not her own flesh and blood, and there was nothing they can do about that.

So, Reuben went out one day and found some mandrakes. It's a kind of root, kind of fruit, supposedly a kind of fertility fruit, and so he found those, and he brought them to his mother, Leah. So, Rachel says, *"Give me some of your son's mandrakes."* And she said *"No. Is it not enough to have taken my husband that you should want to take my son's mandrakes too?"* Well, in those days, they just about bargained for anything, and as you can see tonight, this particular incident looks a little bit raunchy. Rachel says, "Okay, then, you can sleep with my husband tonight." You look at that, and you say, "What are we talking about here?" Again, you have to go back to where they were in the desert. A very, very, very, very, very primitive people. Without the light, without the law, without the knowledge of what was right or wrong. Barely knowing the Lord God, Yahweh. And I think sometimes we are almost angry because God was so patient with the primitive people. But I think today with all the light we have, I wonder if we're not just as primitive in today's age. Everybody's sleeping with everybody else. It seems to be nothing wrong in their mind, there seems to be no sin anymore. I wonder if we have advanced any at all. It's disheartening to think that we have literally pushed ourselves back in some kind of time tunnel to the morals or a lack of morals of the people who never knew any better. It's like being seventy years old and then shrinking yourself down to a baby.

How do you think you can find fault with them? I really don't. And when you hear sometimes priests and ministers advise young couples of birth control, all kinds of things that they know in their heart are not right, you just have to wonder if we're not just taking all the light out of the gospel and of the life of Jesus and just saying, "Look, take it back." Think of that. I don't know. It does get you.

And of course, she conceives and bears another son and names him Issachar. Well, Leah, bears a sixth son and names him Zebulun, and then a daughter Dinah. You have to remember, now, that all of this time there is this constant anger in Rachel. Everybody is having children but her. And so, she prayed and prayed and prayed. It said: *God opened her womb, and she conceived and gave birth to a son, saying, "God has taken away my shame." So she named him Joseph.*

Joseph. We're beginning to see God fulfilling His promise to Abraham. These were Abraham's great-grandchildren. He said, "I will make your descendants like the sand on the seashore, the stars in the heavens." And Abraham never saw that happen. But the Lord never said he would. He gave him a promise about his descendants. And Rebecca and Isaac certainly didn't see too much happening.

But now it's Jacob. And the Lord is using all this turmoil in a family and the jealousy between two sisters. He didn't ordain it; you've got to get that in your mind. But He used the weaknesses of human nature for a greater good.

You know, you read about that in the New Testament, you read about it in St. Paul, you hear me say it, you hear ministers say it, your priests say it, and they will continue to say to the end of time that God brings good out of our mistakes and everything. And all of the tragedies and the pain in our life, He brings good, and we don't see it. Well, we don't see it sometimes like Abraham didn't see. Those of you that are praying for your children or your parents, relatives, and they don't seem to be really corresponding, and you think, "Well, they'll never be saved, or they'll never know God, they'll never know Jesus," and you just go on and on and on, and you get discouraged. But you see, you may not see it. You may be like Abraham, and your faith will save them. You may go to the Kingdom before they do, and you've got to trust. If there's one thread that goes through all of this, it is a necessity to trust and not jump the gun on the Lord.

We see here what happened. God used all these children for each of the tribes, and yet He chose Leah's son, Levi—all the Levites were priests of the Lord. But He chose Joseph, Rachel's son, to save the people from starvation, from extinction. It's good to go back, and as you read the Scripture, you go back, and you see God working in such a beautiful way with these jigsaw puzzles. These little pieces that look all crumbled, and maybe this crumbled jigsaw piece will make a mountaintop in your life. And there's another one that looks so black and beaten up, and maybe that makes a valley that you go through to climb the mountain. And so, all these little pieces that we mess up, God puts just in that spot. And this should give us hope. This should give us great hope, because it's the same God. It doesn't work any differently now. It's the same God.

Now, *when Rachel had given birth to Joseph, Jacob said to Laban, "Release me, and then I can go home to my country. Give me my wives for whom I have worked for you, and my children. You know very well the work I have done for you." So, he says, "If I've won your friendship ... I learned from the omens that Yahweh has blessed me on your account. So,"* Laban said, *"name your wages."* I'd be afraid if he told me that again. Well, once before he said, "What are your wages?" and Jacob got into a lot of trouble.

Well, we look at Jacob. He's worked hard. He has many children now. He's got two, four wives. So, he says, "Oh, Laban, I think it's time. I'm getting various omen signs that I need to go home and see my father. I think I need to go." So, Laban says, "All right. What are your wages?"

Well, I think Jacob has learned a little bit about Laban over the years. He says, *"You will not have to pay me anything, if you do for me what I propose. I will be your shepherd once more and look after your flock. Today I will go through your flock and take out of it every black animal among the sheep and every speckled or spotted one among the goats. Such shall be my wages. And my honesty will answer for me later when you come to check my wages. Every goat I have that is not speckled or spotted, and every sheep that is not black, shall rank as stolen property."* That's a kind of odd bargain, isn't it? So, he wants every speckled or spotted goat and every black sheep. Every black animal among the sheep.

So, Laban said, *"Good, let it be as you say."* I would suppose Laban thought: "That's pretty cheap wages. I mean, how many black sheep do I have? How many speckled or spotted goats do I have?" Well, you have to realize that Jacob was really blessed by God and his shepherding paid off, because Laban had grown enormously in wealth. *But, that same day Laban took out the striped and speckled he-goats and all the spotted and speckled she-goats, every one that had white on it, and all the black sheep. So, Laban handed them over to his sons, and put a three-day's journey between himself and Jacob. And Jacob took care of the rest of Laban's flock.*

Now, I'm not too sure about the rest of this because it's kind of difficult to understand how what Jacob did had anything to do with the fertility of these goats and sheep, but anyway, you have to realize in those days, again, he did something very, very primitive. *Jacob gathered branches in sap, from poplar, almond and plane trees, and peeled them in white strips, laying bare the white on the branches.* Well, I think what happened here, if I'm not mistaken, at least that's how it sounds, there must have been a particular odor about these poplar, almond, and plane trees. The sap was running through the bark of these trees. And when you peel that off, all that gooey stuff was there, and I would imagine it had a terrific odor. *He put the branches he had peeled in front of the animals, in the troughs in the channels where the animals came to drink; and the animals mated when they came to drink. They mated therefore in front of the branches and so produced striped, spotted and speckled young. Moreover, whenever the sturdy animals mated, Jacob put the branches where the animals could see them, in the troughs, so that they would mate in front of the branches.* As a result, he got a fantastic flock of sheep and goats. I mean, if he had been living today, he'd be a multimillionaire. This man was very, very clever and very astute. And of course, *he became extremely rich and became the owner of large flocks and had slaves and camels and donkeys.* He got extremely rich.

You know, I don't know why this reminds me of this, but this great need for people to have more than they need, to me is, well, you wonder sometimes if we're just not rushing headlong into disaster. When we encourage children, and that's when they are nine, ten, eleven, twelve years old, to be so involved in making money. I just wonder if we're not just taking all the adolescence and the childhood away from children and we're just pushing them forward to being adults as fast as possible. And you read about kids that have big corporations already, or at least they're making more money than their parents make, and you just wonder what's happening to the soul. What's happening to our minds? When this one kid, ten years old, said, "Money is power." Money isn't power. Whatever can be taken away from you tomorrow is not power. Whatever eats up your soul and possesses your mind until that's all you think about is not power. Whatever happens that you think of only satisfying yourself and getting one million after another million and one million after another million until you walk on people and there's just nothing in your heart but a dried-up heart that's filled with money. I don't think that's power. I think that's slavery. But in the days of Jacob, and today's day, it hasn't changed much.

Now, I'm not against anybody having money. If God has given it to you, God bless you. Use it well. The problem is the possessiveness we have for power and glory that we think only money can give us. Because when you die, and then what? I had a man who would ask a friend of his, who was always talking about all the things he wanted to do: "Then what?" "Well, I'll go to college, I'm gonna get a good job, I'm gonna own my own company." And then what? "I'll get married, I'm gonna have cars and boats." And then what? "I'll go on trips and enjoy myself." And then what? Maybe this is a good place to stop for a minute and ask yourself the question: When I have all the things I have ever wanted, then what?

Well, Jacob learned that the sons of Laban were kind of criticizing him. They were watching him from afar, and they said, "*Jacob has taken everything that belonged to our father; it is at our father's expense that he's acquired all this wealth.*" So, Jacob began to see the writing on the wall, and he said, "Well, I better go." *So, he says to Rachel and Leah, "I have lost favor with your father. I can see by his face that things are not the way they should be. I have worked hard for him. Your father has tricked me, ten times changing my wages."* Ten times. Laban tricked Jacob ten times. "*But whenever he said,*

'*The spotted ones shall be your wages,*' *all the animals produced spotted young; whenever he said, 'The striped ones shall be your wages,' all the animals produced striped young.* God has blessed me."

And he said to them, "*In a dream, the angel of God called to me, 'Jacob!' And I answered, 'Here I am.'*" It'd be wonderful if you and I could imitate Jacob in that and say, "Here I am, Lord." You say, "Well, God doesn't speak to me." Oh, yes, He does. He's speaking to you all the time. He's always speaking to you in some way.

So, he says, "Here I am." God said, "*Look up and see: all the males covering the females of the flock are striped or spotted. I have seen all that Laban has done to you. I am the God of Bethel.*" Remember Bethel is where Jacob poured oil on this rock and made a monument. He says, "Now get ready and move." So, God was with Jacob through all his sufferings. And those of you that maybe are suffering — you drank a lot, and now you've got cirrhosis of the liver or whatever — if you can give that to God and say, "Lord, I am sorry." If you can use that to be repentant. Not resentful. Not rebellious. But repentant. "Lord, I have sinned against You and Heaven and earth. Have mercy on me." So, this is what has happened to Jacob.

He paid dearly for the trick he had played on his brother and his father. In fact, he paid ten times. But it didn't keep God from blessing him, as he was repentant and sorry and paid his dues. The Lord waited until Jacob became a humbler man and knew that, whatever he had, it was from the Lord God.

And you can become holy even though you may have been the cause of the pain and the suffering that you have at this moment. God can turn it around for you. It's what He wants to do. That's how you glorify God.

So, Rachel and Leah, in this hour of trial, go together and said to Jacob, "*Have we any share left in the inheritance of our father's house? Does he not treat us as foreigners? For he has sold us and gone on to use up all of our money. Surely all the riches God has taken from our father belong to us and to our children. So do all that God has told you.*" Now, you could see Laban was being kind of punished by God too. But you know, I don't like the word *punishment*. I think we become the victims of our own sin. We're the cause, and we become the effects.

So, if you drink too much, you get cirrhosis, or you get hepatitis, and you get a venereal disease—well, you can't blame God. But you can use that to become holy by being repentant. You just give that pain and suffering to God for your soul, for the salvation of souls, and turn it around.

FIFTEEN

Genesis Chapters 31–34

We're going to continue on with Genesis. Before we begin, though — as we study human nature and how God acts within human nature, within human events brought on sometimes by our own weaknesses and mistakes, sometimes sins — I want to remind you again of God's great goodness to us.

God is calling us to do great things, and as I've said many times before, I think time is very short. No, I don't mean the end of the world's coming, but there are just so many things happening that force us to want to reach out, do more and more to save souls.

So, let's turn to Genesis 31:22. Now, you have to recall that Jacob left — took his wives, all his children, and fled. He began to realize that his popularity with his father-in-law was beginning to wane a little bit. So, he began to accumulate great wealth and takes off. Now, you've got to put this in your family situation, and some of you may have had something at least similar to this.

Well, it says: *Taking his brothers with him, Laban pursued him for seven days and overtook him. God came by night in a dream to Laban.* Now, Laban was about to do great harm to Jacob, but God intervened. He came to him by night and said, *"On no account say anything whatever to Jacob."* Well, that probably meant do him no harm, because when he caught up with Jacob, he did say quite a bit. He said, "*What have you done? Tricked me and driving my daughters off like prisoners of war? Why did you flee in secret, stealing away without letting me know so that I could send you on your way rejoicing?*" Now, we know that wasn't true. Laban would have never sent him away rejoicing. So, he said, "*You do not even let me kiss my sons and daughters.*" That's all his grandchildren. "*You behave like a fool.*" I would imagine there were some other words that were exchanged and not written in this book. You can imagine what they were.

Laban said, "*It is in my power to do you harm, but the God of your father said to me last night, 'On no account say anything whatever to Jacob.'*" Well, what he was really angry about was that somewhere along the line some of his little gods were stolen. That was his security. And Laban, even though he knew that Jacob had the God Who was Father, he said, "Why would you take away my gods?"

Jacob said, "*I was afraid, thinking you were going to snatch your daughters from me. But whoever is found in possession of your gods shall not remain alive.*" So, he didn't steal any gods. So, he asked him to go around and examine everybody. *Now, Rachel had taken the household idols, and put them in a camel's litter and was sitting on them.*

Well, you could imagine what that was like. You know, you have here a real family squabble. And I think sometimes we think that family squabbles somehow take away holiness. Well, I think there's no question that if we had a real family love, if we really knew what it meant to love each other, we wouldn't have all this hatred. And certainly, this is not any Christian example, but still in the midst of a non-Christian example, at least Jacob knew the Lord God. His grandfather, Abraham, was chosen by God to begin this new nation. And these are very important men. It was from Jacob that came the twelve tribes of Israel. And so, it's difficult to understand sometimes that even within holy households, there are holy terrors. There are sometimes occasions when our human nature seems to forget its destiny of becoming holy. Seems to forget what God has called us to, and as a result, we go down.

So, Jacob begins to defend himself and took Laban to task. *Laban gave Jacob this answer: "These daughters are my daughters, and these sons are my sons; these the sheep are my sheep, and all that you see belongs to me. But what can I do today about my daughters, and about the sons they have borne? Come, now let us make a covenant, you and I."* So, they made a covenant.

The difference, I think, between this and other family squabbles — and you wonder why today in Christian families there should be such a difference since we have so much more grace — the difference is that they had a pretty big argument and a lot to quarrel about, but they came to a conclusion. And you have to wonder how people who know so little about God, so little about His mercy, His love, never even the prophecies of the coming Messiah — there was nothing — but the little they had, they used so well that in the midst of this, they could resolve their differences. And so they made this covenant, they told each other what they would do and what they wouldn't do. *And then Laban rose early the next morning, and kissing his sons and daughters, he blessed them and left to return home. And when Jacob was going on his way, angels of God met him, and on seeing them, he said, "This is God's camp."*

Isn't that an example of how we should act? How many of you out there have feuds? I mean real feuds with various families or races. We call that prejudice. You never make peace, there's always a war in your heart, and yet you have much.

You've got Jesus, you've got salvation, redemption, Resurrection, Ascension, you've got the gospel, you've got the whole thing written out, you've got a Church that explains it to you, have the Eucharist. You've got so many things. You can understand why God held this generation so responsible. When we've been given so much, yet we practice so little. It is astounding to me that we never seem to come up to the level of spirituality and grace that God has given us. And so, if you hate a family or a member of the family, it's years and years and years, you never speak to each other. And it's usually some little, bitty thing. And most of it, not half or even a third of what happened to Jacob and Laban. Some little thing. "You didn't come to my shower," so the families are angry for years. "You didn't come to my wedding." "You didn't do this." Or just little things that create such deep-rooted hatred. You've got to wonder, do we understand Christianity?

And it's even worse when something is imagined. When our imagination works overtime, and we go along and imagine in a rash judgment. Do you know what a rash judgment is? It's when you imagine some motivation that somebody has, and you imagine that motivation. "I know why he did this. Why he did that. He hates me." He may not even know you exist. So, you just have to kind of sometimes sit down in awe at the little we seem to understand Christianity. And how much these men seemed to bear fruit in all of their sinful human nature, their crudeness, they just had no advantages at all. Living in deserts as nomads, just a very difficult life, very difficult. And yet they have a sense of a Father's presence and lived by it. Can you imagine a world with as many Christians as there are in it, if we all lived our full faith? The whole world would be changed.

We'll go on here to Genesis 32. We find that Jacob's problems are not over. Far from it. First, he had to deal with his father-in-law. Now he's getting close to the area where his brother, Esau, lives. And you remember what he did to Esau.

He took his birthright for a pot of lentils. Really. He took his inheritance by putting on a false skin so he'd have a lot of hair and make enough venison — really a goat that he pretended was venison — and he got the will, got the inheritance, then he fled. So, when he left, Esau was crying and begging for just some kind of blessing. Well, if I were in Jacob's shoes, I would be scared to death. And he was. We're looking at something I think is so absolutely necessary and important today. I want you to imagine that your brother lies and cheats and takes away your entire inheritance, and let's say fourteen, twenty, twenty-two years pass somewhere in there. And all of a sudden, you see him coming down the street. What would your reaction be? Well, Jacob sent instructions, and the instruction said, *"Say this to my lord Esau."*

Now he knows, and he's beginning to kind of bow down a little bit. He's scared. There's a great difference there. He said, *"Here's a message of your servant Jacob."* So, all of a sudden, he calls him "lord Esau." And he said, "I am your servant Jacob." So, right off the bat, he's kind of calming things down. *"I've been staying with Laban until now. I have acquired oxen, beasts of burden, flocks, and men and women slaves. I send news of this to my lord in the hope of winning your approval."*

But when these people went to Esau, they saw Esau coming with four hundred men. Well, they go and tell Jacob, and he is scared to death. I mean, he thinks: "He is after me! He's gonna destroy everything I have." So, what does he do? Exactly what you and I do when we're scared. We pray very hard. You think ahead. And we find this very human thing going on. It says: *He was greatly afraid and distressed. So, he divided the people with him, and the flocks, into two companies.* "Okay, Leah and all of you on this side, and Rachel and all of you on that side." He's thinking to himself, that if Esau comes to one of the companies and attacks it, the other company will be left to escape. But then he prays. Let's see what Jacob prayed. Maybe there's got a secret here, maybe something that we never thought of, for when someone has hurt you this bad, and they're coming to get you, or you think that.

So, he says, "*Oh, God of my father Abraham, and the God of my father Isaac, Yahweh, who has said, 'Go back to your country and family, and I will make you prosper.'*" So, he is bringing up a promise that God made to his grandfather Abraham and his father Isaac. He said, "*I am unworthy of all the kindness and goodness you've shown me.*" He's getting to be humble. "*I only had my staff when I crossed the Jordan, and now I can form two companies. I implore you, save me from my brother's clutches, for I am afraid of him.*" You know, now instead of just running, he prayed. And he had a humble prayer. He was not afraid to admit to God that he was afraid. He wasn't afraid to admit he was a sinner and did not deserve all of this attention or this particular favor. He said, "*I implore you to save me from my brother's clutches, for I'm afraid of him. He may come and attack us and all mothers and their children. Yet it was you who said,*" — he's remembering again, he's reminding God of that promise — "*It was you who said, 'I will make you prosper and make your descendants like the sand on the seashore, so many it cannot be counted.'*"

And Jacob slept there that night, praying. *From what he had with him, he chose a gift for his brother Esau. Two hundred she-goats* — I don't know if you and I would consider that a gift, but this was money — *twenty he-goats, two hundred ewes and twenty rams, thirty camels in milk with their calves, forty cows and ten bulls, twenty she-asses and ten donkeys. He put them in the charge of his servants, in separate droves. He gave the first this order: "Go ahead of me, leave space between each drove and the next. And when my brother Esau meets you and asks, 'To whom do you belong? And*

*where are you going? Whose are those animals that you are driving?'
you will answer, 'To your servant Jacob. They are a gift sent to my
lord Esau.'"*

He has depended upon the Lord, he has humbled himself,
he knows who he is, and he knows what he did. And he's
sorry. He's got gifts. But he's still not sure those gifts are going
to mean anything. *And he gave the same order to the second and
the third group: "You must say, 'Your servant Jacob himself is following.'" For Jacob argued, "I will conciliate him by sending a gift
in advance; so when I come face to face with him he may perhaps
receive me favorably."* You know, there's a lesson here. When
we're angry with others, especially when we have family feuds,
people haven't spoken to aunts or uncles or brothers and sisters
for years, and your children don't speak to them either, and
their children don't speak to them, and nobody really knows
why anymore. But you gotta hand it to Jacob, with the very
little light he had, he prayed. He admitted. He was humble
enough to admit he was scared to death. He offered a gift. He
was seeking forgiveness. He said, "This is terrible. I did a terrible thing. But I make reconciliation."

*That same night he rose, and taking his two wives and two slave
girls and his eleven children, he crossed the ford. He took them and
sent them across the stream, and Jacob was there left alone.* And
this is something that we've heard of. It says: *And there was
one that wrestled with him until daybreak, who, seeing that he could
not master him, struck him in the socket of his hip, and Jacob's hip
was dislocated as he wrestled with him.* There was somebody very
definite here. *He said, "Let me go, for day is breaking." But Jacob
answered, "I will not let you go until you bless me." He then asked,
"What is your name?" "Jacob," he replied. And he said, "Your name
shall no longer be Jacob, but Israel. Because you have been strong
against God, you shall prevail against man."* Well, you wonder

what in the world does that mean? Well, you could give all kinds of interpretations, but the one I like the best is that Jacob wrestled with God. He wrestled with that deep reality that he was nothing. He persevered, he was strong, and in spite of the obstacles facing him, in spite of the fact that there was every chance that his brother would annihilate him and his wives and his children and take all his possessions as spoil, he knew that his chances without God were nil when it came to being reconciled to his brother. But he kept on all night long. And then Jacob said this: "*I beg you, tell me your name.*" But he replied, "*Why do you ask my name?*" And then he blessed him.

Jacob said, "I have seen God face to face, and I have survived." And the sun rose. And he limped. And this is strange. *That is the reason why to this day, the Israelites do not eat the sciatic nerve, which is in the socket of the hip.* All you that have sciatic nerve trouble. I have it. I'd say I have sympathy for Jacob because that is some kind of pain. It says that he struck Jacob in the socket of the hip. Why would he do that? As a reminder. You say, "That's a pretty painful reminder." I think a lot of us need painful reminders of God's goodness to us, and that certainly was a lot less than being utterly destroyed with all his possessions. It's an amazing phenomenon, and this is a kind of example—even way, way back there before Jesus came and suffered so much for us—of preventive suffering and redemptive suffering. I'm sure that a dislocated hip and that sciatic nerve caused him problems the rest of his life. That's just nothing to make you happy, and it's a pain you can't get rid of. Just always there. It was a constant reminder of the battle between the inner man and God, between our sinful nature and what God wills for us, between the effects of bad decisions that we make and how we ask God to "get me out of this thing." A constant reminder to Jacob that he would never repeat that deceptiveness again.

Sometimes, you and I need pain and suffering. So many people are against it. "No, God doesn't want you to suffer, God doesn't want pain." You aren't scriptural when you say that. You're not looking at your Scripture. You're not really looking at the essence of pain that never goes away. This is that cross that never seems to change. The one that you feel sometimes, "I can't endure this any longer," but it gives on and on and on, and you think you're at the end of your rope, and it still goes on, but you still go on. There's a purifying essence of pain, purification and holiness and all that wrapped together.

I think you and I have learned a lot, and I think we need to know now what happens when finally Esau and Jacob meet. Remember, he's got his wives and children and everything across the stream. And he's standing there alone, this great moment that he feared, dreaded, prayed over, got struck in the hip with. *Looking up, Jacob saw Esau arriving with four hundred men. He divided his children between Leah, Rachel, and the two slave girls. He put the slave girls and their children in front, with Leah and her children following, and Rachel and Joseph behind.*

You know, you look at this, it seems so unfair, and it's obvious, and you just have to feel sorry for Leah. He figures if anything's going to happen, it can happen to her first. You know, with all the prayers, with all the repentance, with all the everything that Jacob had and God protected him and all, he's still got that thing in for Leah. He puts that poor woman first, and then Rachel and Joseph behind. If anything is going to happen, at least he can save Rachel and Joseph. *He himself went ahead of them, bowing to the ground seven times before going up to his brother.* He's really scared. But you know, in a family feud, we wouldn't do that. I'm not suggesting you go around bowing down to your enemies by any means. But I mean, there is an attitude here of humility. Humility and a lot of these virtues are kind of mixed in. It's like a marble cake. Y'all make marble cakes? Fascinating to me — a marble cake. It has chocolate and white or chocolate and yellow. They don't mix to make a tan cake, they just each stay in their little separate sections, and they just swirl around. You get ice cream. It's half chocolate and half vanilla. And they just kind of swirl around.

Well, that's how holiness is. I'm not saying — and please understand what I'm saying — I am not saying that you're holy a minute and you sin a minute, and you're holy a minute and you sin a minute. This is not a sin, what Jacob's doing. They're imperfections. They're weaknesses. They're frailties. Not committing any sins.

And so, he bows down to his brother in great humility seven times. And here is the surprise. With all the graces that Jacob had — he's been chosen by God to be the father of the twelve tribes of Israel, his name was changed from Jacob to Israel, just like Abram to Abraham — well, here is Esau. *He runs to meets Jacob, took him in his arms and held him close and wept. Then looking up, he saw the women and children. "Who are these with you?" he asked. "The children whom God has bestowed on your servant." The slave girls then came up with their children, and they all bowed low. And Leah came up along with her children and bowed low. Finally, Rachel and Joseph came up and bowed low. And Esau asked, "What is the meaning of all the company that I have met?" And Jacob says, "It is to win my lord's favor."*

So, all those goats, donkeys, and all the rest — he says, "What is this?" And Esau surprises us again. He said, *"Brother, I have plenty. Keep what's yours."* Jacob's guilty, though. He doesn't feel too hot about this thing. I mean, Esau was so great. Have you ever thought of making an attempt at least to approach the family next door that you stopped talking to a year ago? Or your uncle or your aunt or somebody that the whole family is against? Have you ever stopped and approached? You say, "Oh, I know what they're gonna do, they're gonna get so angry, they're gonna say this." How do you know? Are you like Jacob? Well, there's no question here that God answered his prayers. He did wrestle with God, and he did win. But still, you know, we don't give God the opportunity of softening hearts. We already know the whole thing; we make our own decisions. And so, we lament all our lives that "so-and-so doesn't speak to us." But have you ever tried to speak to them? Have you ever said, "Lord God, I am a sinner, and I have also been responsible for this feud and for this ill will, and I want to have reconciliation. Before I die, I want to be reconciled with my brother." Have you ever thought of just keeping on praying and praying so God can soften that person's heart? How do you know they wouldn't be just like Esau, that they would come up to you and hug you and kiss you and hold you close and just cry because you're friends again?

Well, Jacob says, *"To speak truly, I came into your presence as into the presence of God, but you have received me kindly. So, accept the gift I have brought for you, since God has been generous to me. I have all I need." And he urged him, and Esau accepted.* There is something in here now that is very interesting. I hope you got it. I'm going to go back to verse ten. Jacob is saying to Esau, now: *"To speak truly, I came into your presence as into the presence of God. You have received me kindly."* See, what he is saying right here is that the Lord was present at that meeting. Do you think that the Lord is not going to be present when you meet your enemy, when you want a reconciliation, with all the graces that you have, with the ability to call down the power and the Blood of Jesus and the power of the Spirit? Do you think you have less fruit than Jacob?

No way. I think you and I learned a great lesson from Genesis 32–33. I want you to think about the person that you haven't spoken to for years or months or weeks or days. I want you to go back to that person and try for reconciliation. I want you to think of that.

Wouldn't it be great if a person that you haven't been speaking to were to suddenly become your friend again? Think about it. Let God have the joy of that miracle. The person you've had an inner anger about, or the person you've never forgiven for whatever they've done, be it ever so small or ever so big. The person that made you so angry one day, that you said, "That was unfair, unjust, and I just don't want anything to do with them. They can stay where they are, and I'm going to stay where I am, and we'll just be friends from far away."

Maybe you were friends one time, dear friends who shared things together. For some reason, it all seems to be gone. Whenever you meet that person, there's a barrier. You chitchat about weather and insignificant things. But the old friendship and everything is gone. What a shame. What a real shame. Something God gave you was destroyed by some misunderstanding or whatever, and so again, we have to look here and say, "What did they have that we don't have?" Well, they didn't have anything. It's a knowledge of Yahweh. You say, "Well, at least God spoke to them once in a while." Oh, lookee here. Look how God has spoken to you. All of this through the centuries, in the life of Jesus, in the two thousand years of Christianity and the lives of holy men and women. If you don't get the picture by now, I don't know when you're going to get it.

Well, as we go on to Genesis 34, we find that human nature is once again at its worst. And Dinah, who was the daughter of Leah, was raped. And as we read this story, we realize that the boy loved Dinah and wanted to marry her, and so they said, "Well, all right, you can do that. But this whole tribe will have to be circumcised." And they said, "Okay." But then a very treacherous thing occurred. When the men were suffering and weak, Dinah's brothers, Simeon and Levi, sons of Israel—we don't say Jacob, now we call him Israel—killed them. And there again, you see this deceit and revenge. And Jacob is appalled. He said, "Oh, you do me great harm."

See how our human nature is so prone to revenge, resentment, anger, and deceit? And although we have much more grace than anyone ever had before, we still fall into that pit. You know why? We call this the consequences of Original Sin. The tendencies we have to evil, at the drop of a hat. It's easy for us to do the wrong thing, difficult for us to do the right thing. But since Jesus came, it should be the opposite. Why? Because you've got God within you, you've got the Father, Son, and Holy Spirit. When you were baptized, this miracle happened. The God of Heaven and earth came and lives within you. He lives within you. Why, then, don't we act more saintly and holy?

You and I have to ask ourselves some pretty hard questions sometimes. We must. And we've got the grace. We won't be perfect, but we don't need to fall into these grave, grave sins that are deadly. They deal us the death blow that's the only death blow, and that is damnation. That's what Jesus always called death. The death of this body He merely called sleeping—transition from one life to the other. Real death is if you lose your soul. That's the only kind of death there is.

Well, I hope we've learned a lesson. If any one of you ever gets reconciled, this lesson will have been worth it. This whole network would be worth it. If one of you, by reading this, decides, "I'm going to put an end to all this foolishness and hatred, backbiting and coldness. I'm going to go and hug my friend and say, 'I'm sorry, I want to be friends again. I want the past to be buried in the past, and I want to be your friend again.'" I think that's the proof of God's grace in us, and the proof of Jesus's salvation, redemption, and the power of His Precious Blood. We prove we are servants of God by the way we suffer and the way we forgive.

SIXTEEN

Genesis Chapters 35–41

We're going to continue our lesson in the book of Genesis. We want to look at an event in salvation history that is, well, not only interesting, but it depicts human nature again in its struggle. It's a struggle to be like God, to be holy. So, if you remember, Joseph and Benjamin were the children of Rachel, and she was undoubtedly Jacob's favorite wife. Now, in Genesis 35, we saw that Rachel died during childbirth, and so, Joseph and Benjamin were very, very special to Jacob, who is now called Israel. And we begin the story of Joseph.

It says here in Genesis 37:2 that Joseph was seventeen years old. *As he was still young, he was shepherding the flock with his brothers. And Joseph informed their father of the evil spoken about them.* So, these other brothers were not doing too good. So, I think Joseph kind of tattled on them. *Israel loved Joseph more than all his other sons.* You know, you just hate to see that. I don't know of any big family where that doesn't happen. I don't think you can really help it. Personalities kind of appeal to one parent over the other parent, and sometimes it's the firstborn, sometimes you just don't know.

And I'm sure Joseph had an edge on everyone else because he was Rachel's son. And the thing is that Israel never tried even to hide it, tone it down a little bit. In fact, he gave Joseph a coat with long sleeves made just for him. That was very unusual. It was a big gift, showed a love of preference. It's very, very difficult not to show any love of preference, and it's not bad, as I said a minute ago, it's just sometimes you get along with someone better or they're more fun or you like the way their hair is, some kind of crazy reasons why you may love one child more than another.

Well, Joseph showed it. Joseph showed that he was the favorite, and he kind of, well, bragged about it a little bit. And naturally, the other brothers came to hate him. And Joseph was a dreamer. I don't mean that in the worst sense of the word, but he had what we call prophetic dreams. We see that in the life of St. Joseph, who was told it was okay to marry Mary, it was okay to flee into Egypt and get away from Herod, it was okay to come back. So, he got all of these revelations in a dream, and now we find Joseph had a dream where he went wrong. That's what you see here, a lack of the virtue of prudence.

Sometimes, you think the virtue of prudence isn't even known today. There is very little prudence practiced sometimes in our lives because we don't even know what it is. Prudence is that virtue by which we know how and when to be moderate. When to keep our mouth shut and when to speak, when to share something and when not to share something. We seem to get very mixed up. Somebody will just blabbermouth whatever's on their mind. You say, "That's a lack of prudence." Because some people are not ready to hear what you want to say so frankly or bluntly. Prudent people are never blunt. Prudent people think before they speak. They think: "I have to be careful. This person isn't ready for this." They don't say in their heart, "Well, ready or not, here I come." No, what they say is, "Well, I think I'll wait." Sometimes, parents, you have to be prudent in correcting your children because if you correct sometimes when you're very, very angry, you probably will correct in the wrong way, and there would be no good fruit from it.

Sometimes, you have to hold your anger till that specific time and place when it's really going to go a long way. You just be careful. You say, "Well, I can't keep my mouth shut, it's too hard." Well, maybe it is difficult, but prudence doesn't always come easy.

And so, we're going to see what it costs Joseph for one imprudent thing he did. He told his dreams to his brothers. Now, you have to realize this man must have known that his brothers hated him. You can't keep hatred back. Ten brothers, keeping hatred back? No way. They must have given him looks. So, he said to them, "*Listen to this dream I have had. We were binding sheaves in the countryside, and my sheaf rose up and stood upright, and then I saw your sheaves gather around and bow to my sheaf.*" Poor Joseph. What a thing to tell people that were jealous of you! And they thought: "*So you want to be king over us?*" They got the point. They got it. Loud and clear. "*You want to lord it over us?*" *And they hated him still more.* Then this man just couldn't keep his mouth shut.

He had to have that deep realization that his brothers hated him — even worse than before — after the first dream. But this was a man that was absolutely, totally imprudent. He said, "Listen, I've had another dream." You just imagine anybody being a glutton for punishment. *And he said, "I saw the sun, the moon, and eleven stars bowing to me.*" Well, they all got the message that time. *He told his father and brothers, and his father scolded him.* They got the message. Easterners speak in riddles. They're very attuned to riddles, and so they understood the sun was his father, the moon was his mother — of course, she was dead — but it meant all of Israel's wives, and all his brothers — all eleven of them. *And his father scolded him: "A fine dream to have. Are all of us then, myself, your mother and your brothers, to come and bow to the ground before you?"* And his brothers were jealous of him. *But his father kept this in mind.* And he wondered, "What shall this child be?"

Think about it. Try to look into your own life for a minute and see where you've been imprudent. Maybe you've been imprudent with your children, showing more love for one than the other. Maybe you don't see the jealousy, but it's there. Maybe you don't see that inner hatred, but it's there, I'll bet it is. And you don't realize it. See where you've been imprudent, talking to your neighbor. Some woman comes down, and she has a kind of real bright red hat, and you don't like red, and you just blurt out, "Oh, what a terrible-looking hat." That's imprudent. What do you think about the times you've been imprudent? I hope you found some incidences in your life when perhaps you were just a little bit imprudent. And you don't need to be discouraged about them, you don't need to worry about them. Just say, "Well, Lord, I'm so happy now I know that I shouldn't be imprudent."

Well, Joseph has been asked by his father to go out and find his brothers. He said, "Go out to where your brothers are tending sheep and see what they're doing." You know what's strange here is that Israel would not allow his son Joseph to go and tend sheep. So, that's another sign of being a favorite. *He said to him, "Go and see how your brothers and the flock are doing and bring me word.* See if they're goofing off."

Well, they weren't where he thought they were, so he went to Dothan, and he found them there. As he was afar off, as Scripture says, they saw him coming. Well, they about had it with this young kid, probably, oh, maybe eighteen now, protected by his father, having on this fine coat with long sleeves, and there they were, in the meadows, day in and day out, pastoring sheep, and their clothes were dirty, and they smelled bad. And here comes this beautifully dressed young brother with this fantastic coat of many colors, and the long sleeves depicted authority. They just couldn't stand him. And they saw him coming from far off, and they said, *"Come on, let's kill him and throw him into some well. Then we shall see what becomes of his dreams."* Now, Reuben heard this and wanted to save him, and Reuben was no saint. Reuben had committed incest with one of his father's wives. And so, he was a man with a lot of problems, but somehow, he felt sorry for Joseph. And he said, "Well, we must not take his life. Throw him into this well in the wilderness, but let's not be violent." But he said this because he wanted to save Joseph. He thought: "Well, I'll come back later on by myself and pull him out."

So, they pulled off Joseph's coat. I mean, this was their day. Here is the dreamer that they were going to bow down to. Here is this beautiful cloak. They took off his cloak, threw him in an empty well with no water in it. Then they sat down and ate. They were just going to let him starve to death down there. It shows the awesome, horrible effect of jealousy. It says: *They threw him in a well*—intending to kill him in some bloodless fashion—*and sat down to eat.* Unbelievable coldness of heart! Well, looking up, they saw a group of Ishmaelites, and their camels were laden down with all kinds of spices, going to Egypt.

So, Judah said—and read the Gospel of St. Matthew, and you see that Jesus' ancestry came from the line of Judah; "the Lion of Judah" the Lord is called—*"What do we gain by killing our brother? Come, let us sell him to the Ishmaelites."* They were the sons of Ishmael, the son of Abraham's slave girl called Hagar. *"Let us not do any harm to him,"* he said. *"After all, he is our brother, our own flesh."*

So, they sold Joseph to the Ishmaelites for twenty silver pieces. Our Lord was sold for thirty. Joseph, a kind of figure of the Lord, was sold for twenty. Sometimes, though, you look back on this situation. Well, I wonder if Israel wasn't really responsible for all of this. You just have to wonder. He was imprudent too. He must have known his sons were jealous, and he created a situation by being imprudent, by manifesting the fact that Rachel's son meant much more to him than the sons of anyone else. And that's unfortunate. That was his weakness, just as it was Joseph's weakness to brag about his visions. Well, what did they do? Well, they slaughtered a goat, and they took this cloak, and they dunked it in the blood of a goat, and they sent it to their father with this message: *"This is what we have found. Examine it and see whether or not it is your son's cloak."*

Now, we find another evil: hypocrisy, lying. See, they had sold someone to slavery. They intended to murder, and now they lie. So, it shows that one evil follows another. If your conscience does not prick you and make you feel a little guilty or very guilty about something or very uneasy, and you kill that conscience at that moment, you go from bad to worse, and you can see this. Their intention was to murder, but for twenty pieces of silver — that's greed — they'd sell their own brother. You see how all these sins go hand in hand, and once you start, it just seems like you've got to go to the next one, otherwise you can't ever get out. That's what's so bad. And it's the same way with good. Once you begin to be like Jesus in one thing, it begins to follow. Good builds on good. Evil builds on evil.

So, some Midianite merchants were passing, and they sold him for twenty pieces of silver, told their father he was slaughtered by some animal, and Jacob began to tear his garments. That was a sign of great grief. *And all his sons and daughters came to comfort him, but he refused to be comforted.*

And he said, "No, I will go down in mourning to Sheol beside my son." And he wept. There's another sign of hypocrisy. All of his sons who were the cause of Joseph being sold into slavery tried to comfort their father, pretended that it was just too bad that he was eaten up by some wild animal. Unbelievable. There comes a time, I think in all our lives, when you have to kind of take stock. You just have to say to yourself, once in a while, "Why am I so miserable? I mean, why is it that I can't get along with anybody or everybody? What's wrong with me that I can't control myself or I don't have self-discipline? What is that?" Most people today are afraid to death of looking into themselves or acknowledging their weaknesses. You have so much positive thinking and looking around for your dignity, and we have all of these things today. They want to keep building you up, but they build you up on clay feet. The dignity you have comes from Jesus, from your Baptism, from the indwelling of the Trinity, from the grace in your heart. That's where your dignity is from. That's your source of dignity. Think about that.

I'm going to go on now to chapter thirty-nine. Chapter thirty-eight is about Judah, and again, we said Judah had some very serious moral problems, and so did his sons, and so we find in that chapter human nature at its worst.

And so, we find here in Genesis 39 that Joseph was taken down into Egypt and became one of Pharaoh's officials. And he did very well. It says: *Yahweh was with Joseph.* I remember in the monastery in Cleveland, Ohio, where I entered, there was a huge inscription on the wall, and it said, "Ite ad Joseph," which means: "Go to Joseph." And of course, it was speaking of St. Joseph, Jesus' foster father. But Yahweh was with Joseph, and everything went well with him, and he lived in the house of the Egyptian master. And he succeeded. Everything he touched succeeded. Every single thing he touched succeeded. So, the master put him in charge of everything.

Well, here it comes again. The master's wife took a liking to Joseph. He was well built, he was strong, he was young, and he was handsome. And so, she begins to make a pass at him. Well, it doesn't take much imagination to figure out what she was asking for. But he's very moral about it, and he says no. He said, "My master is not home. He has put me in charge of his household. I cannot do this thing."

So, he began to ignore her. He just wouldn't commit that kind of sin. Well, she was a pagan. She didn't understand the laws of God. She had no idea of Who Yahweh was. And so, she began to yell and scream, and so they came in, and she accused him of trying to rape her. But now poor Joseph becomes the victim again. First, he's sold into slavery unjustly, almost murdered by his brothers. Now, it looks like everything is going pretty well. His master's wife takes revenge on him because he refused to have an affair, so she just gets him arrested, committed to jail. And there he stayed.

Now you can see God working. You remember the vision he had, how his brothers and even his father and all his stepmothers bowed down before him, and the sun and the moon bowed down? And you say, "Well, why did God just push him practically to the end of extinction? Almost let him get murdered? Permit him to be sold into slavery?" But all of this was a preparation for that dream to be realized.

Isn't that strange? But isn't that how it works with you and me? I couldn't even begin to tell you how many, many times Jesus has done almost the same thing with us. It just looked like everything had gone down the drain, everything we worked for was just going to go to nothing, till we got to a place where we said, "Lord, what's going on?" And yet those particular tragic moments were a definite part, without which something greater would never have happened. And that's why all of us, or all of you that may be in the midst of a crisis, in the midst of a tragedy, midst of a heartache—the very things you don't want, those things may be the stepping stones. Now, you don't see them. I never see them. And that's why there're so difficult. You endure these things in the darkness of faith, and that's why it's so hard. And you see this in Joseph, two years later. Well, we'll go over to what happened to Joseph before we go into that.

It says, *It happened sometime later that the king of Egypt's cupbearer and his baker offended the master.* You didn't have to do much to offend the master to get put in jail. If Henry VIII didn't like his chicken, he'd throw the cook in jail. Behead him. Absolute authority. Must have been awesome. Must have swelled people's pride to an awesome degree. So, Pharoah was angry with his two officials and put them under arrest in the same jail where Joseph is. So, Joseph is a kind of assistant warden. These two prisoners are under him.

Now, it seems like everybody had dreams in those days that told them the future. So, both of these men had dreams. So, Joseph said, "Why do you look so bad today?" They said, *"We have had a dream, and there's no one to interpret it."* "I'll do it," he says. So, you see, God gave him some very definite gifts. I want you to see yourself and see how God has given you very definite gifts to cope with your situation. He didn't want to be in jail, Joseph didn't want to be locked up. He made the most of it, and God was good to him. The prison official took a liking to him and gave him a certain amount of freedom and made him head of some of the other prisoners. So, his life wasn't torture, he wasn't in a concentration camp.

So, Joseph said, "Tell me." So, the chief cupbearer said, *"In my dream, I saw a vine in front of me, and on the vine were three branches. No sooner had it budded than it blossomed and its clusters became ripe grapes. I had Pharaoh's cup in my hand, and I picked the grapes and squeezed them into Pharaoh's cup, and put the cup into Pharaoh's hand."* And Joseph said, "Well, I'll interpret that for you. *The three branches are three days. In another three days, Pharaoh will release you and restore you to your place. Be sure to remember me when things go well with you."* The poor Joseph is thinking: "Well, maybe he can get me out of here."

So, the chief baker now tells his dream: "*There were three trays of cakes on my head, and in the top tray, there were all kinds of Pharaoh's favorite cakes, but the birds ate them off the tray.*" And Joseph gave him this answer: "*In another three days, Pharaoh will release you and hang you on the gallows, and the birds will eat your flesh.*" What a dream. And it all happened just as Joseph interpreted. Well, as it happened, Pharaoh released the cupbearer, and he hanged the baker. But you know, it's so strange a phenomenon, and it's way back here in Genesis. We never hardly remember something good that either God does for us or someone else. I wonder if we've forgotten the phrase: "Thank you."

We take everything for granted. It's one of those elements of pride — "Whatever it is, whatever I have, I deserve." That is terrible. You don't deserve it. You can't attribute all these good things to yourself. You say, "Well, I worked hard." God gave you strength. "I was lucky." No, it was His Providence. You didn't create yourself, you didn't put yourself in those situations, you didn't open the doors that allowed you to walk in, and you were there at the right time, right place. God did that for you.

Well, the chief cupbearer did not remember Joseph. He forgot him. Can you imagine anybody forgetting someone who had just told you you're going to be released from prison in three days? Can you imagine that? It happened. And I know it happens here. Sometimes, people have asked for prayers from the sisters for brain cancer and prayers for every single thing, and they never write again. And we take for granted that they died. And you hear three, four years later, they're married, they have children. Never said even thank you for your prayers. Oh, that's horrible.

Look in your own life. Do you thank your husband for working at an office or in construction? It's hard to make a living today. Do you ever thank your children for all the things they do? Do you ever thank your pastor or your minister for a job well done? So, you don't like his sermons. We can't all be Bishop Sheen. Did you ever say that it was a great sermon? Maybe you didn't like it, but that doesn't mean it wasn't a great sermon. The virtue of prudence and thanksgiving are so necessary in this life. I want you to think about that.

Do you see yourself a little better? You say, "Yeah, I don't like what I see, though." Never worry about self-knowledge. That's half the battle. Maybe more than half. I think it's two-thirds of the battle. Once you know what you do wrong, don't worry about what you've done. Start doing it right. That's the important thing. Now, you can be more like Jesus. Now, you can imitate Jesus. And that's so important.

Well, two years pass. Can you beat that? Two long years. And Pharaoh had a dream. Everybody in those days dreamed a lot. *He was standing by the Nile*, it says, *and there, coming up from the Nile were seven cows, sleek and fat, and they began to feed among the rushes. And seven other cows, ugly and lean, came up. And these went over and stood beside the other cows, and the ugly and lean cows ate the seven sleek and fat cows.* Well, you have to wonder sometimes how God's wisdom works. We just can't comprehend. It's two years since this man remembered Joseph. And the Pharaoh is very upset. He doesn't understand about these fat cows and lean cows. He knows it means something. But then he has a second dream: *There, growing on one stalk, were seven ears of corn, full and ripe. And sprouting up after them came seven ears of corn, meager and scorched. And the scanty ears of corn swallowed the seven full and ripe ears.*

Now, Pharaoh woke up, and he was petrified. He was distressed. You have to kind of wonder sometimes how you discern whether a dream is a prophecy, whether it's just indigestion, maybe he had too much cheese. But I think in a prophetic dream, first of all, you never forget it, you remember every detail, and you know there's a hidden meaning for you. Most other dreams, well, they come and go. But this one stayed. Not only did it stay, but it disturbed, and he knew there was something he was supposed to be doing. So, he got up all his magicians. Nobody could tell him. But the chief cupbearer said to Pharaoh, "*Today, I must recall my offenses. Pharaoh was angry with his servants and put myself and the chief baker under arrest in the house of the commander of the guard. We had a dream on the same night. There was a young Hebrew with us. We told our dreams to him and he interpreted them. It turned out just as he interpreted for us: I was restored to my place, but the other man was hanged.*" So, Pharaoh said, "Well, get him."

So, it says: *Joseph shaved and changed his clothes and came into Pharaoh's presence.* So, the Pharaoh tells him his dreams, and Joseph said to him, "*Pharaoh's dreams are one and the same: God has revealed to Pharaoh what he's going to do.* You're going to have seven years of bumper crop, much cattle, many, many herds, one after another, all kinds of animals. And then you'll have seven lean years, seven years of famine. Seven years are coming, bringing great plenty, and seven years of famine will exhaust the land." He said, "*The famine that is to follow will be so very severe that no one will remember what plenty the country enjoyed.*"

Well, Pharaoh was scared. And Joseph said, "*You should choose a man who is intelligent and wise to govern the land of Egypt. You should take action and appoint supervisors over the land and impose a tax of one-fifth on the land during the seven years of plenty.* Collect the food produced. Store it. And then you'll have something." When everybody had to give one-fifth of everything they raised and everything they had, that's a lot. In those days, you didn't have a choice. If the king said a fifth, it was a fifth.

Joseph went along, and he governed Egypt. He was prudent, he was loyal, he was a great administrator. And Pharaoh even took the ring from his hand and put it on Joseph's hand, and he cloaked him with his own cloak. And people had to bow down before him. We are beginning to see the prophecy come true. And yet it was such a roundabout way.

Isn't God wonderful? But He acts that way in your life. If you look back, and you're very honest, you'll see that God made you go through—or permitted you, not made you, and didn't ordain either—some tragic things. But yet in the end, it gave you great graces, greater appreciation for Himself more than you ever desired. So, the suffering was a preparation to bear the fruit. And I think you and I must look at God and thank Him for trusting us enough. To put us through all the problems He's had to put us through to make us grow. He had to have faith in you. That in the midst of those tragedies and darkness and heartache, you would not desert Him.

And so today, we learned some lessons. That we must be prudent. We must see God's action in our lives. Even in the midst of its tragedies.

SEVENTEEN

Genesis Chapters 41–45

We're going to look at Genesis 41:50. You know we spoke of Joseph. Do you remember the dreams he had? Well, he had a few dreams, and he made the mistake—we call that imprudence—of telling his father and his brothers that one day he saw these sheaves of wheat bowing down before him. He had two dreams, very similar. Well, the brothers didn't like him anyway. He was Joseph's favorite son. Favorite because he and his brother Benjamin were Rachel's children. And it was no question in anybody's mind that Jacob loved Rachel more than he did Leah. So, you had this rivalry, jealousy, whatever. So, the first opportunity they had, they sold him, told their father that he was killed, put that beautiful cloak of many colors in the blood of one of the goats, and just lied. Well, as you remember, Joseph was brought to the house of Pharaoh and then put into jail and then released.

You know what's remarkable about all this is that from hindsight I'm sure Joseph saw, as we can see, that God used his imprudence to accomplish the very dream he had. And sometimes in your life, and my life, it just looks like God is working backward, and that's where we get tripped up, we get discouraged, we get disheartened. We say, "Lord, I wanna go to New York, and you're pushing me to California." But maybe the only way for you to get to New York is by first going to California. See, you just have to trust the Lord. That's what's so important. You just have to trust the Lord.

And here now, we're going to see Joseph, who interpreted a dream that the Pharaoh had. All the magicians in Egypt could not interpret Pharaoh's dream. He had dreams of fat cows, skinny cows, and so these dreams were something that distressed him and disturbed him. And Joseph came along, and he said, "Well, I know what God is telling you." Pharaoh said, "What?" Joseph said, "Well, you're going to have seven years of bumper crop, lots of wheat, lots of corn. And seven years of famine." So, Pharaoh said, "Well, what do you think we ought to do?" "Well, if I were you, I would find somebody that can store all the excess grain and wheat for seven years, and then when the famine comes, you'll have something to eat."

Sounds logical. Well, Pharaoh was just excited. And he said, "Okay, since you're the man that God has enlightened, you will be the one." So, suddenly, Joseph is raised up from a prisoner unjustly in prison, but nonetheless in prison, to a position of second to Pharaoh. And it says here: *Pharaoh took the ring off of his own hand and put it on Joseph's. He clothed him in fine linen and put a gold chain around his neck. He made him ride in the best chariot he had after his own.* He became governor of Egypt. And the Pharaoh said to Joseph, "*I am Pharaoh. Without your permission, no one is to move a hand or foot throughout the whole land of Egypt.*" Which means he had total absolute control of all of Egypt. He was under Pharaoh. That's a high position. Well, he was thirty years old, he was a young man. Pharaoh even gave him a wife. He had two sons, Manasseh and Ephraim.

Well, it's very interesting because you can see God's hand. And you know, it's a wonder to me that we can read this story, we can read this whole thing, and we can see God so visibly in the life of Joseph, the life of Jacob, the life of Abraham, but when it comes to seeing God in our own life, it's like we're deaf, dumb, and blind. We just don't see it.

But you see, that is the merit, and that's the beauty of Christianity. You have Jesus, Who paved the way, Who went ahead of you, Who said to His apostles in a boat that was shaking and blown about by the wind, "Why are you frightened? Why are you afraid? Am I not with you? Am I not with you in this darkness? In this uncertainty? Why do you fear?" So, now, Joseph suddenly responds to the gift of God in the present moment, and he goes from being a very kind of arrogant, imprudent young man to a very prudent young man. He learned by suffering. It was imprudent of him to be boasting of his dreams. And yet God used that imprudence to fulfill the dream.

You wonder, though, how God would have fulfilled it if he had not opened his big mouth. You can't always say, "Well, I did this, and that was a good thing I did. I made this big mistake." Well, God used that big mistake. But you wonder what He would have done without it. So, God in His infinite love and goodness will use our mistakes. He certainly used this little kid that just couldn't keep his mouth shut, but suddenly through suffering, injustice, and pain, through the hatred and jealousy of his brothers, through all of that, the injustice and lustfulness of his master's wife that got him in prison in the first place — all of this pruned Joseph, made him wait before he spoke, made him weigh what he said, made him prudent. And you can see that the hand of God using the injustices, the anger, the hatred of other people, the jealousy. And that's where you and I get tripped up, and we say, "Oh, this is unfair, unjust." And it all is, and we don't go beyond that. And as a result, we slip, we fall, we become sad, we become discouraged, and we lose faith. Think about it, will you? Think about how this has affected your life and how you answer to God. Have you improved? Have you become more prudent or have you become bitter?

Isn't it wonderful how God works in our lives? He uses all the mistakes we make. That's no excuse to make more mistakes, but when we've made them, He uses them just like scrap. He takes all these scraps, and He makes a beautiful building out of scraps. In your life, in my life, we just have a lot of scraps, we have faults and weakness and sins, things we wish we had never done, things we're absolutely sure were just great, big mistakes. And yet, sometimes, as much as we did make big mistakes and suffer from them, still God uses those very mistakes to sanctify us, to make us holy. This is what happened to Joseph.

Well, let's go on. There was a famine, and it says here the whole world, but you have to realize the whole world is whatever they saw or knew about. So, two sons were born of Joseph—Manasseh and Ephraim. And so, the seven years of plenty came. And when Joseph went all over the country, storing corn and wheat, it got so wonderful that they just couldn't even count it. But when the famine came, it was everywhere, and Joseph began to open the granaries and began to sell corn and wheat. Not to mention how wealthy the Pharaoh became during the time of famine.

Well, as it would, Jacob was also in this famine with his sons, and he saw that there was grain in Egypt. *And he said to his sons, "There is grain for sale in Egypt. Why do you stand looking at one another? Do something."* So, *ten of Joseph's brothers went down.* Now, it's another very interesting thing. It shows you how Jacob was really so prejudiced, he wouldn't let his youngest son go with them. That was Rachel's son. He had already lost Joseph. He wasn't going to lose this one. So, he sends ten of his sons down to Egypt. Benjamin—no way. Benjamin had to stay.

It was Joseph, as the man in authority over the country who sold the grain. So, Joseph's brothers went and bowed down before him, their faces touching the ground, the very dream. Can you imagine that? That scene? Here is Joseph, he's very busy. He's selling grain to this one and to that one. And all of a sudden, he sees ten men from Canaan, and he recognizes them. Suddenly, after all these years, he looked at these men, and he recognized them. And they come, and they bow down, touching their heads to the ground, and his dream comes to him. Oh, can you imagine what he felt? I think it's very easy to imagine what he felt. Well, he decided, though, he was going to come on rather gruff, and he did. So, you can see these ten men, and they're there, and they're bowing to the ground to a man, an Egyptian to their mind, and you have to recognize the fact that Joseph looked Egyptian. You have only to look at pictures of King Tut and all the others. He was dressed as an Egyptian. He looked Egyptian. So, there was no way the brothers could recognize Joseph, but Joseph knew the language. He recognized his brothers, and he looked so different, he was dressed so different, and many years had passed. He was a young, young man, so he had great development yet in store, so there was no way they would recognize him.

He said, "Where have you come from?" And they said, "From the land of Canaan to buy food." And he said, "No, you are spies. You've come to discover our country's weak points." So, they're scared. I mean, they're beginning to say, "Oh, what did we get into?" They said, *"No, my lord, your servants have come to buy food. We are sons of the same man. We are honest men,"* —he must have swallowed hard when he said that—*"your servants are not spies."* And Joseph looks at them hard, and he says, *"Not so. The country's weak points you have come to discover."* Now here comes what he's waiting for. One of the brothers says, *"Your servants are twelve brothers."* He said twelve. There are only ten there. *"The youngest, we should explain, is at present with our father. The other is no more."*

That's what Joseph wanted to hear. They literally did think that he was dead. Joseph answered, "No, you are spies." Well, he tied them up for three days in custody; he put them in jail so he could think this thing over. On the third day, he said, "Do this and you shall live. If you are honest men, let one of your brothers stay here, and then you shall bring me your youngest brother." You know, they never caught on. The thing that's interesting is what's coming. *They said to one another, "Truly, we are being called to account for our brother. We saw his misery."* They're talking, they're going back to that day when they decided to kill him. *"We saw his misery of soul when he begged for mercy, but we didn't listen to him, and now this misery has come home to us."* And they said that in their own language, having no idea that Joseph understood what they said. You see, it's an amazing phenomenon. They were so blinded and so guilty. I mean, years have passed — years. They're still guilty over their brother's death, or at least they thought he was dead.

Well, Reuben is the one who told them to put him in a well instead of killing him. Reuben said, *"Did I not tell you not to wrong the boy? But you wouldn't listen, and now we are brought to account for his blood."* You know, it's another phenomenon here. Isn't it strange that they took this as a kind of rendering account for what they did to their brother?

Now, I want to make that very, very clear. I don't believe that everything you do, God will hit you on the head with a kind of hammer. I don't believe that God punishes you for everything you do. I think what you do, you punish yourself. If you drink too much or you take drugs or whatever, you destroy your body, not God. If you lie and cheat and steal and get caught, you destroy your body, not God. So, many, many times we blame God for things that are our fault. What I like to look at in this situation is not so much personal as general. Now, it just seems to me that God gives us many warnings. We pollute the air, we know it's polluted. Well, do we work at it? We kill little babies every day, make it a law. What do we do about it?

And then when terrible things happen, the worst thing is that we don't even think like they did. At least they said, "We have committed a grave sin, and now we're suffering for it." That never dawns on us. It never dawns on us if you keep polluting the air, there's not going to be much air left after a while. It never dawns on us that if you drink and drink and drink, you're going to pickle your liver. There seems to be no end to your life. There *is* no end to your eternal life, but the body just decays when it's not treated well. And so, we lose the signs today. We're accustomed to tragedies and earthquakes and tornadoes and destruction and war and hatred. And so, it doesn't even make news. And good news, something wonderful that it happened, isn't news at all to a newspaper or a news program. It's just not news. See how far we've fallen?

So, in times when we should take a hint from the Lord, we don't. But then we go and blame Jesus or the Father or the Spirit for every little fiddle-faddle. "God's punishing me. I did this, and God's punishing me." How much do you blame God for things that are really your fault? And then how do you turn these things to good? That's what we've got to do, turn everything to good. Be like God. Turn your mistakes into good. Humility. Maybe that's the only good you can get out of it. "I'm sorry, Lord. I just am nothing without You. I'm full of weaknesses and sins and imperfections, and I acknowledge that, and I glory in Your beauty and Your holiness." If I can get that out of a mistake, I've gotten a lot. So, you and I have to work with God as Joseph did, and his brothers learned the hard way that to those who love God, *all things* turn into good.

Joseph said, "All right, I'll let you go, and I'll give you some grain. But you're gonna keep Simeon here." Joseph gave the order, though, to fill all their bags and baskets and whatever they had with corn, *and to put back each man's money in his sack, and to give them provisions for the journey.*

So, they loaded the grain on their donkeys and went away. But when they camped for the night, one of them opened his cornsack to give fodder to his donkey and saw his money in the mouth of the sack. He said to his brothers, "My money has been put back; here it is in this cornsack." Their hearts sank, and they looked at one another in panic, saying, "What is this that God has done to us?" These men were scared. Returning to their father, Jacob, they gave him a full report: *"The man who is the lord of the land spoke harshly to us.* And they thought we were spies, and we told them we were honest men and that we are twelve brothers and have the same father. *But the man who was lord of the land said to us, 'This is how I shall know if you are honest. Bring back your youngest brother.'"* Oh, can you imagine? These men were so confused. They emptied all their sacks, they discovered that every sack had their bag of money left in it. They were scared to death, and so was their father. *Jacob said, "You are robbing me of my children. Joseph is no more. Simeon is no more. And now you want to take Benjamin."*

See, these Old Testament people always seem to be talking to God. "What are You doing to me?" God was in everything. "God, when are You going to deliver us?" It was God they went to. And today, we don't go to God, we go to science, we go to men, we go to political parties, we go to ourselves, we go to power, we go to rich, wealthy people, we go everywhere and anywhere *but* God. We don't want to think that the visible is in the power of the invisible.

You know, if you can learn one thing from Scripture, God to these people was in everything. Today, we never say after a sin, "Oh God, I am so sorry. Please forgive me." We just say, "There is no sin." And when you do that, you are pushing God out of your lives and out of society little by little by little by little. And then we wonder why things are not going well, why there's no peace, why there's just evil, you can't walk the streets at night, old ladies get mugged.

So, we wonder why these things happen, and still, we get further and further away from God. At least these men, who were not too hot—they were immoral, many of them, they committed incest, they were terrible people sometimes—but they kept going back to God. Do we? Do you?

Well, let's see what happens. So, *Reuben said to his father,* "*You may put up my two sons to death if I do not bring Benjamin back to you. Put him in my care, and I will bring him back.*" But *Jacob replied,* "*My son is not going down with you, for now his brother is dead he is the only one left.*" Kind of a hard saying since he had nine sons looking at him. "*If any harm came to him on the journey you are going to undertake, you would send me to my death.*"

But the country was hard pressed from famine. When they finished eating the grain they bought from Egypt, their father said, "*Go back and buy us a little food.*" But *Judah told him,* "*The lord of the land said, 'You will not be admitted to my presence unless your brother is with you.'*" So, Judah was very hard on him. "*If you are ready to send our brother with us, we are willing to go buy food for you,* but we will not be admitted to his presence unless he is with us." We find here a very delicate situation. They had eaten all the grain; they were starving again. There was no place to go. And they knew it. They didn't dare go before Joseph without Benjamin. You and I, I think, have just as hard a time as Jacob here, in releasing those we love to the Lord, of looking at the present moment and saying, "Lord, I just don't understand what's happening." That's okay to say that. It's okay to be humbled and say, "Lord, I just find this situation impossible. I find it very difficult. I don't understand. But Thy will be done." And it took more hunger and more of the cross to get Jacob to say that to God.

He said, "*Why did you bring this misery on me by telling the man you had another brother?*" His sons replied, "*He kept questioning us, 'Is your father still alive? Have you a brother?' How could we know he was going to say, 'Bring your brother down here'?*" We've got us a little family squabble. The father said, "You dummy! Why did you tell him you had a brother?"

It's a regular honest family squabble. *So, Judah said to their father, "Send the boy with me. Let us start off and go, so we can save our lives and not die. I will go for surety for him, and you can hold me responsible for him. If I do not bring him back to you and set him before you, let me bear the blame all my life."* Well, Jacob's looking at his sons, and he's trying to think so hard, he's saying, "What can I do in this situation?" But isn't it marvelous you see God working in the midst of it? You know what's happening here? These nine men — remember, Simeon is in with Joseph, he's been held captive — these nine men, their souls are beginning to be repentant, self-sacrificing, they're willing now to admit they are and have done some terrible things. They're willing to say, "We're sorry." They're willing to say, "Lord God, what is happening to me is just. I have deserved this." I mean, this comes a long way for these men. They couldn't have cared less before. And you know, Jacob is beginning to realize he has other sons besides Joseph and Benjamin, and they mean a lot to him too. It took him a long time to know that these other sons are his sons and they should mean a lot to him. So, all through this, suffering has done what meditation didn't do or probably couldn't do.

Well, we see Jacob beginning to change in his old age. Well, he said, "If you have to do this, *take some of the land's finest products, carry them to the man as a gift, a little balsam, a little honey, gum, resin, pistachio nuts*" — one of my favorites — "*and almonds. And take double the amount of money, and return the money put back in the mouths of your sacks; it may have been a mistake. As for me,*" he said, "I must be bereaved until you get back." So, he's going to act like they were all dead. He was in agony. Well, you see your whole family wiped out.

The men took his gifts and doubled the amount of money. They presented themselves to Joseph. *When Joseph saw Benjamin* — that's his real brother — *he said to his chamberlain, "Take these men to the house. Slaughter a beast and prepare it, for these men are to eat with me at midday." Now, the men were afraid of being taken to Joseph's house, thinking: "We're being taken there because of the money replaced in our cornsacks the first time. Now they will make us slaves."* All the time, they're guilty over what they did to Joseph. It just gnaws at them.

So, they went up to Joseph's chamberlain and spoke to him. "By your leave, sir," they said, "*we came down once before to buy food, and when we reached camp and opened our cornsacks, there was each man's money in the mouth of his sack. But we have brought it back with us, and we brought more money to buy food. We don't know who put our money in our cornsacks." And the man said, "Peace be with you; do not be afraid. Your God and your father's God has put a treasure in your cornsacks. Your money reached me safely." And he brought Simeon out to them. So, the man took the men into Joseph's house. He offered them water to wash their feet.* I mean, they're really getting first-class treatment. They arranged their gifts while they waited for Joseph. When Joseph arrived, they offered the gifts, bowed down to the ground again, just like he said in his second dream. *He greeted them very kindly, asking, "Is your father well?" And they said, "Your servant, our father, is well. He is still alive." And they bowed in homage.* I mean, they're going to make this fellow feel real good. They acknowledge his superiority, and there's no question in their mind, and they have no intention except flattering him and bowing down and saying, "Everything you say is okay with us."

Looking up, Joseph saw his brother Benjamin. He said, "This here is your brother." And then he said to him, "God be good to you, my son." And Joseph hurried out, for his heart was moved at the sight of his brother. He began to cry and bathed his face. Human nature has just been the same from the beginning, hasn't it? Did you ever need to cry but you didn't want anybody to know you were crying? And what's the first thing you do? You are going to wash your face with cold, cold water. It doesn't help, everybody still knows you're crying. They did it way back there.

So, after bathing his face, he returned and gave the order to serve the meal. *He was served separately and so were the Egyptians who ate in his household, for Egyptians cannot partake food with Hebrews. So, they were placed opposite him, each according to his rank, from the eldest to the youngest, and the men looked at one another in amazement. He had portions carried to them from his own dish, the portion for Benjamin being five times larger than any of the others.* So, they had a great party, they ate, and they drank, and they figured, "What is going on?" They still never caught on who this man was.

You say, "Well, why?" Don't you see what's happening to their souls all this time? They're thinking over and over what they did and how they're really suffering for what they did, and they know it's right, they know it's just.

So, Joseph gave the order. He said, *"Fill these men's sacks with as much food as they can carry, and put each man's money in the mouth of his sack. And put my silver cup in the mouth of the youngest one's* sack as well as the money." So, when morning came, it was light, the men were sent off on their donkeys. *They had scarcely left the city before Joseph said to his chamberlain, "Away now and follow those men. When you catch up with them, say to them, 'Why did you reward good with evil? Is this not the cup my lord used for drinking? What you have done is wrong.' "* And so, when he caught up with them, he repeated these words, and they were astounded. They said, "What are you talking about? We didn't steal any silver cup." "Yes, you did." *"Are we likely to have stolen silver or gold from your master's house? Whichever your servant has found to have it shall die, and we also shall be your slaves."* They were so sure they didn't steal anything. They just went there and had a great dinner party. So, he searched, beginning with the eldest. He was going to really play this. And chamberlain was smart too. He knew what Joseph was doing.

And when he ended up at the youngest, there was the silver cup in Benjamin's sack. And they tore their clothes, and when each man had reloaded his ass, they returned to the city. And they said, "What are we going to do?" So, they had to go back to Joseph's house. *And Joseph said, "What is this deed you have done? Did you not know that a man such as I am is a reader of omens?" They said, "What can we answer, my lord? What can we say?" Joseph replied, "The man in whose possession the cup was found shall be my slave. But you can go back safe to your father."* A hard way to get your brother to stay with you. You say, "Boy, that Joseph is a hard man." I think he was finally getting smart. He realized that his brothers had to learn the hard way as he had learned the hard way. He realized the only way to get his father there was to keep Benjamin. He didn't care if they went, he wanted his brother, his mother's son, to be with him.

Well, Judah went up to Joseph and said, "May it please you, my lord, let your servant have a word privately. Do not be angry with your servant, for you are like Pharaoh himself. My lord questioned his servants, 'Have you a father, a brother?' And we said to my lord, 'We have an old father and a young brother,' and we told you that the boy cannot leave his father. If he leaves him, his father will die." Do you see the compassion coming in these men? Isn't that tremendous? That one brother they mutilated almost and threw in a well, and this one here, there's so much compassion. They're willing to give themselves for their brother. Look how far they have come through this trial from absolute hatred, ambition, jealousy, indifference to concern, self-sacrifice. *"You see, when we went back to your servant, my father, we repeated it to him, and he was just distraught. He said, 'You know, my wife bore me two children. When one left me, I said that he must have been torn to pieces. If you take this one from me too and harm comes to him, you will send me down to Sheol.'"* And he says, "Look, you're going to kill my father. And I, your servant, am surety to my father for the boy. I said to him, 'If I don't come back, let me bear the blame. So, let your servant stay in place of the boy.'"

Isn't that amazing what suffering can do in life? Even guilt over something we did wrong, God can use to mellow us, mold us, change us, transform us if we use it right. These men are getting humble. They would have never offered themselves in place of Benjamin or Joseph before. They didn't have that kind of concern for their father.

And then Joseph could not control his feelings in front of all his attendants, and he says, *"Let everyone leave me."* And then he asked for his brothers to come, and Joseph said to his brothers, "I am Joseph."

Can you imagine what that meant? It must've been like a bolt of lightning. This tall, handsome Egyptian, next to Pharaoh, looks at these men and says, *"I am Joseph. Is my father really still alive?"* And they couldn't answer him. They were shocked.

He said, "*Come close to me. I am your brother Joseph whom you sold into Egypt. But now, do not grieve or reproach yourselves for having sold me here, since God sent me before you to preserve your lives.*"

So, the trials and the heartaches and the frustrations that you and I have day after day, and the things we don't understand, God has sent before us to save our lives, our souls.

Well, quite an event. Read it yourself, see what the Lord tells you in your particular circumstances in life, and then the Scriptures will be alive to you, and you'll be one with them.

EIGHTEEN

Genesis Chapters 45–50

We're going to continue with Joseph. You know, we saw how Joseph took his brothers in, forgave them, kind of tricked them before he let them know that he knew who they were. And you kind of see a new Joseph. He was a man before that was extremely imprudent, he was rash, he was a little bit arrogant. Then we saw how God, through all this pain and suffering, made a new man out of Joseph. Wise, prudent, intelligent, shrewd. So, when we left off, we found out that Joseph told his brothers who he was. You can kind of imagine that moment when Joseph looked at his brothers and said, "I'm Joseph." I bet they almost died. Can you imagine somebody in your family that you've been mourning or thought they were dead? Especially guilty because they thought they killed him. All of a sudden, he's next to Pharaoh. Just see the shock of it. Sometimes when you read the Scriptures, you just read them so fast, and as a result, you don't get the whole essence of the emotion in Scripture. We've gone through the book of Genesis. We're not finished yet, but we've gone through pretty much all of it. We've got a few chapters yet to go.

But there is in every book of the Scriptures a kind of thread—the human thread and the divine thread mixing together. And you say, "Well, I can see that in Scripture." But it doesn't matter, it's the same in your life. It really doesn't matter whether it's the Scriptures or your life. The same thread is together. There is God and man, and God uses every single thing that you could possibly think of. The most insignificant thing, like the hairs that fall from your head, He uses all of that to change, to transform, to make you over. And so, you can see this now as we've gone through this book. So, we're going to start here at Genesis 45:9.

So, Joseph says to his brothers, *"Return quickly to your father and tell him, 'Your son Joseph says this, "God has made me lord of all Egypt. Come down to me at once. You shall live in the country of Goshen, where you will be near me, you, your children and your grandchildren, your flocks, your cattle and all your possessions, and I will provide for you there, for there are still five years of famine." ' "* All this happened in the first two years.

So, he knew there were going to be seven good years and seven bad years. Well, he said, *"You can see with your own eyes, and my brother Benjamin can see, too, that it is my own mouth speaking to you. Give my father a full report of the honor I enjoy in Egypt."* What a reunion that was. But you know what's so strange about this? When you and I forgive somebody, we always bring up the thing that we're forgiving. Joseph never said once, "You dogs, you pushed me in a well, and I had to suffer all these years, and God rewarded me." He didn't go through the whole thing. But you and I, even in the act of forgiving, make each other angry. It looks like we are never satisfied until we put all ten fingers in some garbage, stir it up, and then we end up very generously forgiving. These men didn't have the grace that you and I have. Didn't have it at all. But they were able to forgive just by looking at each other. Nobody said anything here about "I'm sorry." Their love said, "I'm sorry." The brothers had said before, "We're being punished, that's why we're starving, for our brother's blood." But you have to admire Joseph, the way he forgave. So magnanimously.

Now, I gotta ask a question. How is it that Joseph — with very little knowledge of God, with very little grace, didn't have the grace you had, didn't have the Spirit living with him — was able to forgive so magnanimously? Don't you wonder why we can't forgive like Joseph did with great love? Look what he did for his brothers. He didn't say, "Go and starve. Go to the desert. That's your problem." He's going to give them the whole land of Goshen. He's going to give them a place where they can live for five years and have enough wheat and corn for themselves and their cattle. It's almost like a reward. That's why I say if you can read the Scriptures, you gotta read it in such a way that you can say, "Well, how do I do this?" How do you forgive? Got to rub it in? You know what, some people, when they forgive, they forgive for the moment, but sometimes a year later, they'll bring it up again. Ten years later, bring it up again. Twenty years later, bring it up again. I don't know, I wonder if we read this book sometimes, and we think we need forgiveness, we want God to make our garments white as snow, and we just get so caught up in the parable of the Good Samaritan and the lost sheep, and the Prodigal Son, and we get all enthused because we're thinking, "Oh, God's going to forgive me. Look how great is our God." And He is. Well, I've got news for you, sweetheart, you've got to forgive like God forgives. You say, "Well, I don't believe He expects that much." Well, then you stop saying the Our Father because the Our Father says very explicitly: "Forgive me as I forgive those who trespass against me." You ever say that? You better know what you're saying because you're asking God to forgive you in the same way you forgive. So, you want to learn a lesson in forgiveness, I would read the story of Joseph, because he had a lot to forgive. Most of us forgiving don't have half of this.

So, let's go. News reached Pharaoh's palace that Joseph's brothers had come, and Pharaoh was pleased to hear it. It was a different Pharaoh all those years later when they were in the desert after they fled from Egypt. So, they were in Egypt a long time. And forty years later, after the exodus, only then did they go to the Promised Land. But here, it says this Pharaoh was a good Pharaoh. He had great admiration for Joseph because Joseph saved all the Egyptians. And he made Pharaoh very, very wealthy. Because all the money that came from selling this wheat and corn went to Pharaoh. I want you for a few minutes to think about two things. First, how do you forgive? And second, when you forgive, can you forgive in a way that you never mention it again? And then do you forgive in a way that makes your brother feel good? You do something nice? We don't expect you to give him a city or feed him for five years. Do you have lunch together? You have a little celebration that this is over with? What do you do? How do you forgive? Think about it.

Well, I hope you got some light. We all have to, once in a while, sit down and examine our conscience. So, Pharaoh was extremely kind to Joseph's brothers and father, and he said, *"Take wagons from the land of Egypt for your little ones and your wives. Get your father and come. Never mind about your property, for the best that the land of Egypt offers is yours."*

Now, there's another lesson here. There're so many lessons in Scripture that it's really hard to pick them all up. But isn't it strange how famine and suffering and pain made people kinder? Pharaoh was extremely generous. And so is Joseph. And it used to be that way. That's what's so strange. It used to be that in a tragedy, people just worked together. You didn't become enemies. Everybody pitched in, and everybody helped along. And now if there's a tornado, you've got to put soldiers out so people don't take everything that's there. If there's any kind of a tragedy, they got to bring in the National Guard just to keep the few possessions that people have left from being stolen. And last year when there were some very severe tornadoes, they had to get psychiatrists on the speaker in some of the shelters to keep the people from killing each other. You've got to ask yourself: What happened to us? What's happened to mankind that we're so selfish and self-oriented and angry all the time and all the things that we are? What is it about suffering today that's so different than suffering yesterday, that it doesn't bring people together? But Lord, we're children of the New Testament. We should have more love for each other in tragedy and heartache and suffering. Why? Because we got grace, we've got the Spirit. It seems to me like the world wants possessions, ambition, desire for glory, material things, that constant need for more and more and more and more. Something has happened to us. I'm not sure what it is. Either we don't pray enough or something, but we're not getting less selfish, we're getting *more* selfish. So, I think when you look at this, you read it by yourself, sometimes you've got to say, "Well, I've got to do better."

Let's look and see. We're going to finish the book of Genesis. I didn't think we would, but I think we will.

Joseph brought his father down. And it was remarkable to me. He was stunned, for he didn't believe when they said his son lives. But they told him all Joseph had said. Now, you have to realize now they had to tell their father what they did. Because he'd have to say, "Wait a minute, you brought me a coat that was full of his blood." Then they had to say, "Well, it really wasn't. I mean, we were jealous of Joseph, and we were going to kill him, and then Reuben said, 'Well, why don't we wait?' And he really wanted to go and free him, but then we thought he'd die in that well, so we sold him for some silver, but we thought he died." Now they had to admit a whopping lie.

You know, everything comes out in the wash. You get away with something once in a while, but it's gotta come out. I don't care what it is, you can be sure God knows it. If you've got the humility at one time to say, "I did it, I'm sorry, and I want to go on from here." And so, Jacob, I suppose, was so elated over the fact that his son still lived and he was the lord over Egypt that I don't think he cared about anything. I don't think he stomped his feet and said, "You lied to me!" He said, "*My son Joseph is alive. I must go and see him before I die.*" And you can just imagine — some of you men especially — you could imagine what must have happened when he met Joseph. Israel, or Jacob, left with his possessions and reached Beersheba, and there he offered sacrifices to God. *And God spoke to him in a vision: "Jacob, Jacob." And he said, "I am here."*

You know, the old prophets, they had a connection with God. If you heard somebody say your name out loud, the first thought would be, "I must be going wacko. There's nobody in this room with me." We wouldn't say, "I'm here, Lord." We wouldn't even probably think it's the Lord. But these men were so attuned to the presence of God in their life that they heard His voice. They said, "Yes, Lord," just as calmly as if they were speaking to somebody in front of them, a friend — and they were.

The voice said, "*I am God, the God of your father. Do not be afraid of going down into Egypt, for I will make you a great nation there. I myself will go down to Egypt with you. And I myself will bring you back again, and Joseph's hand shall close your eyes.*" What a promise. All those years. Jacob, who's now called Israel, had to think God had abandoned him. At some point or other, he lost his son, he lost his favorite wife, he was starving, his cattle were starving, children and his family, grandsons—everybody seemed lost, everything seemed lost. And suddenly, the very thing he thought was gone forever was about to stand right before him—Joseph.

When you get in those spells in your life or times in your life when everything seems wrong, everything is going downhill—I get them often. You can't run a television network like we do and the way we do it without having—*woooop!* It's the way it goes. But God is in it. See, if we could remember God is with us going down, then going up. It isn't like all of a sudden He leaves us, and that's why we go down, and then He picks us up. That's not how it works. If you're going down, God is with you. He says right here, "I will go with you into Egypt, and I will bring you back." That was a long time. And Moses had to bring him back. But God was with him. "I am with you. When you are going down and when I bring you up, but I am with you all the time." There is no such thing as God just leaving you to yourself when you're miserable and then He finally says, "Oh, you miserable, old wretch." He's with you all the time. So, that's another lesson we could learn. Well, if you go down to verse twenty-eight, it says: *Israel sent Judah ahead to Joseph so that the latter might present himself to him in Goshen. Joseph had his chariot made ready.*

Can you imagine that meeting? I get excited over that. Went up to meet his father. As soon as he appeared, Joseph threw his arms around his neck, and for a long time, wept on his shoulder. Can you imagine that? Some of you who have lost your children, they run away or maybe had bad marriages and moved to other states, and you don't know what they're doing. Oh, there're just so many things that break parents' hearts today. Imagine them all. All of a sudden, the doorbell rings, and you open the door, and there they are. And not just all disheveled, but handsome or beautiful, strong. You just can't imagine what that would be like.

So, you wonder if Israel even remembered at that point all those years of heartache. You know, they say if a woman gives birth, she doesn't remember. I don't know if that's true or not. My mother never forgot because I was eleven and a half pounds, and I can tell you she never forgot. But anyway, it's true that sometimes when you've had just a hard, hard time, and then it just all blossoms out, and the Lord just makes everything move—you forget.

Joseph said to his brothers and his family, "I will go up and break the news to Pharaoh. I will tell him, 'My brothers and my father's family who were in the land of Canaan have come to me. The men are shepherds and look after livestock.' And when Pharaoh summons you and asks, 'What is your occupation?' you shall say, 'We look after livestock,'" which is the same as a shepherd, but for some reason the Egyptians had a horror of all shepherds. You say, "Why?" Because they were thieves, they were bandits. They're up there all night long, watching sheep. Well, they had a few pasttimes where they would go out and raid and rob. Everybody was scared to death of a shepherd, that's why when the angels appeared at the birth of Jesus to shepherds, you say, "Oh, Lord, You seem to go around looking for the worst." But isn't it wonderful that He does that? Most of us are the worst. We're all sinners in the eyes of God—all of us. No matter who you are. Except for Mary, our Mother. Just the rest of us. So, it's so wonderful when God, in His infinite love and goodness, takes us out of garbage heaps and raises us on high.

So, Joseph went on and told Pharaoh about his relatives being there, and they said, "Yeah, we take care of livestock." He got kind of shrewd in his old age, Joseph did. It's really the same thing. We begin to learn something about Joseph. You see, for the first two years of this famine, people paid money for grain and corn. Well, there's so much you have. The money started going down. So, what happened was that they didn't have any more money. But Joseph had a lot of grain and a lot of corn. I bet he was a hard businessman. You know, some men are hard businessmen. They're great at home, they're great with their family and friends, but when it comes to business, oh, they get a lot done. So, Joseph was pretty rough with all the money in the land of Egypt.

In Genesis 47:15, they said, *"Give us bread. Have we to perish? Our money has come to an end."* So, Joseph said, *"Hand over your livestock."* If you wanted a bag of corn, you had to give him a cow. If you wanted a bag of wheat, you had to give him two sheep. Well, that was great for a while. First thing you know, a whole year passed, and they didn't have any livestock. So, now Pharoah had all the money, thanks to Joseph, and Pharaoh now had all the livestock, thanks to Joseph. So, the people were saying, "Hey, you've got our money, you've got our livestock. What do you want now?" Let's see what he wants. *They said, "There's nothing left for my lord except for our bodies and our land." So, they said, "Buy us and our land in exchange for bread." Then Joseph acquired all the land in Egypt for Pharaoh since, one by one, the Egyptians sold their estates.* They had some pretty big estates too. And they really gave up everything they had for food. *As for the people, he reduced them to serfdom, from one end of Egypt to the other. The only land he did not acquire belonged to the priests.*

Then Joseph said to the people, "This is how we stand. I bought you out with your land on Pharoah's behalf. Here is seed for you so that you can sow the land. But when your harvest comes, you must give a fifth to Pharoah." You wonder why he didn't give them that seed before he got the land. All of a sudden, he comes up with all this seed. *"The other four-fifths you can have for sowing your field to provide food for yourselves and your household and food for your dependents."* They said, *"You have saved our lives."* So, Joseph made a statute concerning the soil of Egypt: a fifth goes to Pharaoh. A fifth—that's a lot. So, we've realized that there was in Joseph shrewdness but honesty, and that today seems to be an almost impossible combination. If people are hard and shrewd in business, almost all the time or at least much of the time, they become dishonest. Because the temptations are there. So, you see, Joseph didn't keep any money for himself. All went to Pharaoh. The lands, the estate of the people—everything went to Pharaoh. He worked honest and hard, and that's another thing today we wonder about. That's why I thank God for my sisters in my crew, all the people who work here—they work hard.

But do you know there're many things many times you call for some service—plumber, electrician, anybody—you wait days. You call him up, and they say, "Yep, he's on the way." He's no more on the way than a man on the moon. Call up the next day. "Well, he left a half-hour ago." He must've went by way of California, he never showed up. Now, when he comes, he's got his tools but no parts, and then he's going to go back and get the parts, which will be next week. Well, then you gotta wait another week. And it seems to go that way in so many, many areas that it gets absolutely frustrating. And you wonder.

I had an employer talk to me not too long ago, and he said, "You know, the first thing people ask when they come to my establishment to apply for a job is they want to know when is their vacation and what are their fringe benefits. They never tell me their talents, they never tell me what they can do or what they want to do for the business." So today, our standards and our values and our sense of responsibility are all just messed up. Sometimes, I think we don't have that sense anymore of wanting to do a good, hard eight hours of work for an employer, knowing that it is part of God's will that if I get money for my work, I've got to work to get the money.

By the time we get long lunches and coffee breaks and all this, you wonder how much does an employer get? Does he get six hours of work, seven? And of those seven, are you really putting in your effort — your very, very best? See, work is a gift from God. If we don't work with a sense of responsibility and honesty, then we are not accomplishing God's will. And if we don't accomplish God's will in the present moment, then you gain nothing all day long. It's a kind of stealing. Did you know that? When you don't do your best at work, when you loiter, you gossip, you talk, you take a lot of time off and all this — it's stealing. You are stealing from your employer time and work that doesn't belong to you, it belongs to your employer. You're being paid for that, and if you're being paid for it, and you're not giving him a good day's work, then you're stealing. It's dishonesty. Today, we don't even think of that. And I wonder how many of us would be like Joseph, or would we take a little bit off for ourselves? So, we take the cream for us, take a little bit off the top, a little bit of kickback. Still stealing.

I heard a man say, "Well, I can get something under the table if I get the job." It's dishonest. God sees you. It doesn't matter if anyone else sees you. God sees you. If you're going to be dishonest, that's all written up there. So, when you're reading this, you have to really look and say, "Wow, Lord, I'm not even as far as Joseph." But we can be. You can just say, "Jesus, I want You to give me light. I want You to give me that sense of responsibility where I can be strong, responsible, honest, so I can love my work and do a good day's work. Where I can go home and know I have for eight hours done my very, very best, and I did it for the Lord. I did it for the Lord."

Well, let's go on. The Israelites stayed in the land of Egypt, they acquired property, they were fruitful, increased in numbers, and Jacob lived seventeen years in the land of Egypt. That's a long time, considering how old he must have been. *And the length of his life was 147 years. And when his time to die drew near, he called his son Joseph and said, "If I enjoy your favor, place your hand under my thigh and promise to be kind and good to me; do not bury me in Egypt. When I sleep with my fathers, carry me out of Egypt and bury me in their tomb."* Well, Jacob adopts Joseph's two sons, Manasseh and Ephraim. If you want to learn something about family, you've got to look at the Old Testament. Family ties were extremely important, and they clung together no matter what. Why don't you think about that for a minute? I want you to think about how you stand. How close are you, how honest? How responsible in your work?

We're going to go through this a little bit quickly because we're going to finish Genesis in the next few paragraphs. In chapter forty-nine, Jacob blesses his sons, and he gives a blessing to each one, and then there is his last moments in that chapter.

Turning to chapter fifty, which is the end of Genesis, you'll find Jacob dying. And Joseph covers his face with tears and kisses him, orders the doctors of Egypt to embalm him—and you've seen Egyptian mummies, and I'm sure they did the same with Jacob—and it took forty days to embalm. Aren't you glad it doesn't take forty days now? Oh, wouldn't that be a tragedy. But it took forty days, and then they had seventy days of mourning. That's over two months of mourning.

So, Joseph goes to Pharaoh, and he tells him that he's got to go back to his own land and bury his father. And all the chariots and horsemen went up with him, a very large retinue went with Joseph to bury his father. Now, his brothers are beginning to wonder. It says: *Seeing that their father was dead, Joseph's brothers said, "What if Joseph intends to treat us as enemies now that our father is dead, and repay us in full for the wrong we did him?"* They never got over the fact that they had committed a pretty big sin. They were guilty even now. *So, they sent this message to Joseph: "Before your father died, he gave us this order, 'You must say to Joseph, "Forgive your brother their crime and their sin and all the wrong they did you."'* Now, therefore, we beg you, forgive us this crime."* First time they said that. They acted like they were sorry. Never said it.

You know, a lot of people do that. Do you do that? A lot of people will, instead of saying, "I'm sorry," they'll send you a box of candy, flowers, or just come in and do something nice or speak nicely to you. And that's great. I'm not against that. But I gotta ask myself, "Why does it take so long to say, 'I'm sorry'?" Two little words. *I'm. Sorry.* And I'm sure the candy, the flowers, and all the rest go a long way. Many years it took for them to say, "I'm sorry." Well, their love showed they were sorry. Joseph's love showed he forgave. What did Joseph say? His brothers came to him, fell down before him and said, *"We present ourselves before you as your slaves."* And Joseph said, *"Do not be afraid. Is it for me to put myself in God's place? The evil you planned to do to me has, by God's design, been turned to good."* You know, if you and I can only think in our lives how God planned that to save the Israelites from extinction — as painful as it was, as dishonest as it was, as brutal and tragic, God used it to save His people.

And Joseph knew that. His brothers never caught on. He knew that, and he said, *"That he might bring about, as indeed he has, the deliverance of a numerous people. So, you need not be afraid. I myself will provide for you."* In this he reassured them *and touched their hearts.* What a man was Joseph. The kind of prototype, I think, of St. Joseph, the foster father of Jesus. A prototype of Jesus Himself, Who was so maltreated and so wronged and yet said, "Father, forgive them, they don't know what they're doing."

So, you can see Joseph is that example that the Father has put before you and before me. Of learning, overcoming our weaknesses, that beautiful gift of the ability to forgive and be so magnanimous after you forgive. And most of all, I think, the most magnificent part of this whole thing is this sentence: *"Do not be afraid. Is it for me to put myself in God's place? The evil you planned to do me has, by God's design, been turned to good, that he might bring about the salvation of many people."*

Well, I think you and I have learned a lot in this book of Genesis. At one time, then, Joseph said, *"I am about to die, but God will be sure to remember you kindly and take you back from this country to the land he promised."* And he said, "When He does, take my bones from here and bury them in our land."

So, Joseph died at the age of 110. They embalmed him and laid him in his coffin in Egypt.

Well, that's the book of Genesis. It didn't take us too long. You know, I hope you've learned a lot. I have. We can begin to apply the lessons to our life and see the Providence of God working then and now. He works the same in your life and in my life. We have our ups and our downs, and we have our struggles, and we have people to forgive, and we have people to forgive us, and God just uses it all—even our mistakes. Anytime you're discouraged, you just have to read the story of Joseph to really get a boost and know that the presence of Jesus is within you, around you, and what are you to fear?

So, I hope you've enjoyed this Scripture series on Genesis. I have enjoyed giving it to you. I've enjoyed the light that God gave me to give to you. I learned as much as you did, and I thank God for the opportunity of this network, just to sit down and be able to talk to you about the Lord.

To me, that's the most wonderful thing in the world.

Mother M. Angelica
(1923–2016)

Mother Mary Angelica of the Annunciation was born Rita Antoinette Rizzo on April 20, 1923, in Canton, Ohio. After a difficult childhood, a healing of her recurring stomach ailment led the young Rita on a process of discernment that ended in the Poor Clares of Perpetual Adoration in Cleveland.

Thirteen years later, in 1956, Sister Angelica promised the Lord as she awaited spinal surgery that, if He would permit her to walk again, she would build Him a monastery in the South.

In Irondale, Alabama, Mother Angelica's vision took form. Her distinctive approach to teaching the Faith led to parish talks, then pamphlets and books, then radio and television opportunities.

By 1980, the Sisters had converted a garage at the monastery into a rudimentary television studio. EWTN was born. Mother Angelica has been a constant presence on television in the United States and around the world for more than forty years. Innumerable conversions to the Catholic Faith have been attributed to her unique gift for presenting the gospel: joyful but resolute, calming but bracing.

Mother Angelica spent the last years of her life cloistered in the second monastery she founded: Our Lady of the Angels in

Hanceville, Alabama, where she dedicated herself, alongside her Nuns, to prayer and adoration of Our Lord in the Most Blessed Sacrament.